Cesare L...
The Father of Criminology
Redefined

Randall R. Butler, Ph.D.
R. Steven Jones, Ph.D.
Alejandro del Carmen, Ph.D.

Kendall Hunt
publishing company

Cover image Courtesy of Museo di Antropologia criminale "Cesare Lombroso," Università di Torino, Italy. Photo: R. Goffi. Photographer: Randall Butler

Kendall Hunt
publishing company
www.kendallhunt.com
Send all inquiries to:
4050 Westmark Drive
Dubuque, IA 52004-1840

Dedication

To Our Children

Rich and Laurie Butler,
Evan and Leslie Jones,
and
Gabriel and Gemma del Carmen

MAP OF ITALY

Contents

Preface

There is probably no other figure in the history of criminology as a field of study that has captivated the attention of those that concern themselves with the causes of deviance than Cesare Lombroso. Unfortunately, as it is often the case with historical figures, Lombroso is often misinterpreted by those that minimize his personal life and the impact it had on the major contributions he made to the field of criminology. In fact, most of us criminologists, learn very little about Lombroso other than a few historical anecdotes and perhaps a cosmetic discussion on his works.

Perhaps the most significant challenge in the field of criminology is that we seem concerned about modern and contemporary themes without paying much attention to the historical heritage and meaning of the works of those that provided the foundation to the study of deviance. This is further enhanced by the fact that most of us criminologists lack the academic training in the application of the historical techniques that are appropriate for the study of historical figures like Lombroso.

Therefore, what makes this book unique from all others that have attempted to define Lombroso from a personal and professional perspective, is that it was written by two historians and a criminologist. That is, the historical research efforts employed have uncovered a great deal about Lombroso that was not known prior to this writing. Not only are the personal anecdotes interesting, but throughout the book, it is highlighted how Lombroso's major personal life events marked, defined, and influenced his works. In the case of Lombroso and after reading this book, you will agree with the concept that it is impossible to separate the man from his works. In fact, it is the work of Cesare Lombroso that has undoubtedly left behind a rich contribution to the field of criminology; thus, revolutionizing and affecting even today's modern way of thinking about the causes of deviance.

— Alejandro del Carmen
August, 2017

Acknowledgments

If it takes a village to raise a child, the same is true for writing a book. The authors are deeply indebted to a group of wonderful scholars and friends for their contributions that made this book possible. We want to especially thank Dr. Silvano Montaldo, Director of the "Cesare Lombroso" Museum of Criminal Anthropology at the University of Turin and Professor of Contemporary History, and Dr. Cristina Cilli, Curator. Drs. Montaldo and Cilli are also professors at the university. They generously opened the museum and its archives, and most important, allowed the photography of the unpublished biography of Cesare Lombroso prepared by his daughter, Gina Lombroso-Ferrero, a singular gesture that literally made this book possible. They also provided interviews and responded to countless email questions.

We also wish to acknowledge the assistance in translating Italian materials by Mrs. Sandra Lapini-Lozzi, a native of Florence, Italy, and currently an Administrative Assistant at Tarleton State University. The staff in Special Collections at the Columbia University Library in New York City was also invaluable in finding various miscellaneous Lombroso materials.

We owe a debt to several people at Southwestern Adventist University for their help. In order to obtain a better understanding of Lombroso's mental state of mind, we are particularly indebted to Dr. Mark Aldridge, Professor of Psychology at Southwestern. His observations provided invaluable insights and opened potential new avenues of research. Dr. Amy Rosenthal, Academic Dean at Southwestern, was a constant cheerleader and secured research and travel funds. Cristina Thomsen, Southwestern library director, and her staff ordered many obscure books on Lombroso and made many similar interlibrary loan requests. Also, a special thanks to Kaitlyn Warman, student assistant in the Southwestern Adventist University History Department who downloaded and emailed countless photographed documents, and copied, collated, and bound version after version of our manuscript-in-progress.

The authors also wish to express our gratitude to the administration, faculty, and staff at Tarleton State University. There is no question that without their support, our ideas and efforts would have never materialized in the form of a book. Special thanks to the faculty at the School of Criminology, Criminal Justice, and Strategic Studies at Tarleton State University.

The past two years of research and writing would not have been possible without the encouragement and loving support of our wives and families. They have graciously forgiven us for our travel and writing schedule.

This book would never have reached the press without the enduring service and support of Ms. Bev Kraus, Project Coordinator for Kendall Hunt, and Lara McCombie, Senior Author Account Manager, for Kendall Hunt who visited the authors at just the right moment to provide encouragement. To Bev Kraus and all the good editors at Kendall Hunt, we extend our sincere appreciation. Of course, any omissions or commissions are the solely the responsibility of the authors.

Introduction

Cesare Lombroso's face floats in a jar at the Museum of Criminal Anthropology in Turin, Italy, the Piedmontese city where Lombroso made his scientific reputation. His skeleton hangs on an armature in another part of the museum.

Fittingly, the skulls and death masks of hundreds of Italian convicts are on display near Lombroso's preserved remains. Together they create a historical tableau of 19th-century scientific investigation; of scientist and subjects; of professor and lecture topics; of criminologist and criminals.

When Lombroso (1835-1909) published *L'uomo delinquente* (*Criminal Man*) in 1876, no one would have called him a criminologist. The term simply did not exist. And yet Lombroso was indeed that, the first criminologist. Today, a criminologist is someone who analyzes "data to determine why . . . [a] crime was committed and to find ways to predict, deter, and prevent further criminal behavior (Become a Criminologist)."

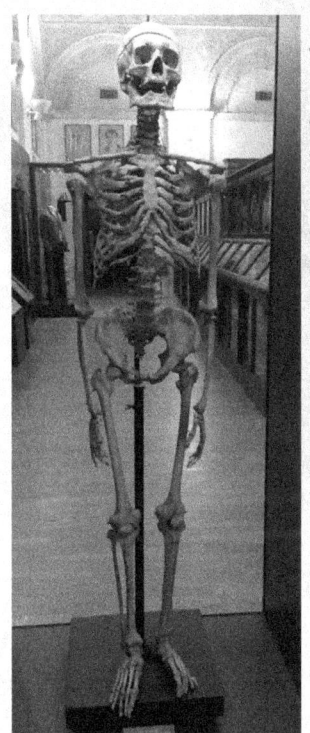

Lombroso's skeleton

Museo di Antropologia Criminale "Cesare Lombroso," University of Turin, Italy; Photographer: Randall Butler

Lombroso, a quasi-historian, psychologist, and patriot in the cause of Piedmont-led Italian unification movement, became fascinated, perhaps even obsessed, by finding the causes and motives of criminal activity. Once discovered, those results could in fact lead to predicting, deterring, and preventing criminal activity.

Lombroso created his field. He worked with no template, no mentors, no professors to follow. By 21st-century standards, Lombroso's science was shoddy, frequently based more on anecdotal evidence and assumptions. When he

Partial collection of death masks and skulls in the Cesare Lombroso Museum

noted that many convicted criminals had "sloping foreheads" or "jug ears," he ran with it, making broad categories of criminal types and classifying criminals even more broadly. When Lombroso satisfied his own bias that Romagna Italians — gypsies in the vernacular of the time — were inherently prone to crime, he stated it as scientific fact.

Forget what you know about DNA evidence in modern investigations. (And by all means, forget what you've learned on the many TV variations of CSI!) Scientific knowledge of DNA was nearly a century beyond Lombroso's career. Accepted scientific psychological inquiry was in its infancy. Lombroso had the theoretical works of Darwin, Spencer, and others and to go by, that is all. Knowing that science required quantifiable evidence, which, through repetition, can be trusted, he turned to the only evidence available to him. Those were the non-normal visual and physical characteristics — anomalies — of criminals. Those anomalies included low foreheads, jug ears, swollen temples, square jaws, an excessive desire for sex, a propensity to wear jewelry, and a tendency to get tattoos. Lombroso could categorize those characteristics, then match them with the crimes of corresponding criminals and thus create file upon file of quantifiable evidence. As Lombroso scholars Mary Gibson and Nicole Hahn Rafter note in their edited edition of *Criminal Man*, "Because anomalies can be examined, counted, and classified, Lombroso promised to turn the study of criminality into an empirical science" (Gibson and Rafter, 1).

Lombroso's work was the direct product of the confluence of three European academic and philosophical movements — naturalism, materialism, and positivism.

A fourth "ism," this one political, also fueled his career. That was nationalism. Lombroso applied his life to the observation of natural phenomena in humankind, whether determining the cause of cretinism and pellagra, mental illness, or discovering and explaining the criminal type. Both observations on health and crime were central to his vision of a new, unified Italian state. Nationalism and its emphasis on unity, identity, and geo-political boundaries provided Lombroso with a cause of intrinsic national interest. Italian national aspirations were the over-riding interest in Lombroso's public life. He understood that the foundation for nation building began with the people, their cultural identifications and social institutions (S. Montaldo, personal communication, September 20, 2016; Horn, 2003).

Lombroso attempted to apply *science* — that foundation of the rational age — to a sociological problem, crime. The hard science would have to wait for other practitioners after Lombroso, but he laid the groundwork of inquiry. Cesare Lombroso was indeed the first criminologist.

This study of Lombroso does what many others have not. That is, simply, to place Lombroso's work, research, and theories in the context of the political and scientific world in which he lived. Such is true, obviously, of any historical figure. As we mention in the acknowledgments of this book, material from the Museum of Criminal Anthropology was invaluable to its creation. Some of it, we are sure, historians have not used in a century.

Was Lombroso groundbreaking? Was he controversial? Was he eccentric? Was he influential? The answer is to all of those questions is "Yes!" This volume hopes to offer a fuller, more nuanced biography of the Father of Criminology.

"How to Become a Criminologist." Http://www.criminaljusticeusa.com/criminologist/. Accessed July 13, 2016.

Lombroso, Cesare. *Criminal Man*. (1876). Mary Gibson and Nicole Hahn Rafter, eds. Translated with new introduction. Durham: Duke University Press, 2006.

About the Authors

Dr. Randall Butler, PhD, is Program Coordinator for the School of Criminology, Criminal Justice and Strategic Studies at Tarleton State University. He has published in several fields including criminal justice and history. Butler is a Master Peace Officer in the State of Texas. He has a special research interest in Native American law enforcement.

Photo © Randall Butler

Dr. R. Steven Jones, PhD, is the Chair of the History and Social Science Department and Professor of History and Political Science at Southwestern Adventist University. He has published on the American Civil War, U.S. military history and foreign policy, and criminal justice.

Photo © Steve Jones

Dr. Alejandro del Carmen, PhD, is Professor and Executive Director of the School of Criminology, Criminal Justice and Strategic Studies at Tarleton State University. He has published extensively in the field of criminology and criminal justice and is recognized as a national expert on racial profiling and the use of force in law enforcement. He is currently part of the federal monitoring team in the Puerto Rico Police Department Reform Agreement.

Photo © Stacy Bogan

Lombroso Chronology

1807   Aronne Lombroso, Cesare Lombroso's father, born

1814   Zefora "Nina" Levi, Cesare Lombroso's mother, born

1815   Congress of Vienna

1816   David Levi, cousin of Nina and supporter of the *Risorgimento*, born

1831   Giuseppe Mazzini established "Young Italy" independence movement

1833   Samson Ercole Lombroso, brother of Cesare, born
            Young Italy coup in Sardinia fails

1834   Pasquetta Lombroso, sister of Cesare, born

1835   Cesare Lombroso born, November 6, in Verona
            (Two more Lombroso children, birthdates unknown, followed Cesare)

1840   David Levi journeys to Paris to help Mazzini's Italian independence movement

1843   Renewed Italian independence uprisings

1844   Fratelli Bandieri incident

1848   Liberal revolt in Sicily
            Charles Albert signs *Statuto*
            Piedmont begins war against Austria
            Cesare Lombroso in attendance at Veronese gymnasium

1849	Austria defeats Piedmont
	Charles Albert abdicates in Piedmont; son Victor Emmanuel II takes throne
1850	Siccardi Laws in Piedmont put constraints on Catholic Church
	Lombroso seeks tutoring outside of the gymnasium
1851	Lombroso publishes review of Marzolo's *Historical Monuments*
	Lombroso enters Pavia University
1853	Crimean War begins
1854	Lombroso enters Padova University
	Lombroso writes "Lunacy of Cardano"
1855	Lombroso enters University of Vienna
	Piedmont sides with France and England in Crimea
1857	Lombroso tours Lombardy in first effort to find cause of cretinism
1858	Lombroso receives doctorate from University of Pavia
1859	France supports Piedmont in new attempt to oust Austria from northern Italy
	Lombroso joins Piedmontese army
1860	Much of Italian peninsula united under Piedmont in *Risorgimento*
	Lombroso writes on military injuries and traumas
1862	Lombroso stationed in Calabria during Italian army's fight against brigandage
1863	Lombroso, while still in army, begins studies in psychiatry at University of Genoa
1864	Lombroso teaches briefly at Pavia
1865	Lombroso recalled to military service, finishing in 1866

1868	Lombroso begins to focus research on pellagra
1870	Lombroso marries Nina de Benedetti Italian unification completed, Rome becomes capital
1871	Daughter Paola born to Cesare and Nina Lombroso Lombroso discovers *median occipital fossa* in Villela skull
1872	Daughter Gina born to Cesare and Nina Lombroso Lombroso makes presentation on pellagra at Turin Medical Academy
1873	(date uncertain) Son Arnaldo born to Cesare and Nina Lombroso
1875	(date uncertain) Son Leo born to Cesare and Nina Lombroso
1876	Lombroso becomes head of Legal Medicine and Public Hygiene at Turin University First edition of *Criminal Man* published.
1877	(date uncertain) Son Ugo born to Cesare and Nina Lombroso
1878	Second edition of *Criminal Man*
1880	Lombroso's parents, Aronne and Nina, die within a week of each other
1882	Lombroso's son, Leo, dies Lombroso begins tangential work on spiritualism
1884	Third edition of *Criminal Man*
1885	First conference of International Congress of Criminal Anthropologists, Rome
1889	Fourth edition of *Criminal Man*
1891	*Man of Genius* published

1892   Lombroso begins research observation of spiritualist medium Eusapia

1893   *Criminal Woman* published

1894   Lombroso's oldest son, Arnaldo, dies

1896   Fifth edition of *Criminal Man* published

1897   Lombroso visits Russia

1909   Cesare Lombroso dies, October 19
        Lombroso's final book, *After Death – What?*, published

CHAPTER 1
Lombroso: Young Academic

"I must do good for the good."
—Cesare Lombroso

Cesare Lombroso was born at a time of political and intellectual turmoil. At the time of his birth on November 6, 1835, Europe was in transition from the Age of Enlightenment to the Age of Nationalism. The Enlightenment had flourished for 200 years (1600-1815) and provided the foundation for modern European commerce, scientific innovation and technology, industrialization, arts and literature, political systems and philosophy. The "rational man" was champion of the age. The Enlightenment was a liberal movement for modernity that challenged church and crown alike. It also stirred a new introspection on the ills of society, especially poverty, crime, and the disparity in wealth and power between classes (Mishra, 2017).

The Enlightenment was not a set of dogmas but rather a movement against superstition, metaphysical ideas, and religious authority. It challenged the status quo and conventional wisdom regarding nature, man, society, and government. Freedom of speech, thought, and individual liberty were at the very core of the Enlightenment. Followers, as Lombroso would be, regarded those ideas as intrinsic values; they were natural laws. The behavior of man under those laws intrigued Enlightenment thinkers. They also believed science held the key to discovery of those natural laws. Scholars wielded empiricism and the power of reason against the fundamental tenets that Europeans had held

1

for centuries. Lombroso would pride himself in his use of scientific methodologies to unlock the secrets of nature, whether on issues of health or crime.

Before the Enlightenment, western philosophy sought to explain the natural world within the realm of the supernatural. From earliest Christendom, the Catholic Church held that God created and ruled the universe and all behavior in the natural world was subject to Him. To know God was to know the universe; to transgress God's dominion was a sin. The Enlightenment turned the God-centered world on its head. To Enlightened thinkers, natural laws rather than ecclesiastical or metaphysical forces governed the universe and man. Furthermore, man could discern these laws through science and the senses. Science and reason were a continuum to understanding the universe.

All of these forces would frame Cesare Lombroso's life and scholarly work. Like those social forces, his studies reflected a sea change in European thought and gave way to modern Europe.

******

Cesare Lombroso, who championed Italian nationalism and made his reputation as one of united Italy's first noted social scientists, was born an Austrian. At the time of his birth in Verona, his home province of Venitia was under Austrian control (Kurella, 1). So was the region of Lombardy, west of Venitia, and they had been since the Congress of Vienna in 1815. Then, Austrian Foreign Minister Klemens Von Metternich had orchestrated the restructuring of Europe after Napoleon Bonaparte's defeat at Waterloo and the collapse of his French empire. In fact, Italy as a nation did not even exist; it was simply a collection of states — from Piedmont in the northwest, south down the Italian peninsula to the Mediterranean islands of Sicily and Sardinia (Craig, 186).

Lombroso was also a Jew. As a result, he had to wend his way through the various pockets of anti-semitism that peppered northern Italy. He also benefitted from a fluke of history.

When Napoleon controlled Lombardy and Venitia, France had extended full equality and legal rights to Jews. Local Jews knew that as the "first emancipation." That ended, however, when Austria took over the regions; save for Verona. That city, and other areas in Venetia, had experienced great traditional tolerance for Jews. Many had landed in Venice when Spain expelled them after completing the Reconquista in 1492. Later, in 1574, Solomon of Udine, the Jewish ambassador to Venice from Turkey, helped end orders expelling Jews that were pending in several Italian kingdoms. He also secured long-lasting rights for Jews, which ultimately would benefit the young Lombroso. Verona was one of a few cities where Jewish children could attend the gymnasium — or public school — that Jesuits operated. Lombroso's parents, Aronne and Zefora Levi, made their home in Verona for just that reason (Kurella, 2).

Zefora — usually called "Nina," in fact, laid the foundation for everything that her son, Cesare, would do and become. Nina, born in 1814 to Levi and Sara, who ran various factories that made fabrics and soaps, (Curi, Lombroso e Verona) possessed a great intellectual curiosity, an "idealism, intelligence, and passion" for learning, according to her granddaughter Gina Lombroso-Ferrero (Lombroso-Ferrero, Chap. I, 1).

David Levi, a cousin two years younger than Nina who lived near her family in Chieri, peaked her interest in things cultural and intellectual. David and Nina were both descendants of a Jewish line of Levis, influential in northern Italy. Levi biographer Alessandro Grazi explained some of the Levis' situation, as well as that of other well-to-do Jews in the northern Italian regions:

> David was a member of . . . an important and wealthy family, part of Piedmont's emerging middle class, which would become on of the pillars of the Italian Bourgeoisie. David Levi Senior, his grandfather, was a successful businessman, who combined an elevated education with a keen interest in politics. His good economic condition assured him and his family privileges that were denied to most Jews in Piedmont and in the rest of the Italian peninsula. They owned land and houses, in spite of the prohibition [against such Jewish ownership under Austrian rule], and ran successful companies. During the so-called 'first emancipation', David Levi Senior served as a mayor of Chieri and was Piedmont's Jewish representative at the Sanhedrin in Paris, the famous institution established by Napoleon (Grazi, 8).

Early in life Levi showed a quality of stubborn intellectualism and insatiable desire for learning that became a common denominator in the Levi descendants. He was also raised by a strong mother, another trait common in the family. Like other Jews in Piedmont, David could not attend public schools, and David learned elementary education from a rabbi at a private school. He was restless, however, and his parents soon put him in a series of private tutorships, but, according to Levi biographer Helen Zimmern, "what knowledge these could supply did not suffice to satisfy his hot thirst for learning" (Zimmern, 364).

Levi's family had an extensive library, though, which he capitalized upon. "The Levi house was the center of a small intellectual coterie, who would meet there at stated intervals to discuss current events, literary and political, as well as the inner affairs of the synagogue," writes Zimmern. Discussion there "was calculated to awaken reflection in the mind of a naturally thoughtful youth . . . [and] there was evoked in David Levi the conviction that the troubles of his co-religionists and those of his fatherland flowed from the same source," writes Zimmern (365). That source was tyranny, and tyranny was Austrian rule. "There sprang up in his heart a twofold love for Israel and Italy, which was destined to affect his whole life, career, and labours."

David Levi also used the family library to inculcate Nina Levi in academic, intellectual, and cultural thought. David taught her to "read and appreciate Omero, Sofocle[s], Tito Livius . . . and . . . Italian and Latin classics." That education imbued Nina "with a mixture of rigi[d] Jewish moral[s] and Rousseauian" thought (Lombroso-Ferrero, Chap. I, 1-2). Given his bent toward an independent and unified Italy, Levi could not help but pass that enthusiasm on to his cousin as well.

Not only did David Levi inspire Nina, he would greatly influence her third child, Cesare, in liberal intellectual and patriotic directions. He also became one of the intellectual founders of the Italian unification movement. In frequent absences from Chieri, David Levi would become friends with, and an ardent follower of, Guiseppi Mazzini, who would be a driving force in the unification of Italy.

Nina's cultural and historical studies gave her an awareness of regional anti-Semitism, as well as a very clear idea what she wanted in a mate. Lombroso-Ferrero wrote, "[Nina] declared that she would only accept a husband who lived [in the part] of the country where her children would be able to go to school and take part in the civil life, where there was . . . justice and equality for the people of the race to which she belonged" (Lombroso-Ferrero, Chap. I, 2).

Her family agreed, and ultimately they found her a husband in the Lombardy-Venitia region, which Lombroso-Ferrero described as one of the most culturally rich regions in Italy. "It was under Austria, and Austria had many of the excellent reforms brought about by the [French] Revolution. School had remained lay and Jews [were] under the same laws as the other citizens."

The man they found was Aronne Lombroso, small with tiny feet and hands, high eyebrows, and blonde hair, which he parted "the Russian way, in the middle." He was "sincere, delicate, affectionate [and] lively," his granddaughter reported, but he was also "very, very shy, without practical sense," afraid of people and disorderly (Lombroso-Ferrero, Chap. I, 2).

Aronne was also rather immature. His parents were Samson and Pasqualina Lattes Lombroso. They owned "a number of houses and shops in Verona," according to Ettore Curi. The two had an older son who, however, died at the age of 10. The parents no doubt heaped upon Aronne the affection and dread of a couple who has suffered the death of their first-born, making his childhood, perhaps, fearful. Then, Samson died earlier, further fragmenting Aronne's young life. Pasqualina married again, this time a man named Samson Del Grego. There is no hint of Del Grego abusing Aronne, but neither did he help him. While Del Grego, from Trieste, was also "wealthy and affluent," (Curi, "Lombroso e Verona") he did not bother to teach Aronne the family business or the ways of personal enterprise. The fact that he was ten years older than Nina put his relative immaturity in greater relief.

[Lombroso writer Ettore Curi, suggests that Aronne was not as financially clumsy as Lombroso-Ferrero and her sister, Paola Lombroso, indicate. He says they display a preference for Nina, their grandmother, and an "inexplicable contempt" for Aronne. Instead of being financially inept, Curi says, he bought and restored houses, shops and villas, and was able to increase his own family's wealth.] (Curi, "Lombroso e Verona")

The marriage of Aronne and Nina was not one of love, but of practicality. Certainly Aronnne was, as Gina wrote, the "inferior" member of the pair, both in "character and education." Nevertheless, the marriage was "not an unhappy one." Aronne was "good, affectionate, and loved immediately [and] intensely the wife, he adored her with the intensity of the shy who finally find somebody on who to lean after having for many years felt as a leaf in the wind." Truly, Nina was sturdy enough for Aronne and their children to lean upon (Lombroso-Ferrero, Chap. I, 3).

Aronne and Nina went to live with his mother, Pasqualina, and stepfather, a man named Del Grego. Their time with Aronne's parents were difficult for Nina, who eclipsed both them in education and character just as she did their son. Pasqualina was born in 1764 and lived in Venezia before the French Revolution. She was haughty, proud, aristocratic, "attached to etiquette," and she "adored . . . form more than substance." Nina found Samson Del Grego even more "arrogant and contemptuous . . . than his wife." He had hobbled Aronne's maturation, and did not let him "learn a profession or even get acquainted with [the family] business" (Lombroso-Ferrero, Chap I, 3).

Not surprisingly, Nina escaped the Lombroso-Del Grego home frequently. She returned to Chieri often, and she frequently went on to Padova and Venice to visit other relatives and friends. When she was in Verona, however, she found that the intellectual atmosphere "compensate[ed] her for the family clashes" with the Lombroso-Del Gregos (Lombroso-Ferrero, 5).

In 1833, Nina began having children, and she had them in rapid succession. That year she had a son, Samson Ercole; in 1834, a girl named Pasquetta. In 1835, Cesare arrived. Such a relentless progression of pregnancies and births would certainly have taken its toll on Nina. Her mother-in-law did not help matters. When Samson was born, Pasqualina forbade her from nursing him per some "etiquette prejudices" (Lombroso-Ferrero, Chap. I, 4-5).

Nina was in Chieri — no doubt by design — when she gave birth to Pasquetta. Free from the dominating Pasqualina, "[Nina] nursed her with all the volupty given by nursing, and [she] became terribly attached to that girl, the desperate affection of a person who is not happy." When Pasquetta contracted tuberculosis, Pasqualina quickly blamed Nina's nursing for the disease. Pasquetta died in 1836 (Lombroso-Ferrero, Chap. I, 7; Curi, "Lombroso e Verona").

By the time Ezekia Marco "Cesare" Lombroso was born, in 1835, Nina was ensconced in Verona. It was a place she loved, and she passed that love on to her descendants. Years later, writing her father's biography, Lombroso-Ferrero said "there is no city better than Verona to enchant and calm the pain of an artistic and culture[d] soul." The city had lost none of its intellectual or cultural allure, even though the Austrian army had quartered its cavalry in one of its theaters. Neither had "the place of Guilietta [the supposed home of Juliette from Shakespeare's *Romeo and Juliette*] closed the lively ogival [a Gothic arch that culminates in a narrow point] windows and romantic balcony although it had become a stable." She continued, "such a town that seems to live and laugh with passing generations must have a great fascination on such a sensitive nature as that of young [Nina]" (Lombroso-Ferrero, Chap. I, 7).

Cesare was not the last of the Lombroso children: Nina bore a third son, Romolo and another daughter, Chiarina. The most precocious of them, by far, was Cesare.

Later, when recalling memories (which he called "souvenirs") of his childhood, Cesare claimed to remember an event from when he was 10 months old. Nina set a "pepper pot" in front of him while he was sitting in his high chair. Thinking it was chocolate, he stuck in his finger and then licked it off. "I can perfectly well remember the burning feeling and the fear I had," Lombroso said (Lombroso-Ferrero, Chap. I, 8). From the age of 2 he could remember someone pulling a dead cat from a well; from age 4 he could remember a friend carrying him past a hedge. He remembered the friend "had a long blond beard, [it was] at noon time, and then nothing else." (Lombroso-Ferrero, Chap. I, 8)

Lombroso also connected many of his memories to smells. "That means that my olfattive memory must have been strong," he said. He remembered the smell of violets from a meadow in Chieri where he used to play, and the smell of baking bread at his grandmother's house in the same town. (Lombroso-Ferrero, Chap. I, 8)

Fears, too, dogged him. In a diary entry he wrote, "I have observed on me all kind of mania: Since I was 4 I have been haunted by the idea to be drafted [into the army]. At 8 I had visions of angels. I had all kind of fears going to bed and turning out the light" (Lombroso-Ferrero, Chap. I, 9). He also had a fear — a mania, he called it — of "breaking things." His little sister, Chiarina, said Cesare later attributed these fears to a parasite in his bowels, something Gina would call a "rebel solitary worm that made him sick for many months. The worm forced him to lie on his stomach while reading, suffering cramps all the while. When getting up he was . . . cranky." (Lombroso-Ferrero, Chap. I, 12)

Those fears may point to other aspects of Lombroso's adult life. Silvano Montaldo, director of the "Cesare Lombroso" Museum of Criminal Anthropology at the University of Turin, Italy, said that Lombroso was prone to depression, perhaps even bipolar disorder. "He had mood swings," Montaldo said, "Gina also said he was moody — he changed his mind very easily. He [could be] happy and then depressed" (S. Montaldo, interview, September 20, 2016).

Dr. Mark Aldridge, professor of psychology, in reviewing these observations suggests several things in Lombroso. First, he was probably hypersensitive to stimuli, such as environmental change and certain triggers. That could certainly account for his sensitivity to smells. Daughter Gina's recollection of moodiness also points to recurring depression. (Aldridge, interview, June 13, 2017)

In 1840, when Cesare was 5, crisis hit his family. Aronne's stepfather, Samson Del Grego, died unexpectedly and left the family in financial chaos. Del Grego had supported Aronne and Zefora's family. But his estate was "complicated," probably because Del Grego and Pasqualina had had other children (Curi), and Aronne saw little benefit from it. Ultimately, according to Lombroso-Ferrero, Aronne took a job at a "Spanish Temple," doing clerical work. He also moved his family into small quarters at the temple, a dramatic change from the large home in which Del Grego had established them.

Cesare stayed with his mother's family in Chieri while Aronne and Nina attempted to resettle their life. As one might expect, Cesare became the darling of the household. "Everybody went crazy over the little guest, who with his blue eyes, blond[e] hair, red lips, and little body, affectionate, sociable, [and] smiling [demeanor] conquered all the heart and seemed to fit perfectly in the house," Gina said.

"He soon became the beloved of all the family and the affection [and] the happiness of those years [would] be for him later a wonderful [memory]."

At the same time, though, Cesare got his introduction to Italian patriotism, with a little intrigue thrown in.

David Levi, the cousin who had helped Nina discover intellectualism, had become enmeshed in Giuseppe Mazzini's *Giovine Italia* (Young Italy, a youth-based Italian independence movement). With skills as a writer and law school experience that his parents had insisted upon, Levi became "a very apostle of conspiracy, a link, a mouthpiece" (Zimmern, 370) was in and out of Cesare's early life. In 1840, Levi left Chieri at about the time Del Grego's death caused trouble for Cesare's parents. He traveled to Paris, where, according to Lombroso-Ferrero, he became part of Mazzini's "ground movement." She said, "He had been part of the conspiration [sic] in France, in England, in Switzerland against Austria" (Lombroso-Ferrero, Chap. I, 10).

The "conspiration" in which David Levi became enmeshed was long in coming. It was part and parcel of a series of risings that would lead to Italian unification.

As early as 1794, liberal plots grew to overthrow local governments in Naples and Turin (Lombroso's future home). While those failed and led to the executions of their leaders, the plots laid the groundwork of Italian liberalism (Collier, 23). Chief among liberal goals was the expulsion of Austria from the northern Italian provinces. A secret society known as the Carbonari (Charcoal Burners) agitated for that to no avail (Collier, 25; Craig, 188).

In 1831, Giuseppe Mazzini, who had been jailed for his work with the Carbonari, conceived of Young Italy, which he intended to lead the unification of not just northern Italian states — where most of the liberal movements had begun — but all of Italy. In 1833, Young Italy attempted to stage a coup in the Kingdom of Sardinia (which included Piedmont and the island of Sardinia) that ended in abject failure. The conservative government of Charles Albert retaliated with the arrests of nearly 70 insurgents and the execution of twelve of them (Collier, 25-26). The next year, after another abortive attack on the Piedmont government, Mazzini fled Italy. He ultimately arrived in London, where he reformed Young Italy and other such groups on the European continent that supported unification.

Working with Mazzini, David Levi organized a plan to have two Austrian naval commanders, the Flag brothers — who later became known as the "Fratelli Bandieri" — commandeer Austrian ships to support an uprising of the *Risorgimento* in Calabria, the southernmost region of Italy that forms the "toe" of the Italian "boot." The expedition failed, and many of the Flag conspirators were arrested and executed later, in 1844. Lombroso-Ferrero referred to the incident as "the unfortunate expedition of the Fratelli Bandieri" (Lombroso-Ferrero, Chap. I, 10, 16).

Upon Levi's return to Chieri, he worked on a book about the life of Giordano Bruno, an Italian Dominican friar who challenged Catholic authority and dogma by writing a cosmological study of the universe, which he saw as infinite. He also indicated that the Earth was not the center of the solar system. The church burned Bruno to death for heresy in 1600. Bruno's life and thoughts had fascinated Levi since his teens. It is understandable that Levi would pick Bruno to study, as the friar illustrated Levi's own fascination with intellectual freedom and writing. Lombroso-Ferrero said of the biographical work that Levi "was trying to have Bruno tell through his rebellious life, the love and feeling of the revel of the time" (Lombroso-Ferrero, Chap. I, 10) Levi's work would ultimately become his 1887 book *Giordano Bruno; The Religion of Thought; The Man, Apostle, and Martyr* (Zimmern, 366).

Cesare charmed David Levi as he had the women of the family. "[Levi's] young nephew was a relief to him and he passed many and many hours with him. He taught [Cesare] to read, write and love poetry. He made him love Dante. He taught him to despise lies, and vanity . . . . He taught him to love intense freedom, the source of every progress." (Lombroso-Ferrero, Chap. I, 10) With such a tutor, Cesare could not help but grow into a life of intellectual curiosity and freedom, one which would see him question many fundamentals of sociological thought.

When Cesare was old enough, he entered the school in Verona — the gymnasium — that Nina had planned for all her children to attend. The Verona gymnasium proved an excellent springboard for Lombroso. Throughout his life, Lombroso would prove that he was a polymath — someone with an interest in many academic subjects. His daughter also called him an "autodidact," someone who frequently taught himself the things he found deeply interesting. "He was a philosopher," said Silvano Montaldo. "He was not a scientist, but a thinker — a philosopher. . . . He was interested in many things" (S. Montaldo, interview, September 20, 2016; Lombroso-Ferrero, Chap. II, 4).

While Jews were allowed to attend the gymnasium, Jesuits still taught classes there. One such teacher, Don Gaetano Caprara, instructed Cesare in most of his courses, including Latin, Greek, history, geography, and math. Caprara "must not have been too fanatic [in his Catholicism]" as Cesare never mentioned "being scorned." Nevertheless, "he did not feel at ease" with Caprara (Lombroso-Ferrero, Chap. I, 13).

Gina Lombroso-Ferrero described young Cesare as a "visiv" type, someone whom today we would describe as learning through visual cues. "He was not interested in spoken lessons," she wrote, "he preferred books, being very independent in his principles he did not want to accept as divine verb everything he was taught. He was indifferent to be the first of the class and hated to study what was of no interest to him. He hated mathematics and had terrible difficulty in solving the problems" (Lombroso-Ferrero, Chap. I, 13).

Like many children who live much in their own heads, seeking their own interests and exploring their own intellectual leads, Cesare Lombroso had difficulty making friends. "Although he [needed] friendship and affection [he] did not know how to make friends," Lombroso-Ferrero wrote. He did make a friend named Arvedi (who would later become mayor of Venice) and whom Cesare referred to as R.R., or simply R. Lombroso-Ferrero's notes are unclear. Arvedi and R. could be the same person, or they could be two different friends. Nevertheless, R. "loved to have fun," which attracted Cesare. "R. loves me because I am studious," Lombroso wrote in a diary, "I [love him] because he knows how to have fun" (Lombroso-Ferrero, Chap. I, 13).

R., however, would disappoint Cesare. The two liked to walk among the hills near the Adige River and read from a cheap copy of the works of Lucretius. So that they would always have the book when they wanted it, R. and Cesare hid the book in a cache in a rock. But one day they could not find it. After looking for a time, they forgot about the book since it was inexpensive. Several weeks later, however, Lombroso found that very book in a second-hand bookstore. R. had stolen it from the hiding place and sold it (Lombroso-Ferrero, Chap. I, 13).

Cesare later wrote that the experience was "the greatest pain in my life. It was not the loss of the book, but to see me betrayed by my best [friend] from whom I cannot stop loving. It gave me such discouragement of life . . . [that]

I was sick for [a] month" (Lombroso-Ferrero, Chap. I, 14). Lombroso-Ferrero suggests that the betrayal may have sparked Cesare's initial interest in criminal behavior. "It may well have been at that moment that Lombroso had his first glimpse of the monstrosity of crime. Such a [treason] as the one R. did could only be attributed to morbid impulse, as R. was the only son of a very rich family, and the boy always had as much money as he wanted" (Lombroso-Ferrero, Chap. I, 14).

As a teen, Lombroso grew irritated with the Jesuit school. R.'s betrayal certainly did not make him any happier there, but the roots of his discouragement ran deeper. While it afforded him a basic education, Lombroso chaffed against the Jesuit strictures of the Verona school. The Jesuits were firmly sympathetic to Austria at a time when Italian nationalism was rising, and they "deliberately discouraged all advanced ideas." Lombroso and fellow students who sought broader knowledge secretly read such enlightenment work as that of Giambattista Vico, a political philosopher who created the field of the philosophy of history (Kurella, 5).

Lombroso kept a journal, in which he railed against the Jesuits and the Catholic influence of the school. "It may be said of my schooldays without exaggeration that I was thrust back into an environment of persistent medievalism . . . The memory of this forcible discipline, which did violence to the inborn logical spirit, and visited with severe punishment any protests against its methods, is so hateful to me that even now it visits me in dreams like a nightmare" (Kurella, 5).

While Lombroso railed against the constraints of the gymnasium, he assuredly found the political events that whirled about him fascinating. The unification movement provided Lombroso with a political and social education as surely as the university system provided him with one of science. One of Lombroso's first biographers, Hans Kurella, says those events were central to Lombroso's political leanings, which, of course, affected his scientific investigations. "Lombroso's revolutionary tendencies in the field of science, and his small respect for what was traditionally established, were doubtless dependent upon the joint effect [of those political incidents]," Kurella said. (Kurella, 4)

In 1848, while Lombroso and his fellow students inveighed against the conservative restrictions of the Veronese gymnasium, new revolts shook the Italian states. This movement reached back to 1843, when Catholic priest Vincenzo Gioberti (in exile from Piedmont on suspicion of being a radical liberal) wrote that perhaps the Papacy — situated in the Papal States in and around Rome — could unite the Italian states. He said nothing, however, of ousting Austria from the north. The next year, Cesare Balbo wrote in *The Hopes of Italy* that Piedmont, not the Papacy, should lead Italian unification and push Austria from the northern provinces. When he read Balbo's book, the pre-eminence of Piedmont in the movement interested Piedmont King Charles Albert (Collier, 29-30).

The Papacy, however, remained interested in its own role in Italian leadership. In 1847, Pope Pius IX tried to ingratiate himself with Italian liberals by reducing press censorship in the Papal States, establishing a civil Council of State to advise on governmental issues within the Papal States, and creating a civilian guard to protect property within the States (Collier, 33). Austria — invoking a clause of the Treaty of Vienna that allowed them to keep an armed force inside the Papal States — occupied the city of Ferrara, further angering nationalist liberals. That same year, Charles Albert in Piedmont — sensing advantage in courting liberals — fired a conservative minister and allowed other limited reforms, including less restrictions on the press.

In 1848, a spontaneous liberal revolt erupted in Sicily, which had been under the control of Naples since 1816. Poverty and disease, which Sicilians placed at the door of Neapolitan governance, was the flashpoint of the rebellion. By the end of April, Sicilians had wrested control from Naples and created their own Parliament. The movement spread to the Italian peninsula. In Naples, liberals forced a less conservative Parliament; in Piedmont, Charles Albert agreed to a less restrictive constitutional monarchy (Collier, 35).

Charles Albert went further. In signing the *Statuto* of March 1848, he agreed to a lower house of Parliament that was elected — albeit by only two percent of the Piedmont-Sardinian population — and could debate financial matters. He also guaranteed civil liberties, including freedom of religion, to everyone in Piedmont. To the south, in the Papal States, Pius IX also allowed a Parliament but in no way embraced civil liberties as did Charles Albert. While Charles Albert was no liberal, he saw wisdom in meeting liberals half-way. In that, he was paving the way for Piedmontese leadership in Italian independence and unification.

Meanwhile, liberal revolts erupted in France, and in Vienna, the capital of Austria. When iron-handed Metternich — the architect of post-Napoleonic conservatism — resigned as Austrian foreign minister in the face of the revolt, repercussions were widespread. In Milan, in the Austrian-held northern Italian province of Lombardy, engaged Austrian troops in street fighting. When outnumbered Austrians retreated, the Milanese had achieved a minor victory. The insurgency spread to Venitia, which declared an independent republic at the end of March 1848. Both Lombardy and Venitia knew, however, that Vienna would never acquiesce to their independence — and they appealed to Charles Albert in Piedmont for help.

At once reluctant and hopeful that Piedmont might be able to oust Austria and annex Lombardy, Charles Albert and Piedmont declared war on Austria on March 22, 1848. When Piedmontese soldiers invaded Lombardy, troops from Naples and the Papal States marched north to join them. However, the Papal States general, Giacomo Durando, had overstepped his orders from Pius IX, making it seem that the Pope endorsed a war with arch-Catholic Austria.

Pius did not want the war, and he issued what became the infamous *Allocution* to prove his stance. The *Allocution* stated that Pius did not approve of the war; that Charles Albert, not the Papal States, was the aggressor; and that Pius did not approve of a united Italy. The *Allocution*, while it saved Pius' political position for the moment, caused liberals to distrust him. It meant that neither he nor the Papacy would ever be accepted as leaders of unification. Plus, the Papal soldiers withdrew from the front in Lombardy. Then, in Naples, Ferdinand II retook control of his old government. Neapolitan soldiers also left Lombardy, leaving the Piedmontese fighters on their own.

Charles Albert attempted to carry on the war, but after a summer of fighting, Austrian troops overwhelmed his own at the Battle of Custozza. The Piedmontese soldiers withdrew from Lombardy, but Charles Albert tried once more to take Lombardy in 1849. The result was the same, with Austrians defeating the Piedmontese again on March 23, 1849. At home in Piedmont, Charles Albert abdicated the throne, handing it over to his son, Victor Emmanuel II.

Even though Piedmont had failed in its campaign against Austria in Lombardy, it became a beacon for liberals throughout Italy. Charles Albert's *Statuto* remained in force under Victor Emmanuel, and it attracted liberals from places where liberal attempts had collapsed after 1848. In 1850, Piedmont's liberal reputation rose when Giuseppe Siccardi introduced a series of bills to Parliament that put significant controls on the Catholic Church. These Siccardi Laws mandated that special courts for clerics be abolished — those suspected of wrongdoing would be tried in civil courts like everyone else; the church could not offer sanctuary to criminals; the right of religious entities to buy property was restricted; and the number of feast days on which people were religiously forbidden to work was reduced (Collier 48-49).

Obviously, the Siccardi Laws took advantage of the Papacy's diminished position with liberals after the *Allocution*. It also found a fervent supporter in

Count Camillo Cavour, the Piedmont-Sardinian minister of trade and agriculture under Prime Minister Massimo d'Azeglio. While the kingdom was veering left, d'Azeglio was at best center-right. His supporters, plus the Papacy, disliked the Siccardi Laws, but Cavour was able to marry center-right members of Parliament with center-left members in a coalition called the *connubio*. That done, the Siccardi Laws were protected and the government became more liberal than it had been. Victor Emmanuel dismissed d'Azeglio and gave the prime ministry to Cavour. The count was now in the role that would make him the chief architect of Italian unification and independence.

After the liberal failure of 1848, Austria responded in northern Italy with a series of retrenchments that would have hobbled the inquisitive Lombroso as much as the gymnasium. Austria enacted laws that prevented groups of four or more people from walking together on the streets lest they be arrested. If police noticed a person visiting a friend too often, they suspected them of espionage. People could not publicly read a book that the government had not approved. Foreign newspapers were not allowed, and sanctioned Austrian newspapers could only consist of one page. "Everything and everybody was under suspicion," wrote Lombroso-Ferrero, "fashion, gloves, handkerchiefs, hats, and even ribbons (the Italians had fun in mixing the national colors). All coffee houses, clubs, theaters, and especially book shops were always with police supervision" (Lombroso-Ferrero, Chap. II, 1). Punishment for offenses, at least for men, was conscription into the Austrian army, something that must have terrified young Lombroso, who manifested that manic fear of the draft at age four.

Lombroso found a way around the educational strictures, at least, of the Austrian reaction. By 1850, 15-year-old Cesare sought tutoring outside of the school. He studied privately with a Professor Sandri, "an eminent Veronese botanist." However, the most influential group of people in his life — a "cenacle," Gina called them — were, just as in the case of David Levi, a group of strong women. They included, "His mother, who saw in him more than a son but the incarnation of [her] ideals; his sister, Chiarina, always sweet and ready to do what the brother wanted; and three ladies . . . [friends] of the family, Mrs. Jung, a good and calm teacher full of practical sense; Mrs. Levi, wife of Emmanuel Levi, a good writer of that epoch; and Mrs. Kraus, who had come to Verona to be the mother of his nephews, whose mother had died" (Lombroso-Ferrero, Chap. I, 14).

Gina Lombroso-Ferrero called this group of women her father's "first cenacle." It is instrumental in understanding much of Lombroso's life. In the absence of a strong father figure (or at least in the presence of one whose very strong wife eclipsed him), Cesare Lombroso was markedly more comfortable with, and more influenced by, strong women. Certainly, he would have strong male professors who encouraged and directed his career. But it was these strong women, especially his mother, that he always remembered, and another — his daughter Gina — to whom he turned in times of stress.

"He certainly is female oriented," said Dr. Mark Aldridge. "This is not that he has a classical Freudian Oedipal complex, but he looked up to strong women. He got strength from them. He got comfort from them. In the absence of a strong male, women fill up the vacuum" (Aldridge, interview, June 13, 2017).

Buoyed by this "first cenacle," Cesare wrote two monographs, one an essay on the history of the Roman Republic, the other on the agriculture of ancient Rome. In fact, history had become Lombroso's first academic love. Those essays were what biographer Marvin E. Wolfgang called his first "two serious papers." Lombroso-Ferrero said that, after her father's death, those two works "remain [equal with] the best works of Lombroso" (Wolfgang, 1961, 362; Lombroso-Ferrero, Chap. I, 14). He read voraciously, typically in the fields of language and history. His library would grow to include "Arabian, Chinese, Abissinian, Indian, Tartar, Hebraic, [and] Babylonian grammars, . . . dictionaries of Italian dialects, notes on Zend Avest classical books of India, Persia, and Roman histories, Venetian history, research on linguistic philosophy, on religious philosophy, [and] pure philosophy." He also ventured into ethnographical studies of Dakota Native Americans, Mexicans, and Brazilians (Lombroso-Ferrero, Chap. II, 2-3).

Lombroso got a measure of academic recognition the next year, at age 16, when he reviewed the first volume of Paolo Marzolo's *Monumenti storici revelati dall' analisi della parola* (*An Introduction to Historical Monuments Revealed by Analysis of Words*). Marzolo was a physician, but, like Lombroso, had a decided interest in history. He had published the work a year earlier, in 1850, and it met with largely favorable reviews. Marzolo was disappointed, however, that most reviewers, he believed, had not fully grasped his interpretations.

Marzolo saw Lombroso's review of *Historical Monuments* in a Veronese journal, and he believed he had discovered the first Italian academic to understand him. Marzolo biographer Checcarel wrote that Lombroso's comments "Had delighted the latter for the first time in several years, and had at length rewarded him for his long and arduous labours." Checcarel commented that Marzolo "Imagined that the writer of the . . .[review] must be an advanced but lonely scientific thinker, one who owing to his private circumstances or an account of the disturbed times had hitherto lived in retirement" (Kurella, 6). When he requested a meeting with the author, Marzolo was "amazed to find him only 16 years of age" (Wolfgang, 1961, 362).

Cesare Lombroso was "shy and modest" when he met Marzolo, but he had "a soul which was trying to find an ideal to give everything to it, with joy and exuberance," Lombroso-Ferrero said (Lombroso-Ferrero, Chap. II, 1). Just as Count Cavour was ascending to leadership in Piedmont, Cesare Lombroso was finding that ideal, and he gained an academic mentor at the same time — Paolo Marzolo himself.

Lombroso had not intended to study medicine and probably would have remained in the humanities had Marzolo not influenced him to change academic directions. His mother, Nina, hoped he would study law, such as her cousin, David Levi, and her brother, Marco, had. At this point in his Lombroso's academic career, however, Marzolo had more influence than Nina. He wanted to make sure that Cesare remained untainted by "the school of philosophy, which he feared more than anything else" (Lombroso-Ferrero, Chap. II, 3).

In Pavia

Lombroso then matriculated to Pavia University. If he harbored any doubts about his new academic goal, that changed when he met the second of his great mentors, 70-year-old Bartolomeo Panizza. Panizza was both a professor of medicine and the president of the university. He had led a life of adventure, having fought with Napoleon's army on its Russian campaign in 1812, and he was esteemed enough by both France and Austria that he went through the revolution of 1848 professionally unscathed. Panizza biographer Andrea Verga said the professor was electric and captivating in the classroom. He "taught by memory, walked across the room, dramatically, his ways were neat and sincere, sometimes new and strange, but always efficient. Every part of him was talking, his face, his eyes, his gesture, everything helped him in his demonstrations and illustrations — the cape, the room, the table, the chair, the handkerchief, the paper" (Lombroso-Ferrero, Chap. II, 3). With such drama, Panizza made complicated subjects enjoyable and comprehensible. Certainly it is no surprise that the Panizza's academic theatrics would attract Lombroso's unquenchable curiosity. Lombroso later wrote in his diary that, after the "years passed solitarily in Verona," meeting Panizza and getting "in touch with intelligent people, with who[m] to share the flock of ideas coming in his mind," was exactly what he needed (Lombroso-Ferrero, Chap. II, 4).

Pavia enabled Lombroso to make new friends, which had never been easy for the young man who so often dwelt within his own mind. In late 1852, while visiting Milan, 24 miles from Pavia, he wrote to a friend, Ettore Righi, that he was "now in one [of] those condition[s] that you dream more than you think, without worries, without policemen, independent to stay or go as you please." He said he enjoyed the company of "wonderful young people as I would never have found in Venetia." He enjoyed traveling from Pavia to Milan and back, "rooming here and there," going to dances, lectures, and parties (Lombroso-Ferrero, Chap. II, 4).

He also was meeting women. Later, writing again to Righi, he said "Life is good and fun. There was a horse fair here, which was also a woman fair as not one but the most modest girl from Pavia and villages remained in their homes, so the fair was great and wonderful" (Lombroso-Ferrero, Chap. II, 4). In the 19th century, Lombroso would have thought nothing sexist about comparing a gathering of young women to a horse fair.

Lombroso, who obviously lived so much within his own mind, had a desperate need for friendships. His daughter wrote that, after leaving home, Lombroso embarked on an "orgy of friendships." Of course, she did not refer to "orgy" in any sexual sense, but in a quantitative sense. Simply, Lombroso wanted — perhaps needed — many friends. "He wanted to meet every body [sic]," from poets and musicians to professors and students. He apparently had a lengthy list of friends, but their relationships did not last. In the end, they also seemed to tax the young Lombroso mentally (Lombroso-Ferrero, Chap. II, 6).

Writing to Righi in 1855, he apologized that he could not write as a long a letter as he intended. Embarrassed, he explained that "I have 8 or 10 friends as good as you, that I love as much as you, [from whom] flows the swift of the Gran Simpatico [the body's sympathetic nervous system]." He continued, "You will laugh, but I assure it is so, I am exhausted by it as one is exhausted after a long, and so well liked, discussion with people very intelligent. In the brain we probably have the deposit or maybe the machine for ideas, but it is in the Gran Simpatico that is the sublime current that give movement, maybe heat, certainly the disposition and versatility of the ideas" (Lombroso-Ferrero, Chap. II, 6).

Regardless, Lombroso seemed desperate for friendship, someone to write to — with whom to communicate. In another letter to Righi, also in 1855, Lombroso says, "I write you because I need to write, to trust you. . . . You must have felt sometimes this intense need to trust somebody, to confide in him" (Lombroso-Ferrero, Chap. II, 5).

In a diary entry from the same year, Lombroso endeavored to explain friendship in, not surprisingly, by anthropological means. "The difference between love and friendship is one step. It is always sympathy, attraction, and an approach. The great analogy is that between two real friendships is always one that represents the feminine elements and the other the masculine, that is to say the active and the passive" (Lombroso-Ferrero, Chap. II, 5). Gina Lombroso-Ferrero did not know if her father's theory could hold for everyone's friendships, but she applied to his. "It was [true] of the young [Lombroso] who was always in his friendship the masculine element because he liked to love more than be loved. He preferred to show his expansiveness [more] than to receive it from others" (Lombroso-Ferrero, Chap. II, 5). Whether 21st century students would accept Gina's 19th century assessment as correct, or rather as an element of male-dominated relationships is an open question.

In this moment of discovery and transient friendships, Lombroso did make two that were to prove influential. One was Alfredo de Maury. The other was Paolo Mantagazza.

Maury (1817-1892) earned notoriety as both a physician and scholar with studies on dreams and their stimuli (Roland Pec, "Dreaming About Dreams.") In 1850, Lombroso excitedly read Maury's *Les Reves* (*Dreams*). Then he wrote "an enthusiastic letter" exchanging ideas with the author. Their ensuing friendship would be the second that the precocious young Lombroso started by contacting the author of an academic text (Lombroso-Ferrero, Chap. III, 6).

The next of Lombroso's new and important friends was Paolo Mantagazza. (In correspondence with Lombroso, Mantagazza would later refer to himself as "Paolo II" to avoid confusing with Lombroso's first academic friend, Paolo Marzolo.) Mantagazza was four years Lombroso's senior, they being 24 and 20 when they met. Nearing the end of medical school, Mantagazza was "good looking, happy, adventurous, elegant, intelligent, and loving all beautiful things in nature and art and science" (Lombroso-Ferrero, Chap. III, 7). Mantagazza would be the man who got Lombroso interested in the "cell that thinks," — the brain (Lombroso-Ferrero, Chap. III, 7).

Lombroso worked as Mantagazza's research assistant while the latter finished a study on the "Physiology of Pleasure." In a series of diary entries, Lombroso shows that he was examining his own personality as a window into the minds of others. In part, he wrote:

PLEASURE: When I am in [a] state of cerebral well being, even if only a mediocre well being, I have extreme need, while I read or talk, to touch something with my hands, a big knife or a bone . . . knife.

HEARING: I love music and also it excites me much [in] my work — without formulating a thought — but I cannot differentiate between good and bad music.

SMELLS — I love the smell of storm[s], of wet dust, or paper. I am not sensible much to smell of flowers . . . .

GENERAL AND VARIOUS PLEASURES — In certain cases . . . I have immense need to move, to fight, to eat, to . . . dance, and jump. Great pleasure in moving more than running and being uncomfortably seated afterwards.

Pleasure in fresh air and excitement.

Pleasure to expand, to confide to a friend, to be a friend.

Great sympathy towards people with nervous [conditions].

Hate of red hairs and lymphatics [someone who was flabby, or sluggish].

When I am in state of mental weakness I take pleasure in cutting papers, draw lines on the table and copy pictures.

Pleasure of association to see papers and books coming from the library.

Pleasure in seeing some papers and some places without knowing why.

Pleasure in rereading Goethe and Schiller

Pleasure to see one's own writings printed (Lombroso-Ferrero, Chap. III, 8-9).

These entries provide opportunity for some snap assessments. Like his childhood memories of the smell of bread baking, these also show a hypersensitivity to sensations. His remark about being in a "state of mental weakness" points to depression. And, Lombroso's admission that he sometimes wants to fight, jump, dance, or sing could indicate the manic phase of a bipolar condition. Finally, his pleasure in seeing his own writing printed — well, that's no less than a sign of a budding academic!

Lombroso also included in his diary short sayings of the type that Benjamin Franklin or George Washington might have included in their own writings. They include:

> What monotony in the world in the eyes of [the] philosopher, what variety for the eyes who look without seeing!

> There are rich people popular for their meanness and there are well-known people known for their naughtiness.

> A small man goes to visit a big one. And he says I too am big — compared to worms (Lombroso-Ferrero, Chap. III, 10).

While Lombroso's diary shows evidence of deep thought and melancholy, it also shows the beginning of an unfounded worry about his own health — hypochondria. "We find in his diary symptoms of a new sickness that must have been imagined as he was never sick at that time," writes his daughter (Lombroso-Ferrero, Chap. III, 10). Strangely, Lombroso credited this sickness with his early academic interests and abilities, but then blamed it for an inevitably quick mortality. "I have seen in me the beginning of a heart disease and am sure of what I foresaw. I will not live until the age of 40. The excessive development of my cardiac system provoked my precosity [sic] of the intellectual development and now I undergo the metamorphosis." Lombroso was 21 when he wrote that (Lombroso-Ferrero, Chap. III, 11).

The next year he reiterated his claim. "Each year, periodically, I must repeat the well-known lamentation about my decadence, and each year that passes will bring my hand nearer death, the convulsive traits of my organism are getting slower. I will not live long and not happy" (Lombroso-Ferrero, Chap. III, 11).

Lombroso's childhood fears of being drafted and his visions of angels haunted him as a young adult. He credited them to "[hy]pochondria, lipemania, [and] demency." He wrote "I had all instincts of fear in going to bed and turning the light off. The fear of this did not let me sleep" (Lombroso-Ferrero, Chap. III, 11). Without reason, Lombroso confessed he believed he had tuberculosis and would die from it. He also believed he was impotent, had a hernia, and was an idiot.

Lombroso said that, at age 19, he worried that he had chosen the wrong career, that he had bad study habits, and "that I was ugly. Last sad discovery I have yet to make, I am bad, I am bad, I am moved by the great, the good, the beauty but the commotion does not push me to act" (Lombroso-Ferrero, Chap. III, 11).

Lombroso would continue to deride himself in later entries. "I am honest but not good." And, "I am a good studious person, but not a thinker" (Lombroso-Ferrero, Chap. III, 11). Such would have been a torturous thought for someone embarking on an academic career.

Years later, when she was writing his biography, Lombroso's daughter Gina realized that depression had haunted her father for decades. She wrote that she and her family had thought that his periods of depression when they were children were because of the various fights he had to wage against detractors of his thesis of the "born criminal." But discovery of his diaries proved otherwise. Those diary entries "gave us to believe that this melancholy did not come from age or bitter experience of life, but should be attributed to some recurrent discomfort, or some atmospheric causes." Gina noted what was obvious, that Lombroso in Pavia first was gleeful with his new friends, but that happiness quickly gave way to the gloominess of Pavia, "where the mist covers the sun for months at a time" (Lombroso-Ferrero, Chap. III, 12). Lombroso's melancholy, it would seem, was also tinged with what we now call "seasonal affective disorder."

Lombroso was like many a student in college — he had little money. "He was poor," according to Montaldo, "He ate only bread and water." And, in a characteristic that foretold his future studies, "He never drank alcohol, he hated it. He believed it contributed to criminality" (S. Montaldo, personal communication, September 20, 2016). As far as original academic work went, he did little. Perhaps his depression sapped his mental energies. However, he did complete a paper, published in the *Collettora dell'Adige*, in which he attempted to show that "intelligence, instinct, and spirit" were directly related to the "genitals." Essentially, his thesis was that, the more reproductively prolific was an "animal," the less intelligence it possessed (Lombroso-Ferrero, Chap. III, 13).

To Padova

Lombroso's depression made his time in Pavia untenable. When his friend Mantagazza — Paola II — left the city, Lombroso quickly departed as well. He went to Padova, where he enrolled in the university there, in 1854. The change did nothing to brighten his mood, even though Padova was "more artistic and sunnier" than Pavia. Lombroso found his professors not up to par with those in Pavia, and he was isolated from friends.

Given his tendency toward melancholy and his insistence on worrying about his health, it is no wonder that Lombroso was also shy around women. He was attracted to them, certainly, but prone to more drama than love in romance as would befit a poet. "There is a great difference in the effect inspired by the sight of a beautiful woman's face and the theories of an old philosopher. The difference there is between form and reality," young Lombroso wrote (Lombroso-Ferrero, Chap. III, 15).

In fact, a young woman had inspired Lombroso's diary entry. Eloisa Della Zara was a 17-year-old Jewish girl in Padova. Brunette, with a "sweet face, large black eyes . . . and very, very fair skin." She was sweet, cheerful, kind. She lived with her grandparents, and Lombroso visited them in 1855, but apparently he was unable to impress her. His diary revealed his plight.

Lombroso admitted that he was shy, but at the same time he tried to console himself that he was trying to avoid being boastful. He expressed something of Paul's biblical lament when he proclaims that "Often when I want to do one thing I do the contrary. When I want to attract I try to escape. When I want to hide a thing it is just when I express it better and more clear" (Lombroso-Ferrero, Chap. III, 16). In short, he was tongue-tied and stymied in the presence of Eloisa. As he observed, "Young men who would like to talk to a woman start talking when the woman is out" (Lombroso-Ferrero, Chap. III, 16).

Lombroso could not tell Eloisa his feelings. Instead he confessed them to his diary. "Oh how I wanted to kiss you, to press you tight in ecstasy as one's dream only and always the pleasure of vanity and ambition! Oh, to feel your virginal lips give me that oath! It is my conviction and I had to contradict myself, turn my shoulders instead of kissing you."

Cesare Lombroso was definitely in love, but his shyness, his intellect, his worry and tendency to overthink situations cost him the girl. Eloisa married another man several months later. Lombroso became suicidal (Lombroso-Ferrero, Chap. III, 17).

Lombroso returned to the solace of his diary. "There are cases in which the pleasure and love for a woman may take such a specific character in the nervous system as music for the musician so that the individual cannot live without it, as other[s] can eat only one kind of food, in those case[s] both madness and suicide are justified." (Lombroso-Ferrero, Chap. III, 17)

Lombroso continued, "Suicide is coward[ly] say those who do not feel coward[ice]. One must be [a] coward to believe suicide is [not] cowardice" (Lombroso-Ferrero, Chap. III, 17). His inability to attract Eloisa was a "great love defeat and that throws my soul to despair" (Lombroso-Ferrero, Chap. III, 17).

Lombroso apparently wrote several letters to Eloisa, all of them undelivered. He kept at least one, either with his diary or with other papers that his daughter discovered after his death. He wrote:

> This letter is the last one, probably not the first one, I write you. How many times did I ease my soul and painted you my admiration. And something more but all those letters I wrote for me and me alone! . . . The duty of hospitality held me back, and scolded me for my . . . in thought of a friendship that should have been that of friend, and also I was retained because I did not want to trouble you[r] serene and young heart because of a passion I was not able to repress. But you go away now, in the midst of your happiness and of the noise of the world, maybe you can suffocate a little sympathy for me. It would be too hard to leave you without telling you all I feel, and if I was not honest until the end, I do not feel at fault . . . if I was you can punish with your silence.
>
> . . . I studied you very well with intuition and with the analysis of the envious and enemy to try to find a few defects in you so as not to suffer you[r] absence so much but I did not find anything except a very light, a few stroke[s] of non-feminine violence . . . and that's all. I looked at you, here in Padova, as something more of divine reality, a sweet ray of sun in a cave. I looked at you for long moments without speaking. For the first time I felt that there is another love that that of science, which can give joy. I felt it so much that I lost both now.
>
> I never knew what were your thoughts, and I do not know them now. . . But I told too much. I will travel to far away lands. It will be years before I see you again or receive your news (Lombroso-Ferrero, Chap. III, 18).

Lombroso-Ferrero said that her father's romantic wound soon closed "as sadness was not organic with him. He had a temperament "too happy" to allow him not to forget Eloisa. Her words are not convincing, especially since she later admits that she recognized her father's tendency toward melancholy, and that she deliberately stayed by his side, even adopting his interest in criminal anthropology, so she could help keep his depression at bay. And while it may be true that Lombroso could one day speak about Eloisa "with tranquility," it is also true that he kept that last, undelivered letter.

In an effort to forget Eloisa, Lombroso fled Padova for Vienna (Lombroso-Ferrero, Chap. III, 19).

To Vienna

In Vienna, Lombroso found renewal. He left the depression of Padova behind and traded it for the happiness, art, culture, and scenery of the Austrian capital. He also realized that medicine was, indeed, his true calling. Even though Paolo Marzolo had urged him into medicine years earlier, Lombroso was not certain of it, even while attending Pavia and Padova. Professors at both places reduced medicine to theory, to lectures, dusty chalkboards, and readings. Never did they visit the sick or pursue hands-on learning with practicing doctors and ailing patients.

In Padova, Lombroso still clung to ideas that he might be a historian or some other type of philosopher. Perhaps even a dramatist or newspaper publisher. If he chose medicine as a profession, it would only be to support his other interests. In fact, one of the few creative efforts Lombroso produced in Padova sat astride the disciplines of medicine and history. The work was a 40-page monograph on the "Lunacy of Cardano." Girolamo Cardano (1501-1576) was a Pavian physician, mathematician, astrologer, and philosopher. He is well known in Renaissance studies, and suspected of a degree of madness. Lombroso's daughter, Gina, notes that, while the monograph does not have the "synthesis or complexity" of his earlier essays [which may point to his depressed state in Padova], it nevertheless bore the "first nucleus for his *Genius and Madness*," a work he would produce in the heyday of his career as a criminal anthropologist (Lombroso-Ferrero, Chap. IV, 1).

In Vienna, professors turned the stale pedagogies of Pavia and Padova upside down. They took students on hospital visits, allowed them to see and examine patients, and listened as the students offered diagnoses and prognoses. Of course, professorial experience and wisdom could temper youthful diagnostic enthusiasm. "This was . . . the first complete medical school Lombroso would see" (Lombroso-Ferrero, Chap. IV, 1-2). It cemented Lombroso in his desire to pursue medicine.

Lombroso's youthful depression dissipated — although depressive tendencies would follow him all his life. For now, though, he abandoned the diary entries, which were so often simply the repository of his regrets and hypochondriacal worries. To his friend Righi he wrote, "I tell you that I am happy. Here it is for the first time that I really start loving medicine. Half of my day I stay with sick people. I made friends with four or six lovely young men as you cannot find in Italy and I learn a lot from them. A good student here can teach to our professors, and I am far behind them."

In Padova, in the midst of his depression when he wrote the undelivered letter to Eloisa, he had admonished her to "do good for the pleasure of doing it." Including that statement in such a letter made it obvious that it was part of his own fiber. Until his arrival in Vienna he had no way expressing it. Now it was apparent.

"To do good, this is my religion," Lombroso later wrote. "I must do good for the good" (Lombroso-Ferrero, Chap. IV, 6). During his first year in Vienna, amid his medical studies, Lombroso realized that a particular medical problem in his home region was the first target of his quest to do good. He had now dedicated his life to public health and the finding of cures for both the physical and mental diseases that threatened the vitality of the Italian people. Lombroso-Ferrero wrote, "He concentrate[d] all his forces, up to that moment thrown in all directions, to study mental alienation extremely frequent and awful in Lombardo Veneta, what he calls in that part of the country the scorn of the foreigner: cretinism" (Lombroso-Ferrero, Chap. IV, 6).

Cretinism is a disease associated with chronic untreated iodine deficiency or hypothyroidism. It can present with or without a goiter, and may lead to stunted growth and mental disabilities. In 1857, cretinism was frequent in Lombardy. No one knew the cause or remedy.

Lombroso, now afire with purpose, spent the summer of 1857 touring Lombardy, intent on scientifically chronicling the disease and finding its cause. He fired off a note to his friend, Righi. "To give you some news I tell you I am studying the cretins and making observations on them." He did not know it, but the study would dominate much of his early professional career.

Long after his initial foray into the study, Lombroso published *Cretinismo in Lombardia*. In its preface, he harkened back to his original field research in 1857.

> The observer who looks at cretinism not in the quiet wards of an asylum but in city shacks or in village ones is stricken with terrible pain. His soul and his eyes will be tormented by [the] dark hovels, by those dirty roads, those gloomy faces of the inhabitants, by that horrible misery that you see everywhere. He will [be] sadly stricken by those new kind of man beasts who gro[a]n, stutter, squat in the middle of apathetic relatives, on which you see the affinity of blood and of the ailment both on their faces and on their throat. What happens then when you start talking to them and you see that the little ray of intelligence that still lights their little human body is full of the most ignoble form of egoism and wickedness (Lombroso-Ferrero, Chap. IV, 7).

Lombroso visited those shacks and hovels one by one. His daughter and first biographer, Gina, noted that he investigated "the air, the water, the sun, and the sick people" (Lombroso-Ferrero, Chap. IV, 7). She continued, "he will find out that cretinism has its . . . origin in bad water, his immediate reason in goiter, its cure in iodine, its prophilaxy in good aqueducts."

Once back in Vienna, Lombroso wrote his first study on cretinism. It propelled him on to the completion of his medical degree. In his assessments, Lombroso also concluded that "madness" (insanity) was "the bridge between theoretic and practical medicine" (Lombroso-Ferrero, Chap. IV, 6). And, just as he had with cretinism, Lombroso developed a special interest in finding a cure for pellagra (Lombroso-Ferrero, Chaps. IV, 5, 6; XX, 10).

As much as he liked Vienna, Lombroso did not want a degree embossed "with the sad decoration of the hated sovereign," that is, the emperor of Austria (Lombroso-Ferrero, Chap. IV, 10). He returned to Pavia, Italy, for the conferral of his degree. While there, Lombroso had the opportunity to organize the mental ward at St. Euphemia Hospital. The experience gave him additional clinical time to study the correlation between cretinism and insanity, and it gave him his first administrative experience, although unpaid (Lombroso-Ferrero, Chap. IV, 9).

Finally, on March 13, 1858, "on one of those rare sunny days," he received his doctorate from the University of Pavia. Cesare Lombroso was on his way to becoming one of united Italy's most recognized scientists, and one of its most controversial.

CHAPTER 2
In Patriotic Service

"*Lombroso's position cannot be separated from the historical context of Italian Unification.*"
—Dario Melossi

The next phase of Lombroso's young life would impact his career as much as his time in Vienna. He went to war in the name of the *Risorgimento*.

After graduation, Lombroso returned to Torino in Piedmont. He found his brother, Ecole, "tall but looking older." He visited his beloved Chieri. "There I see again, as a man, for the first time that same place that [as an] adolescent in which I felt the first palpitation of love." His daughter, Gina, theorizes that Piedmont also awakened him "a patriotic ardor." That is quite likely, for Piedmont was about to launch the next episode in the epic of Italian unification.

Just as Lombroso's academic career at the gymnasium coincided with the revolutions of 1848, his university career took place as Cavour aligned Piedmont to unite Italy. Cavour understood that any Piedmont-led unification of the Italian peninsula required, first, respect for Piedmont-Sardinia in foreign affairs, and, second, a powerful ally. If the first goal of Italian independence and unification was pushing Austria out of its northern regions, then one of those allies, obviously, had to be either England or France. Luckily for Cavour, a crisis in the Crimea presented an opportunity to achieve the latter.

The Crimean War erupted in October 1853 after Russia attempted to exercise control over Ottoman Turks in modern Romania. After the Turks declared war on Russia, Great Britain and France followed suit in early 1854. Russia moved out of the western Black Sea regions to avoid frightening Austria into the war, but fighting continued around the Crimean Peninsula. In 1855, Cavour and Sardinia sided with France and England.

In negotiations following the war, France's Emperor Napoleon III agreed to support Sardinia in any war to push Austria out of Lombardy and Venitia. Cavour was able to do just that in 1859 by staging military maneuvers and calling for Sardinian volunteers to roust Austria from the north. Fighting wrested Lombardy from Austria; negotiations took the port of Venice from them. As part of a pre-war agreement, Sardinia ceded the region of Savoy and the city of Nice to France. Italian unification, or the *Risorgimento* (or the Rising Again) was under way. In 1860, thanks to an amphibious and mobile land campaign under Guiseppe Garibaldi, Piedmont annexed most of the boot of the Italian peninsula, including the Kingdom of the Two Sicilies, Tuscany, much of the Papal States, Modena, and Parma.

Venitia, which included Lombroso's home of Verona, would not become part of greater Italy until 1866, and the region around Rome not until 1870. Rome, which had until the year before been under a French protectorate became the new capital of united Italy in 1871. The unification of Italy was emblematic of the forces for change in Europe and Lombroso played an important role as a member of the northern Italian intelligentsia. The military campaigns exemplified Lombroso's desire to see a unified nation. They also gave him an opportunity to pursue his interest in anthropology, ethnology, psychiatry and the place and identity of man in a new social environment.

******

In 1859, "without a word to his parents," Cesare Lombroso grabbed up a few books, went to Milan, and sought admittance into the Italian army (Lombroso-Ferrero, Chap. V, 2). Given his hatred of the Austrian occupation of Venitia, his enlightened liberal education, and his schooling in Genoa, which was in the Piedmont region, it is no surprise that Lombroso became fully involved in the *Risorgimento*. In fact, "Lombroso's position cannot be separated from the historical context of Italian Unification in 1861 and the subsequent annexation of large provinces," writes Lombroso scholar Dario Melossi. "This is the not irrelevant backdrop to Lombroso's story." Just out of school in Genoa, Lombroso enlisted as a medic in the revolutionary, pro-unification army of

Piedmont. He displayed not only a proud Italian nationalism, but also began his own campaign to put Italian science at the forefront of European academics (Melossi, 155).

Lombroso-Ferrero agreed. "How could the son of a mother who had voluntarily gone into exile so that her children be free, sit back and wait for the turn of events? [How could] the nephew of David Levi, who had conjured with the Frateli Banderi? His fatherland needed him, too many Italians had left the freedom of Italy go to pieces, quieting their heart and mind with ingenious sophism" (Lombroso-Ferrero, Chap. V, 2). Lombroso's personal maxim — "To do good, this is my religion. I must do good for the good" — must have sounded strongly within the young man's own heart and mind.

Information on Lombroso's military career is spotty. Records for him in the Piedmont army, simply, do not exist. Silvano Montaldo, director of the Lombroso museum in Turin, reports that the museum has no official records of Lombroso's military service. Thus, information on Lombroso's military service must be teased out of other sources, namely his daughter, Gina's, biography. It is ironic that, for a man who would spend so much of his life painstakingly recording research information, so little information exists on this formative part of Lombroso's life (S. Montaldo, interview, September 20, 2016).

However, it is also symptomatic of a casual Piedmontese attitude toward enlistees and volunteers. While Cavour and Victor Emmanuel knew that widespread participation in the army was necessary to put the stamp of legitimacy on Piedmont's victories, they nevertheless did not like the prospect of many non-Piedmontese flooding the army, and thus potentially moving up into the elitist body of its officer corps. What resulted was a mixed series of enlistment terms. In 1854, Piedmont had lofty goals to have most men 21 or older serve in rolling enlistments of five to eight years, with either five or six of those in the reserves. Medical deferments were easy and frequent.

Lombroso, however, was determined. He was mustered into service, and on May 27, 1859, the army assigned him as assistant physician to the Piedmontese Sanitary Military Corps for the duration of the war (Lombroso-Ferrero, Chap. V, 3). Lombroso-Ferrero reports that her father acclimated well to military life, which was so different from that of an academic. "In war, under the tent, in the hospital, in the barracks, there were no anomalies as cretinism on which to study the origin, [or] even lunatics on whom to write the history of man." Rather, Lombroso performed surgeries on wounded men, cleaned bandages, treated men sick with the common camp diseases of typhus and cholera, and "infections to try to stem with the little means of a camp hospital" (Lombroso-Ferrero, Chap. V, 3).

The scientific community was still several years away from accepting that germs and bacteria spread disease. While Lombroso had no part in that process, he did serendipitously discover a connection during his military service. He noticed that soldiers frequently suffered infection — often deadly — after battlefield amputations. Reasoning that dirty bandages might be contributing to gangrene, Lombroso replaced them with cotton saturated in alcohol. "It was a very coarse antiseptic method . . , but very successful in his department" (Lombroso-Ferrero, Chap. V, 3).

From this period exists a lone photograph of Lombroso in uniform. Lombroso, who at most could have been 24, has the angular face and dark hair of youth. The moustache and goatee that would so characterize his appearance are already present. He wears the dark, double-breasted, skirted tunic of a Piedmontese officer, replete with sash and belt. He rests his left hand on the hilt of a dress sword; in his right he holds an indistinguishable piece of paper. His plumed officer's dress hat sits on a prop table, while behind him stands a prop column reminiscent of ancient Rome (Lombroso image). One would like to see the obverse of the photo, if it has any sentiment written by the man himself, for the image is much like the thousands of *carte de visites* (visiting cards) that thousands of American Civil War soldiers — serving at roughly the same time — had taken in camps to send home to their mothers and sweethearts.

Lombroso authority Luigi Guarnieri, in an introduction to Lombroso's short reminiscence *In Calabria*, cites that same, lone photograph. He says that Lombroso "looks like a little man no taller than one meter and sixty," and he wears "his round glasses slipped halfway up the slope of the nose" (Lombroso, *In Calabria*).

While Guarnieri notes that Lombroso worked on "several battlefields" and earned a medal for bravery, (Lombroso, *In Calabria*) it is unclear where he gained that merit.

Lombroso may have been present at the battle of Magenta, June 4, 1859, when allied French and Peidmontese troops soundly defeated Austrians in the penultimate battle of the contest for northern Italy. He could also have attended the fallen from any of the numerous skirmishes as Allied troops negotiated railways, clogged roads, and pontoon river crossings while shoving Austrians incontrovertibly to the east (Schneid, 46-51).

Was Lombroso at the bloody battle of Solferino on June 24, 1859, fought west of his boyhood home, Verona? Perhaps — the battle was savage enough to put any doctor through his paces. There, 138,000 French and Piedmontese troops smashed 129,000 Austrians in a fight that caused nearly 4,700 combined deaths; 23,000 wounded; and some 12,000 soldiers missing. Historian Ciro Paoletti effectively sums up the carnage:

> The fight was terrible and bloody. Stormy weather disturbed operations. At sunset the Austrians were completely defeated. . . . Thousands of wounded and dead covered the countryside. The Medical Corps was exhausted and overwhelmed by the work. All the field hospitals, churches, monasteries, villas, and houses were filled with wounded. Brescia, the nearest city, had no more room in its hospitals. Cemeteries were full and graves were dug everywhere, including along the railway. It was such a horrific sight that a Swiss observer, Henry Dunat, decided to do something to help the wounded and relieve their suffering. After his experience at Solferino, he established the Red Cross (Paoletti, 108).

A historian's job is certainly not to make assumptions. In Lombroso's case, at least with regard to his military career, some assumption — extrapolation, perhaps — is necessary. Magenta and Solferino were the only major battles in the north after Lombroso proffered his enlistment. In 1860, the battles of the *Risorgimento* shifted to the south when Garibaldi's fabled 1,000 fought in Sicily and the Papal States. Montaldo says Lombroso never met or served with Garibaldi, plus Guarnieri suggests that Lombroso spent much of 1860 writing. That year he penned a variety of papers based on military traumas, indicating he had seen plenty of it. There is some safe margin for surmising that Lombroso was present at Magenta and Solferino, or at least cared for the wounded recoiling from those fights.

Among the writing that Lombroso did in 1860 was, according to Guarnieri, the beginning of a study of "medical-psychological fragments" (post-traumatic stress in soldiers, possibly?); a study of the case of a diaphragmatic hernia; and a chronicle of the abuse of "emollient poultices." But what most occupied Lombroso were two papers on battlefield amputations. Rifled, large-caliber weapons of the time — such as the French Minié and the Tyrolese rifles of the Piedmontese *bersaglieri* (rapid deployment, light infantry) — had outpaced medicine, and field doctors could do little with bullet-smashed limbs other than amputate them. Lombroso surely must have done his share of amputations, for Guarnieri says his papers were based on their "macabre memory."

His work was comprehensive enough that the papers received the Riberi Prize, a monetary award from the Turin Academy of Medicine (Lombroso, *In Calabria*). That was the only professional academic award Lombroso ever received (*JewishEncyclopedia.com*).

With the fighting of 1859 over, Lombroso assumed he would leave the army, although he suspected the war was not truly over. After all, Verona and Venezia were still under Austrian control, "Rome was with the Pope, [and] the treat of Villafranca seemed to the Italians more an armistice than real peace." Lombroso's superior officers, noting the recovery of men under his care, asked him to stay in the service. As enticement, they promoted him to medical officer, second class. He accepted. "It was not strange that the young man who had voluntarily entered the army would stay on, waiting for imminent events" (Lombroso-Ferrero, Chap. V. 3).

Surprisingly, given his predilection for youthful worry and hypochondria, Lombroso fit in well in his military surroundings. "He could march without fatigue, did not tire easily, he had minimum need to eat and drink and an extraordinary facility to sleep, study, and think whenever and wherever he had a few minutes free (Lombroso-Ferrero, Chap. V, 4).

"Discipline was compensated for him in the advantage to live among so many young men, all enthusiastic and passionate for a common ideal — the fatherland." Lombroso liked his army friends, and enjoyed typical soldierly pranks and jokes with them. They also liked him. [H]is comrades admired his intelligence and asked for his advices" (Lombroso-Ferrero, Chap. V, 4). Clearly, Lombroso had grown into himself.

Lombroso's stint in the army also did not require him to forego his other interests and researches. Marzolo's tutelage served him well. "Marzolo had taught him how he could from the few words of a child reconstitute some of the laws of the history of humanity; he had taught him to read in the book of nature always open to everybody, everywhere, at every time. He had taught him that wherever you are you can gather stones that will be a part of the mosaic being slowly formed in one's own thoughts" (Lombroso-Ferrero, Chap. V, 4).

Lombroso mixed his military duties with research. He wrote a study of his wartime observations about combat wounds. He stressed that hospitals were best for "preventive" cures, field hospitals best for "operative" cures. Obviously, Lombroso's work relied heavily on the countless amputations he performed. He also noted differences in responses to operations and treatments depending on a soldier's race and region of origin (Lombroso-Ferrero, Chap. V, 8).

The *Magazine of Military Medicine* published Lombroso's study. Its positive reception encouraged the army to give Lombroso another promotion, this time to Medical Officer, First Class.

But the Italian Army had other plans. For three months (at least) in 1862, the Piedmontese army stationed Lombroso in Calabria — the furthest southern region of Italy, essentially the "toe" of Italy's boot. There the army fought "brigandage" — outlawry — as Piedmont endeavored to crush resistance to the northern-led *Risorgimento*. Piedmont soldiers fought Calabrian partisans in a struggle that greatly resembled that of the United States trying to pacify a recalcitrant South after its defeat in the Civil War. The Calabrian campaign included, to a large degree, the hunting down of criminals and their supporting families and friends.

The Piedmontese might have expected the outbreak of violent resistance in the south. Long under the Bourbon dynasty, southern Italy put up a serious fight when Napoleon moved to take the Kingdom of Naples in 1806. Likewise, Calabrians saw the *Risorgimento* not so much as a movement to unite one Italy, but as an invasion from the north. Lower classes in the region — men and women, old and young — took up arms against the Piedmontese. They included individual bandits and their gangs, the Camorra and Mafia. Both the Camorra and Mafia were secret criminal organizations. The Camorra had its origins in the prison system and was strongest in Calabria. The Mafia controlled western Sicily and served as a de facto government in the absence of any real national governmental authority.

Their tactics were the age-old ones of partisans and guerrillas. They would attack regular troops, communications lines, depots, and supporters, then fade back into the mountainous wilds of the south. Without uniforms, they appeared as civilians, and regular soldiers could not easily identify them. Thus, they suspected everyone.

Piedmont, now styling itself the Kingdom of Italy, called this resistance "brigandage;" its practitioners were *briganti*. This Brigands War lasted from 1861 to 1865 in the main, and sparked and sputtered for some years after that. It forced Piedmont to commit 120,000 troops to the pacification of the region. Of them, nearly 1,000 were killed or wounded in action or went missing. In turn, troops killed 2,400 brigands, captured some 4,000 others of whom about 1,000 were executed. A few of those, at least, were executed by a firing squad shooting them in the back, since shooting them front-on was considered too good for such outlaws (Dickie, 122).

Indeed, Piedmont officers publicly staged executions to serve as warnings. Writes John Dickie, "Administering justice to a brigand was something of a spectacle. Executions were often carried out in town squares. Failing that, the corpses or heads of bandits could be put on public display" (Dickie, 124).

Newly united Italy did more than just hunt down and kill the outlaws. It labeled and conceptualized them, cast them in the role of unpatriotic rebels who stood in the way of peaceful unification. The word "brigand" carried more of an unpatriotic, treasonous connotation than "bandit" or "outlaw." Plus, victorious Piedmont intended to write their history and deprive them of any Robin Hood pathos. "For the army, brigandage functioned as a conceptual grid through which a great variety of activities were understood," writes Dickie. "Of these, the first was the anathematization of brigandage as the inversion of the nation, society, or the law; in the minds of the officer class, and of sections of Northern Italian society, the fight against banditry became the battle between civilization and barbarism, reason and violence, humanity and inhumanity, social order and crime. Animality, to give just one example, is a constant theme of writers on brigandage: 'They kill and rape like beasts thirsty for blood and booty and not men created in the image of God'" (Dickie, 121-122).

Frederick Schneid sums the war up well when he writes: "The new Italian government considered the peasant unrest a reflection of both Bourbon sympathies and the backward nature of the people of the south" (Schneid, 88).

Southern Italy was, in the words of Lombroso, a place where the inhabitants "tend to be unstable, and to subordinate the interests of the community and state to the individual" (Lombroso, 1911/2012, 3). Southern Italy was associated with lingering feudal controls over land ownership and governance, subsistence farming, and general lawlessness. Lombroso noted, "the number of crimes increases as we go from north to south" (Lombroso, 1911/2012, 14). The increase in murder rates and violent crimes in general, he explained, "corresponded to the . . . most barbaric parts of the peninsula and, more often, its islands" (Gibson & Rafter, 2006, 316). The southern Italian peninsula to Lombroso was an "extremely primitive" land of inferior people tied to a rural agricultural economy and culture, and given to crime by nature (Lombroso-Ferrero, Chap. V, 9-11).

Certainly the presence of the Camorra and the Mafia contributed to the reality of violence and the perception that southern Italy was out of control and inhabited by a primitive people. How to assimilate and develop or "modernize" this region formed the Southern Question. Lombroso was not a fatalist regarding southern Italy, beyond military intervention he held faith in political and socio-economic reforms that could resolve the Southern Question (D' Agostino, 2002, 322).

Lombroso's new posting was an obvious derailment for his career. Still, he made the best of it. "Calabria became a source for his studies," Lombroso-Ferrero writes. "The little towns were extremely primitive. He [got] a great kick out of his beauty of nature, especially after the horrible villages. His notes are full of description of the beauty and variety of the countryside, where the wheat is grown amid cactus, where the olive is mixed with orange and bergamotto trees" (Lombroso-Ferrero, Chap. V, 9).

Lombroso enjoyed observing the regions' men — "rugged, uncivilized but you can see in the way they carry themselves, in their languages, in their songs, traces of the old races from which they come" (Lombroso-Ferrero, Chap. V, 9). In villages such as Revi, Rocarforte, Cadety, Pondefori, Galige, Korio, and Amenda, Lombroso observed Calabrians and kept journals. His fascination with anthropology and psychology were both at the forefront of his curiosity (Lombroso-Ferrero, Chap. V, 9). The Piedmontese conceptualization of Calabrian brigands and their war, however, would also lend an unintended taint to Lombroso's future signature work.

In his field notes, Lombroso wrote that a keen observer could tell that many Calabrians descended from Greeks. "Their name will tell it, and so will their skull, their high forehead, their straight nose, their large black eyes," he wrote, focusing on characteristics that would be so prevalent in his later work (Lombroso-Ferrero, Chap. V, 10).

In St. Nicola, Spezzano, Celso, Frasinetto, Porcile, and St. Mauro, Lombroso detected signs of "Albanian predominance." He wrote, "Their souls are strong and proud, they are dressed with the costumes of Epirus, and they have the same traditions of their country of origin" (Lombroso-Ferrero, Chap. V, 10).

As he studied Albanian descendants, Lombroso continued his fascination with physical attributes, especially facial characteristics. "They have high stature; contour of the highest head; direction of the horizontal jaw, straight nose, small eyes, lymph-muscular temperament. Excellent runners, skilled [in] hunting" (Lombroso, *In Calabria*, 40).

In attitudes, Lombroso found Albanians of a "proud spirit, fierce indeed, [feel greatly] the duty to take revenge, not [above] murder and domestic theft, least of [all] goats," Lombroso wrote (Lombroso, *In Calabria*, 40). But Lombroso found in the Albanians a great "human contradiction." He said they feel "more delicately [than] us the honor offenses . . . [they are] patient, persistent, and at the same time fantastic and imaginative" (Lombroso, *In Calabria*, 40).

They also had little tolerance for political entities and state borders. And they hated what they saw as "tyrannical policy." He also continued to focus on the physical characteristics, not just of Albanian descendants, but of all Calabrians. He divided them into two categories: Greco-Roman descendants, who he described as bearing a "manly and noble imprint," and the more Slavic Albanian descendants. He described them as having a "Semitic dolichocephalous skull, the arched nose, eyebrows close together and . . . black or brown eyes." He described blacks, coming from North Africa, as having a "protruding upper jaw . . . frizzy hair . . . and dermis bronzino kamitic [bronze skinned African, perhaps Egyptian]." Those, he noted, did not have the "pure oval" face of the Greco-Romans (Lombroso, *In Calabria*, 53).

Lombroso also categorized Sicilians as less meritorious than the Greco-Roman descendants. He said they tended toward "laziness" and "idleness." Calabrians hated them (Lombroso, *In Calabria*, 86).

Lombroso continued to tend wounded soldiers, and perhaps brigands, but the region of Calabria pulled his attention to other fields of study. Luigi Guarnieri says that, while in Calabria, Lombroso was certainly "proud of his military status, but in reality [he had] already taken the irrevocable decision to leave the army" (Lombroso, *In Calabria*, Introduction in e-book version). Lombroso and his indefatigable mind became fascinated with the region, its geography, its resources, and, especially, its people. His short work *Three Months in Calabria* (published in serial form in *Contemporary Magazine* in 1862, then as a single volume in 1863), included chapters on Cal-

Colorful clothing worn by the brigand Gasprone.

Museo di Antropologia Criminale "Cesare Lombroso," University of Turin, Italy]

abria's physical geography; the Calabrian people's literature and folk-songs; the region's schools and public hygiene; their medical traditions; their marriage customs; and their morality and criminal behaviors (Lombroso, *In Calabria*, 47-50). The latter, of course, would consume most of the rest of his professional life.

Lombroso himself called his time in Calabria "one of the most striking moments of my life. . . . When still young, still believing and trusting in the destinies and glories of the fatherland [united Italy], dressed [in a] military uniform, and forcibly detached from books . . . I suddenly found myself face to face with a new world." Lombroso said he was "compelled to scrutinize" this new world, to examine its land and people. Three decades later, when editing his earlier work *In Calabria* with the help of Calabrese Dr. Giuseppe Pelaggi, Lombroso lamented that he had spent only three months in the region (Lombroso, *In Calabria*, iii).

But Calabria also reaffirmed in Lombroso his interest in anthropometry, or the "measuring" of human subjects. Lombroso also discovered that the army in Calabria was the perfect place to begin his studies. As Lombroso authority Mary Gibson writes, "[Lombroso's] genius, in fact, rested on the realization that captive populations could be measured, observed, and interviewed for the purpose of formulating theories based on biological and psychological 'facts.'" Gibson, of course, refers to Lombroso's future work in studying prison populations, but in 1862 a regiment of soldiers would work just fine (Simon, 2142; Gibson, "Prison Science," 31; *JewishEncyclopedia.com*).

Not only did Calabria offer a variety of people for observation, the army did as well. It was a microcosm of all of Italy for scientific study. The mass appeal of the unification movement drew volunteers from all of the Italian regions, and Lombroso took advantage of their proximity. He began a study of some 3,000 soldiers, writes Wolfgang, "seeking to analyze and to express metrically the physical differences which he had noted among the inhabitants of the various regions of Italy." With that information he would begin an "ethnographical-anthropological chart of Italy" (Wolfgang, 1961, 362; *JewishEncyclopedia.com*).

Lombroso literally "measured" soldiers by hand, taking note of their weight, height, skull size, and other characteristics such as endurance and resistance to disease. "He became so good that he was able at first glance to know where the man came from, a Tuscan from a Lombard from a Venetian, a normal from an abnormal" (Lombroso-Ferrero, Chap. V, 5). He also collected skeletons and skulls to further his anthropological studies of human identity and difference. Certainly one area of interest associated with anthropology was the standard of living and issues of health. The overall poor health of southern Italians, particularly in Calabria especially interested Lombroso (Lombroso-Ferrero, Chap. XIX, 1).

Lombroso became so adept at his measurements and observations, that he began making predictions about his subjects' futures. His friends were amazed, and apparently some of his predictions were current enough and accurate enough that they began suspecting him of "strange forms of magic" (Lombroso-Ferrero, Chap. V, 5). When a soldier from Rome, Francesco Siacci by name, had Lombroso measure his head, the surgeon proclaimed it "the most beautiful head he had ever seen." He added that Siacci would be a great man. Indeed, Siacci became one of Italy's best-known mathematicians, a professor of ballistics at the Italian military academy, and a professor in higher mechanics at the University of Turin (Lombroso-Ferrero, Chap. V, 5; "Francesco Siacci," accessed May 15, 2017).

The most obvious characteristic Lombroso observed among the soldiers was their habit of getting tattoos, especially "obscene designs." Men with such body art Lombroso soon categorized as "infractious soldiers." Lombroso said, "I was struck by a characteristic that distinguished the honest soldier from his vicious comrade: the extent to which the latter was tattooed and the indecency of the designs that covered his body." He also began to identify tattooing as "characteristic of criminals" (Wolfgang, 1961, 362, 369).

Lombroso never lost his fascination with tattoos. As late as 1896, writing for, of all publications, *Popular Science Monthly*, Lombroso maintained the connection of tattoos with criminals. He said that, of 2,739 soldiers he had examined (most, presumably, during his time in Calabria), only one to two percent of them bore tattoos. Later, out of a study of 5,000 criminals, he found that nearly 12.5 percent of them had tattoos. That "observation . . . demonstrated to me that this custom is held in too great honor among them" (Lombroso, *Savage Origin*, 8).

Worse, to Lombroso, was that, while soldiers limited their tattooing to their arms and chests, criminals practiced whole-body tattooing. Throughout his career, Lombroso endeavored to illustrate on paper the various types of tattoos he encountered. He was careful to note that many criminals bore tattoos on their faces, backs, thighs, fingers, and penises. Lombroso wrote:

> A certain T——, thirty-four years of age, who had passed many
> years in prison, had not, except on his cheeks and loins, a surface
> the size of a crown that was not tattooed. On his forehead could be

read *Martyr de la Liberté* (Martyr of Liberty); the words being surmounted by a snake eleven centimetres long. On his nose he had a cross, which he had tried to efface with acetic acid (Lombroso, *Savage Origin*, 13).

Lombroso also noted that many criminals wore cryptic sayings on their bodies, many reflecting what the convicts thought of themselves, their lives, and situations. "*Malheur a moi! Quelle sera ma fin?* (Woe to me! What will be my end?)," one man's tattoo asked; another's proclaimed "*Né sous une mauvaise étoile* (Born under an evil star)." Others swore out vengeance or punishment to others: "*Je jure de me venger* (I swear to avenge myself)," one said, while another promised to "*Éventre tout le monde* (disembowel everybody)" (Lombroso, *Savage Origin*, 11).

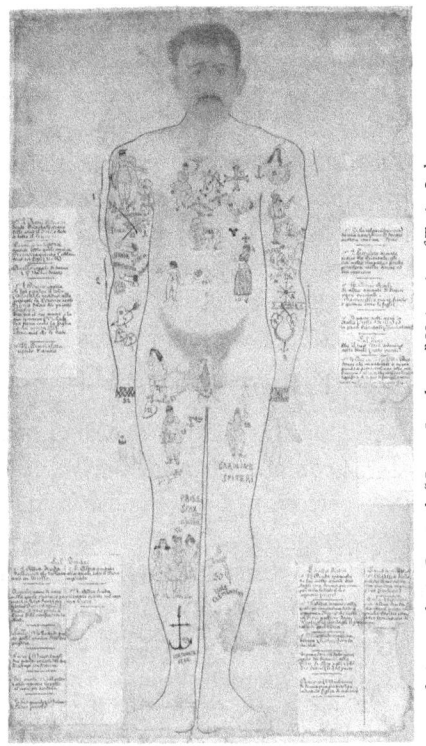

A Criminal's body tattoos.

Muse di Antorpologia Criminale "Cesare Lombroso," University of Turin, Italy

A man whom Lombroso called "Malassen, a ferocious assassin [who was also] an executioner of convicts," bore extravagant illustrations of his life story. He was covered from his feet to his head with grotesque and frightful tattoo marks. On his breast he had drawn a red and black guillotine, with the words in red letters: *J'ai mat commencé, je finirai mat. C'est la fin qui m'attend* (I have begun evil, I shall end evil. That is the end that awaits me). His right arm, which had inflicted death upon so many human beings, bore the terrible device, very appropriate to his hand, *Mort à la chiourme* (Death to the convict) (Lombroso, *Savage Origin*, 10).

Lombroso noted that, as many criminals got their first tattoos between the ages of 9 and 16 years old, the practice might display a spirit of "precociousness." Others got tattooed for "a love of distinction," that is, to make themselves unique. Others were just the opposite, getting tattooed because their peers had done so. Lombroso also saw in various tattooed statements and slogans a type of hieroglyphic that tied together communities — whether regional or criminal.

"But the primary, chief cause that has spread this custom among us is in my opinion atavism," wrote Lombroso. By the time he wrote *The Savage Origin of Tattooing*, the term "atavism" had become especially associated with Lombroso's work. Atavism, simply, was a reversion in man to a primitive state. He tended to classify most criminals as atavistic. Citing prehistoric finds in Europe and Africa, Lombroso said, "Tattooing is, in fact, one of the essential characteristics of primitive man, and of men who still live in the savage state." Including a brief anthropological field guide of Pacific islands (and revealing his own Eurocentric racism), Lombroso said: "I do not believe there is a single savage people that does not tattoo more or less," and "Tattooing is the true writing of savages, their first registry of civil condition." He concluded

> After this study, it appears to me to be proved that this custom is a completely savage one, which is found only rarely among some persons who have fallen from our honest classes, and which does not prevail extensively except among criminals, with whom it has had a truly strange, almost professional, diffusion; and, as they sometimes say, it performs the service among them of uniforms among our soldiers. To us they serve a psychological purpose, in enabling us to discern the obscurer sides of the criminal's soul, his remarkable vanity, his thirst for vengeance, and his atavistic character, even in his writing (Lombroso, *Savage Origin*, 40-41).

Lombroso's adventure in Calabria convinced him that he needed to return full time to science and academia. Conscious that other of his peers, who had stayed in the universities rather than go to war, were already bolstering their careers, Lombroso determined he would leave the army. Guarnieri theorizes that, even while posing for the one extant photo of himself in uniform, Lombroso had already made that "irrevocable decision. . . . [He] does not aspire to the triumphs of war," but rather to the work of science (Lombroso, *In Calabria*, Introduction, e-book version).

The army, however, wanted to keep Lombroso, and it offered him a compromise. In April 1862, the army allowed Lombroso to transfer his military assignment back north to Pavia so that he could present lectures on psychiatry at the university (Lombroso-Ferrero, Chap. V, 13). "The army was doing everything possible to keep [Lombroso] among them," writes Lombroso-Ferrero. But "Lombroso, who seemed happy, still had now had enough of it. He wants more, he is thinking up new theories and wants to do something [else]. All his comrades in school who had not been in the war are all [in] universities making rapid careers. Mantegazza, Tebaldi, Roncati, [told] him that they had been named full professors to Pavia, and Bologna. He did not dare to think [of] such a post but what he wanted was to teach" (Lombroso-Ferrero, Chap. V, 8),

Lombroso worked at the military hospital at Pavia, and he started lectures at the university soon after. In his lectures he stressed what had become his major career objectives, "examination, prophilaxis, classification [, and] cure of mental alienate[s]" (Lombroso-Ferrero, Chap. V, 8). Panizza, by then the president of the University of Pavia, offered Lombroso the chance to not just lecture, but run an entire course on psychiatry. Pavia did not pay Lombroso for the course, and the position carried no academic rank. Nevertheless, the prospect of the course as a career-starter excited the young professor.

Lombroso continued his studies into cretinism and pellagra, and he began pursuing interests in racial theory, the effects of geography and climate on health and race, mental health and "alienation" (insanity), and criminal behavior. These interests culminated in the publication in 1865 of *Studies of Medical Geography of Italy*, which traced pathology related to the environment and climate, illness derived from "food and drink," and the impact of race on disease (Lombroso-Ferrero, Chap. V, 20).

In 1863 the army gave Lombroso temporary leave so that he could attend the university in Genoa to further his study of psychiatry, and present lectures at the University of Pavia on the topics of criminals and epileptics and links between them in addition to questions of insanity and crime (Lombroso-Ferrero, Chap. V, 11, 13). Following this series of lectures, Lombroso published *Introduction to the Clinical Course on Mental Disease*. This was his first publication linking pellagra with insanity, genius, and criminality (Wolfgang, 1961, 363).

On January 1, 1864, Lombroso got leave from the army so that he could teach full time at University of Pavia for the academic year. That same year, Lombroso began his formal study of criminals and criminal behavior in association with his continued study of insanity. The army recalled Lombroso to service in 1865. He served for seven months in 1866 through the renewed war with Austria. Lombroso rose in rank from to First Class Medical Officer at the battalion level. Then he mustered out of military service for good (Lombroso-Ferrero, Chap. V, 3, 8, 17, 18, 21).

CHAPTER 3
The Making of a Criminologist

"In our civilized world, to note the proof of the influence of race upon crime is both easier and more certain."

—Cesare Lombroso

Science in the 19th century challenged the conventional understanding of man, his origin and environment. The 19th century was an era of research on pathologies and their origin. Interest in criminal anthropology was widespread in Europe. Cesare Lombroso was not the first to question the role of man and his behavior within the natural environment, but he was the first to link anthropology, biology and medical-psychology with criminal behavior (Wolfgang, 1961; Gibson, 2002 6; Rafter et al., 2016). In that linkage, Lombroso sought to explain a relationship between criminal psychopathology and a criminal's physical constitution. He was the first to use science in the study of criminals and criminal behavior.

Even though Lombroso was now out of the Italian army, he still wanted to use his medical knowledge to advance the cause of the newly united nation. As he had started in Calabria, Lombroso focused his attention on criminals, or, more specifically, the characteristics of criminals. He believed that dealing with the public scourge of crime was critical to the survival of Italy; plus, it would prove Italy's place among the more established European nations. Of course, Lombroso did not work in a vacuum. The Enlightenment offered Lombroso a milieu of doctrines, theories, and practitioners among which to work. To fully grasp Lombroso's studies and conclusions, one must look at the intellectual mix in which he worked.

Nationalism

The era that provided a home to a range of intellectuals and schools of thought was that of Nationalism. Nationalism began with the collapse of the Napoleonic Empire in 1815, and, as already discussed, sped the desire of peoples to self-identify as independent nations. The Piedmont-led unification of Italy benefitted from that movement.

National identity, social order, and self-determination were powerful forces that animated Nationalism. The era was one of epochal change with rapid population growth, urbanization, an industrial revolution, increased agricultural productivity, mass transportation, improved public health, and cultural identity (Evans, 2016). Positivism and Materialism, and in a subordinate way, Naturalism, with their interest in the interactive role of man and society, and the nature of crime were complimentary and essential to the process of creating new nation states and democratization of the old traditional monarchies. As such, Nationalism presented Lombroso with the opportunity to participate in nation building and in particular the discerning observation of the societal issues of unity and discord reflected in crime and criminal behavior, factors that he linked with public health and the need for reform of the penal system. Just as Lombroso knew he personally wanted to participate in the military efforts to create the Italian state, he also recognized early in his career that science could help build a vibrant and healthy Italy. He wanted to make a contribution to its success (Rafter, Posick, & Rocque, 2016; Gibson, 2006; Melossi, 2000; Ellis, 1890/2010; Lombroso-Ferrero, Chap. X, 7).

Beccaria

Chief among those Enlightenment thinkers working on crime in this era was Cesare Beccaria (1738-1794). Indeed, Beccaria cast a long shadow over everything that Lombroso and his intellectual colleagues would do in the discipline. Students and practitioners of criminal justice (generally referred to as penal jurisprudence in the 18th and 19th centuries), often argued that man was a rational being who through choice informed his actions, for good or evil. Beccaria pioneered the concept linking individual choice and criminal responsibility to criminal behavior in his work, *Of Crimes and Punishment* (1764). With that publication, Beccaria originated the Classical School of Penal Jurisprudence. (In the 20th century that school of thought became the Classical School of Criminology, or simply Classical Criminology. The change in name represented the growing interest and professional preference for the theory of criminality.) His theory was the first modern attempt to explain the origin of crime within a moral system outside the context of religion. The seat of criminal behavior, Beccaria thought, was a question of immorality.

Beccaria's treatise signaled the final shift away from the medieval, Church-supported philosophy that sin caused crime. Beccaria moved it toward the idea that criminal behavior was a conscious choice by the individual. Beccaria's emphasis on the power of choice made individuals responsible for their crimes, but it also put society at great risk. The "despotic nature" and "self-interested passions" of every man, Beccaria argued, "are ranged against the universal good" (Bellamy, 1995, 9). A state "sovereign" was responsible for maintaining order and avoiding "chaos" and "anarchy" through the assurance of punishment (Bellamy, 1995, 9). Beccaria encouraged the state to grade crimes by their severity and punish them with uniform determinate sentences.

Beccaria focused his attention on the crime and the legal side of criminal justice, including the rightful place for punishment. Crime at its core was a juridical problem for the state, with little regard to the psyche of the accused. He emphasized law and punishment as a deterrent to crime. Swift implementation of the law and specific punishments for crimes committed were the deterrence. His interest, therefore, was on the act of crime and not the actor — the criminal.

For nearly a century the Beccarian School was the standard for European and American criminal justice. Individual responsibility placed man in the center of his environment and solely responsible for his actions. Not surprisingly, Beccaria's work created greater interest in crime and punishment. The etiology of crime became the focal point of much discussion and research among 19th century European intellectuals. The roles of inheritance or heredity and degeneracy in crime drew particular attention. For Lombroso, the Beccarian Classical School presented a platform and context for a competing divergent theory of criminality and punishment.

The Other "Isms"

In fact, Beccaria both helped create and worked within a series of intellectual movements that provided Lombroso and others with the tools to unseat the reigning theory of criminology. Those movements were a series of "isms:" Naturalism, Materialism, and Positivism. In the latter, Lombroso would stake his most famous claim.

Naturalism and Positivism shared the belief that natural laws governed the universe. Natural laws were rules of structure and behavior in the natural world. Natural Philosophy was a metaphysical theory about what exists using a cognitive-deductive approach to reality. The acquisition of knowledge was based on an assumed subjective paradigm, since there were multiple realities to choose from. Assembled data was generally non-numeric. The focus of research was descriptive analysis and context. Because of its metaphysical frame of study based on speculation, Naturalism was on the wane by the late 19th century.

The new scientific proof of reality required empirical verification before acceptance as reality. Empiricism, the argument went, simply trumped conjecture and abstract reasoning. Although Lombroso was not the founder of Positivism, his emphasis on inductive reasoning and the belief that knowledge is derived from empirical investigation and observation of "facts" and sensory experiences placed him within the Positivist School.

Positivism has a long history in western thought, but French philosopher Auguste Comte (1798-1857), regarded as one of the founders of sociology, created Positivism's modern method of analysis. Discovery of "positive" data or facts by objective observation, experience, or experimentation was the key to understanding natural law for Positivists. Observation is the cornerstone of original research methodology, and it served as the basis for Positivism. Positivist methodology included the process of identifying a problem or forming a question, conceptualizing a hypothesis, and then testing it for validity through the abundant collection of "facts." Proof was based less on the essential point of fact than on the collection of "facts" or data regardless of pertinence to the question, thus proving by quantity of material the point of the inquiry.

Positivism was an analytical philosophy based on the procedures of inductive reasoning/logic and experimentation. If natural laws could be truly discovered, they exist. Thus, man could predict natural phenomena — or crime. There was a strong deterministic element to Positivist thinking.

Positivists generally quantified data, even if it was descriptive in origin. The use of statistics for building comparative socio-metric models became more common and advanced following the work of Andre'-Michel Guerry, Adolphe Quetelet, and Francis Galton. Both schools of thought, Naturalism and Positivism, exist in the work of Lombroso, although Positivism is expressly dominant. Lombroso made a basic Naturalist's assumption that a criminal type existed, but he relied on the Positivist methodology of empiricism to describe, quantify, and predict the existence and behavior of criminal man.

However, Positivism could often fall into overdependence on a preponderance of "facts." Facts, regardless of specific value, often gave way to speculation and conjecture, even though logic was supposed to steer researchers away from presumptive thinking. Perhaps unwittingly, Lombroso would express the irony in logical thinking in the first edition of *Criminal Man* (1876) when he wrote: "nothing is more illogical than that which tries to be too logical" (92). It seems that in the end "facts" trumped logic and over-thinking the evidence.

A third philosophy gaining popularity in the 19th century also influenced Lombroso. That was German Materialism. To a Materialist, only things that existed *as matter* could be observed and studied. In the abstract, Materialism argued that matter or content preceded thought and ideas. In this simple explanation, the brain exemplified matter from which thought emerged by a biological process. Furthermore, Materialists regarded nature as existing matter, and therefore primary and ethical. A Materialist sought objective facts in contrast to the Positivist's demand for "positive" facts in abundance (Wolfgang, 1961, 52). Lombroso found it easy to infer from Materialistic logic that violence was a primordial reality in the domain of nature, therefore the atavistic or primitive criminal man was predisposed to violence and criminal behavior.

Materialism was in stark contrast to Idealism, which depended only on an idea or perception of reality. An Idealist saw the world as the realization of an absolute idea that was independent and existed before the world, thus an idea existed before matter or content (https:www.marxists.org/archive/marx/works/1886-feuerbach/ch02.hem). In the words of Karl Popper (1972), "only those things exist which can be observed" (295).

Influences and Practitioners

Working within the various theories were the scientists who both founded and expanded them. Not surprisingly, Charles Darwin (1809-1882) heads that list. Criminal anthropologists even before Darwin's publication of *The Origin of Species* in 1859 were exploring the secular idea of man's origin, questions of heredity and theories of evolution. In 1809 Jean-Baptiste Lamarck postulated that from spontaneous generation of life forms there was an inherent linear progression to greater complexity (e.g., man). Knowledge of Lamarck's theory among scholars was widespread and contributed to the discussion of evolution in 19th century Europe. However, it was Darwin who provided a scientific explanation for the theory of evolution, which became publically popular across society.

Darwin was a graduate (B.A.) of Cambridge University in 1831 with special interests in botany and geology. His five-year (1838-1843) voyage around the world on the survey ship the *HMS Beagle* provided Darwin with the observations that informed his theory of evolution. Darwin's *The Origin of Species* (1859) was both a bestseller and controversial. His theory that all species change over time through the process of evolution and that all life forms compete for survival seriously challenged the church's belief in creation by intelligent design. The ascendency of man over his environment was the new mantra for the age. Darwin's theory was deterministic in that the struggle for survival was predetermined internally, a matter of heredity, and yet not necessarily permanently fixed. In his book *Descent of Man* (1871), Darwin applied his theory to the evolution of man specifically.

Perhaps Darwin's greatest contribution was his theory of natural selection, which is a form of adaptive selection. In the evolutionary process of change, certain desirable traits are replicated and built on with each succeeding generation to assure the survival of the live form. Those with undesirable traits die off. He did not have the benefit of a theory of heredity and genetics, but his observations of the natural world opened new areas of study and would be substantiated in just a few short years by the work of Gregor Mendel.

Mendel was a priest in the Austria-Hungary Empire in what is today the Czech Republic. In 1866 after nearly a decade of study, Mendel (1822-1884) discovered the laws of heredity by breeding generations of peas. Lombroso incorporated the theory of heredity to his own definition of criminal man and his prodigy. Darwin's theory of evolution provided a biological basis for Lombroso's development of the criminal type (Mannheim, 1955).

Lombroso, of course, knew of Darwin's theory, but he would not have been able to read *The Origin of Species* until it was translated into Italian in 1876, the same year that Lombroso himself published Volume One of *Criminal Man* (Gibson, 2002). The case has been made that Paolo Marzolo, Lombroso's mentor and teacher, through his own interest in the history and evolution of language, contributed to Lombroso's concept of evolution (Gibson, 2002; Gibson, 2006; Kurella, 1911/2012, 5). It is certainly plausible that Lombroso's concept of evolution originated from their association. Nevertheless, Lombroso was thoroughly versed in Darwin's theory of evolution and natural selection during his university experience. Lombroso acknowledged that he was aware of Darwin's theory and that his own evolutionary theory for criminal man "smacked of Darwinism," nevertheless, he did not consider himself one of "Darwin's acolytes" (Gibson & Rafter, 2006, 236).

The work of Darwin and Mendel provided a biological context for Lombroso's own belief that evolution and heredity explained the origin of criminal man, his unwillingness or inability to change, and the subsequent impact that had on generations. In evolution Lombroso found the empirical evidence of natural laws at work. Criminal man was the product of biological determinism, not his environment; however, in response to both criticism and additional research, Lombroso would later acknowledge the casual effect of social and environmental factors.

Scientists studying the origins and nature of man all sought to identify the causes, manifestations, and structures of the pathological. Once identified, social threats could be isolated from society. For Lombroso and many researchers like him, the evolutionary origin of man was the beginning of knowledge (Mannheim, 1955). Although scholars were discussing evolution in Europe and especially in Italy long before Darwin published *The Origin of Species*, he was the first to give the theory a scientific basis and contextual narrative (Rafter et al., 2016). Lombroso made numerous inferences to Darwin's research conclusions regarding both man and the animal and plant kingdoms.

Herbert Spencer (1820-1903) had a limited formal education and was largely self-taught, nevertheless he became the leading English philosopher of his time. His interests ranged from philosophy, ethics, biology, anthropology, sociology, and political theory. Even before Darwin, Spencer believed that evolution was a progressive force in all nature, humankind and society, and the physical and cultural world of mankind. He coined the term "survival of the fittest" as his own expression of Darwin's use of "natural selection" to represent the struggle for the "preservation of favored races in the struggle for life"

(Spencer, 1864/207. Vol. I, 444). His *Principles of Biology* published in 1864 quickly became associated with Darwin and his theory. While Darwin focused on the evolutionary process of nature and competition for survival through natural selection, Spencer envisioned the same natural progression in a societal context as a struggle for survival.

Franz Joseph Gall (1758-1828) trained as a physician at the University of Strasbourg and in Vienna, Austria. Through powers of observation he deduced that certain behaviors and traits, related to personality and moral judgment, what he called "fundamental faculties," were independently located within the brain. He believed that these fundamental faculties (psychical facts of life) were discernable on the uneven geography or physical organization of the human skull caused by internal pressures (Ellis, 1890/2010). Gall called the reading of the skull Organology. The fundamental faculties where not considered by Gall to be deterministic but rather reflective propensities. Thus he never claimed his "reading" of the skull revealed inherent criminality, rather, it might only show a propensity, but the individual still had the power of choice over his or her behavior. Gall was one of the first to propose the medical-biological link to human behavior.

Gall's collaborator, Johann Spurzheim popularized the new "science" as phrenology. While phrenology was ultimately discredited, Gall is recognized as a founder of psychology and modern neuroscience (Davis, 1955). His concept of fundamental faculties, which is today referred to as localization of function, was a major contribution to the understanding of how the brain functions (Wetzell, 2000).

Lombroso was not convinced of the validity of the phrenological map of the skull per se, but he did adopt the assumption that exterior anomalies mirrored interior moral attributes. He employed Gall's methodology of measuring physical anomalies of the skull. While Gall focused on the geography of the skull, Lombroso adopted the broader principles of anthropometry, which through the taking of scientific measurements of the human body, body parts, and capacities sought to identify body types and identify anomalies in the form of stigmata. Lombroso, like Galton, believed that physical and psychological abnormalities, which he identified as traits, passed through generations of mankind as well as the world of animals, insects, and plants (Gibson & Rafter, 2006, 167-174).

Rudolf Ludwig Carl Virchow (1821-1902) was an acclaimed German physician, pathologist, and politician, who also had a professional interest in anthropology. He is considered the founding father of pathology and social medicine (http://www.famousscientists.org/rudolf-virchow/). His *Cellular Pathology*, published in 1858, concluded that diseases attack cells and cause them to malfunction. Virchow's discovery, including cell division, was one of the most important events in medical history (http://www.famousscientists.org/rudolf-virchow/). He was openly critical of evolution and the concept of atavism. The idea that man evolved from apes, Virchow argued, was a virtual denial of the moral foundations of society (http://www.famousscientists.org/rudolf-virchow/). However, Virchow did denote in man certain physical peculiarities of the lower animals. He referred to these anomalies as theromorphisms (Wolfgang, 1961; Wolfgang, 1972). Virchow was a critic of evolution on moral grounds, but his belief in cellular pathology contributed to Lombroso's concept of atavism or arrested development.

While Lombroso held to his belief that the born criminal was the product of a biological arrested state, which he called atavism, Virchow rejected the concept and explained that criminal behavior was the result of a pathological condition (Bondio, 2006). Nevertheless, Lombroso was influenced by Virchow's theory of theromorphism and the discovery of cellular division and malfunction (Wolfgang, 1961). For Lombroso, these elements helped to affirm his belief in physical stigmata and biological regression or arrested development.

Scottish medical doctor and pioneer criminologist, James Bruce Thomson (1810-1873) served most of his career as physician and surgeon in the Scottish prison at Perth, Scotland. Based on his study of prisoners in the 1860s, he concluded that criminality was closely associated with heredity, physical morbidity, and mental disease (Ellis, 1890/2010; http://bjpsychap.org/content/59/245/354). A similar conclusion was reached by the English psychiatrist and physician, Henry Maudsley (1835-1918). Maudsley believed that crime and madness were the products of degeneracy. Criminal man was "marked by special characteristics of physical and mental inferiority," and represented a "distinct class of creatures doomed to evil" (Mucchielli, 2016, 208). According to Maudsley, "criminals are extremely unlovable beings" who should be separated from the general population and not allowed to marry (Scott, 1972). If born criminals were "not exactly a degenerate species, [they were] at least a degenerate variety of the human species" (Ferri, 1908/2017, n.p.). Lombroso's research followed similar lines of scientific inquiry.

Although it is difficult sometimes to determine whose ideas were original at a time of widespread European interest in criminal anthropology; certainly one idea, the *fundamental biogenetic law*, of organic predisposition, was borrowed by Lombroso from the German biologist and physician Ernst Haeckel (1834-1919). Haeckel's biogenetic law, called monism, proposed that all elements of human identity are implanted in individual cells. Human characteristics thus pass on a cellular level through successive generations (Gibson, 2002). Haeckel's theory declared, "the history of the fetus is a recapitulation of the history of the race" (Kurella, 1911/2012, 118). Spencer and Haeckel both used the symbolism of human growth, from infancy to adulthood to represent the development and perpetuity of civilization and society (Rafter et al., 2016). Lombroso found in recapitulation and Spencer's social evolution theory further support for his belief that crime was a biological predisposition that flows through generations (Wolfgang, 1972; Pick, 1989; Rafter et al., 2016). Haeckel contributed to Lombroso's theory of organic predisposition. Spencer linked both biology and sociology to paint a picture of man and society in a symbiotic yet potentially dangerous relationship.

Francis Galton (1822-1911) was a half-cousin of Charles Darwin and pioneer English eugenicists who believed in particular that certain enduring human qualities including intelligence could be measured through generations by the use of statistics. Galton pioneered the use of statistical correlation and promoted the use of regression toward the mean to analyze demographic information gathered for the first time by the use of surveys. Lombroso preferred direct observation to surveys in his work, and he never adopted the use of regression to the mean or other advanced statistical tools. He appears to have been satisfied with using the average, frequency, and mean as his primary means of statistical measurement. Lombroso, however, certainly shared a belief in Galton's biogenetics theory.

Galton was an early proponent of social engineering who believed that individuals of intelligence and other positive qualities should be encouraged to procreate while inferior (weak) members of society should find welcome refuge in "celibate monasteries or sisterhoods" (Galton, 1869, 362); this in spite of the fact that his research concluded that positive traits and abilities, including intelligence, declined over successive generations in the same family. Galton also developed a method to classify fingerprints (Alphonse Bertillon had pioneered the process of actually *taking* fingerprints).

Lombroso, Gall, Galton, Maudsley, Thomson, and Morel shared a common interest in discovering a "map" (blending physiology and psychiatry), to identify characteristics, traits, and propensities in human subjects. Lombroso, Maudsley, Thomson, and Morel extrapolated from their findings the impact of heredity and degeneration (inverse evolution or regression) on man and society.

Paradoxically, the rise of civilization and modernity provided the basis for decline. Frenchman Benedict Augustin Morel (1809-1873) was a trained physician (Vienna) who turned to psychiatry in his study of man and society. Morel and Theodule Ribot (1839-1916) pioneered the theory of degeneration, but Morel became the more famous. His *Treatise on Degeneracy,* published in 1857, was acclaimed for its biological explanation for generational mental deterioration. This theory is remarkably close to the theory of reversion proposed by Paolo Marzolo.

Morel believed that mental degeneracy was a pathological condition induced by acquired traits (e.g., alcoholism) that were then passed through generations by heredity (Abel, 2015). Heredity and environment interacted to create mental and physical deviations from the norm. These deviations, Morel explained, were expressed in "epilepsy, insanity, mental deficiency, crime, and similar conditions" (Wolfgang, 1961, 366). Lombroso followed a similar train of thought. Morel believed that progress bred decay and social pathology. For Lombroso, degeneration theory was used to provide an alternative explanation for the criminal types beyond the congenital criminal, the original criminal man.

For Lombroso and many of Europe's intellectuals in the 19th century, it seemed logical and easily proven by science that both positive and negative human abilities and faculties regressed over generations. Lombroso's early mentor, Paolo Marzolo described this process as reversion to an earlier stage of civilization (Gibson, 2002; Gibson, 2006). Lombroso often referred to the famous Juke family of New York as an example of the calamity of generational regression or degeneration. The family reportedly produced over 200 criminals through five generations.

Mentors and Friends

Four of Lombroso's professors at the University of Pavia formed the core of his intellectual family. Paolo Marzolo (1811-1867) and Paolo Mantegazza (the Paolo II from his school years) were central to that core. Marzolo, who had given Lombroso direction by steering him both toward medicine and the studies of race, insanity, and the link between insanity and genius, remained a close friend and confidant of Lombroso until his death. Above all else, Marzolo taught Lombroso to keep an open mind to what history and nature could teach him, a lesson that Lombroso exercised to the full in Calabria. Gina Lombroso-Ferrero writes that Marzolo was both an "uncle" and a "guide in life" to her father (Lombroso-Ferrero, Chap. VI, 18).

Mantegazza (1831-1910), the neurologist, pathologist, and anthropologist who was finishing his medical studies when he first met Lombroso, taught Lombroso "the mysteries of physiology" and cellular genesis (Lombroso-Ferrero, Chap. III, 7-8). Also a Positivist, Mantegazza and Lombroso initially pursued similar interests in criminal anthropology, including cranial research and facial stigmata. However, their friendship ended over the results of a study Lombroso made of sensitivity to pain in 1867. Lombroso created an instrument, the "electric algometer," to measure asylum patients' sensitivity to pain, and he recorded the results. Mantagazza argued that Lombroso's findings were inaccurate, even though he found no fault with the device. The "furious" response of Mantagazza "pained" Lombroso and ruined their friendship (Lombroso-Ferrero, Chap. VI, 9). Mantagazza would also later disagree with Lombroso's stress on atavism and the born criminal over mental pathology (Gibson, 2002, 115). While Mantagazza was a highly respected criminal anthropologist, it is very possible that he may have been jealous over the growing success of his earlier student, Lombroso.

Bartolomeo Panizza (1785-1867) the professor and president of the University of Pavia who so enthralled Lombroso and other students with his teaching skill and ability to spark the imagination of his students, was a steady influence on Lombroso. Panizza and his colleague, Agostino Bertani, had published in their "Gazzetta Medico" Lombroso's first major monograph, "Madness of Cardano," and it was Panizza who arranged Lombroso's lectureship during his leave from the army. Alfred de Maury, of course, was among the intellectuals who shaped Lombroso's early work.

There was, however, one more. Max Nordau (1849-1923), who stressed the popular theory of "degeneration," widely accepted through World War I. Originating in France, degeneration explained the generational physical and moral decline of the symbiotic relationship between man and society (Kushner, 2011). The stresses of rapid urbanization and industrialization in Europe saw the rise of crime, public discord, and the pathological criminal type. In his contemporary critique of the 19th-century industrialization and urbanization of Europe, Nordau equated their effects with the creation of an "elegant society" inhabited with "moral and emotional degenerates" given to the latest fad (Nordau, 1895/2016, 9-11). Progress in itself over an endogenous moral defect, Nordau and others argued, created the social phenomenon of degeneracy, which "rendered many people intellectually inferior and socially unfit" (Wetzell, 2000, 69). Lombroso and Nordau were steadfast friends. Nordau attributed his understanding of the psychical nature of the criminal, and particularly the mattoid, to Lombroso. In turn, Lombroso found in Nordau a supportive colleague in his understanding of the influence of degeneration in a criminal and societal context (Lombroso-Ferrero, Chaps. XI, 2; XVIII, 3).

Degeneration was another extension of biological determinism. However, this theory was also used to explain the process of degeneration of both man and society. Degeneration was described as having a cumulative effect over time resulting in the degradation of man and society. Events of the 20th century would reveal the shortcomings of degeneration as a theory, as well as the moral failings of science to engineer society and eliminate perceived "dangerous classes." To his credit, Lombroso would never fully embrace degeneration theory or eugenics as a solution for dealing with undesirables within society.

Family and Assistants

On April 10, 1870, the 34-year-old Lombroso married Nina de Benedetti. They had five children. Two of them, daughters Gina (1872-1944), and Paola (1871-1954), became close supporters and advocates of Lombroso's work. The extended family they created became an integral part of the Lombroso intellectual university.

Following his marriage in 1870, Lombroso's home in Turin was the site of many conversations with men and women of the arts, letters, scientists, and politicians from Italy and abroad. Lombroso was a cosmopolitan man who enjoyed the company of like members from society and Nina helped to make his home a welcome place for intellectual exchanges. These

Paola (L.) and Gina (R.) Lombroso.

Museo di Antropologia Criminale "Cesare Lombroso," University of Turin, Italy informal conversations gave him the opportunity to exchange ideas regarding the future of Italy and its people. He continued this welcome exchange of ideas in the setting of his home throughout his life. Certainly one favored topic was the origin of criminality, the effect of crime on society, and the appropriate punishment for criminal activity. Nina Lombroso was more than a good host; she collaborated with her husband at his urging in his intellectual endeavors, provided advice, and managed secretarial assistance. Lombroso wanted his wife to be a full partner in his life work and she was equally dedicated to his work (Lombroso-Ferrero, Chap. VII, 1; S. Montaldo, personal communication, September 20, 2016).

Nina, Gina, and Paola all assisted Lombroso in his labors. Both daughters shared with their father an intellectual curiosity and desire to learn. Following her marriage to Mario Carrara, a former lab assistant to Lombroso, Paola and her husband played an important role in the family enterprise. Carrara, during his medical training, worked as a lab assistant with Lombroso for several years. He was keenly interested in criminal anthropology, and following medical school he continued to conduct research with Lombroso. Before leaving Turin in 1896 for a professorship at the University of Cagliari, in Sardinia, Carrara organized Lombroso's anthropological museum at the University of Turin. Gina's husband, Guglielmo Ferrero (1871-1942) was also an important partner with Lombroso, providing valuable insights and advice, and using Lombroso's work as a springboard for his own career (Lombroso-Ferrero, Chap. XIX, 4).

Gina Lombroso-Ferrero worked with her father in the creation of *Archive of Psychiatry, Criminal Anthropology, and Penal Sciences* in 1880 and served as editor and contributor. Her articles focused on atavism, epilepsy, and degeneration. She became a physician at a time of limited educational opportunities for women. Gina was fully dedicated to her father's work and continued to defend his work long after his death in 1909. Guglielmo Ferrero was also interested in the female as a criminal type and co-authored with Lombroso in 1892, *Criminal Woman, the Prostitute, and the Normal Woman.*

During his career, Lombroso had the benefit of many interns, lab assistants, and colleagues who assisted him collecting and analyzing data, but none were more important than Enrico Ferri (1856-1929), Raffaele Garofalo (1851-1934), and Sergio Sergi (1878-1972). Lombroso credited them in all five editions of *Criminal Man.* Ferri was a lawyer and ultimately a member of the Italian Parliament. He helped convince Lombroso to incorporate social and economic determinants to the list of causal factors for criminal man. Lombroso credited Ferri as the first to recognize that the congenital criminal "did not form a single species" giving way to new criminal types (Lombroso-Ferrero, 1911/2015, 8). Lombroso's inclusion of the concept of crime prevention to his call for a social defense to crime, may also have originated with Ferri, who believed that crime prevention was key to the work of law enforcement. Ferri was a co-founder of the Positivist School of Criminology, but his interests focused more on social and psychological positivism than on biology, which was Lombroso's main field.

Garofalo was already a magistrate when he joined Lombroso's team in 1879. He joined the jurist Ferri as a fellow advocate for penal reform and reduction of recidivism. They both advocated the principle of "indeterminate sentences," that is, punishment should be proportionate to the crime. Lombroso credited Garofalo with helping him understand the legal implications in the larger scheme of social defense to crime (Lombroso-Ferrero, Chap. XI, 11, 12).

Like Ferri, Garofalo was more interested in the psychological nature of crime and contributed to the Positivist body of work. He was less committed to Lombroso's theory of atavism or the biological origin of criminal man. Garofalo did share with Lombroso the belief that children were born absent of moral values. On this line of thought, Garofalo contributed to Lombroso's belief in moral insanity as separate from organic insanity.

Sergio Sergi, was also a member of the Positivist Modern School and an anthropologist with special interest in human fossils pre-dating Neanderthal man and cranial morphology. He also would work closely with Ferri and Garofalo in creating two criminal classifications which Lombroso adopted, criminals of passion and occasional criminals.

Garofalo and Ferri worked closely with Lombroso as co-publishers of the journal, *Archive of Psychiatry, Anthropology, Criminal and Penal Science*. The journal was divided into two sections, with Lombroso responsible for psychiatry and Garofalo judicial and penal law (Lombroso-Ferrero, Chap. XI, 16, 19).

Lombroso, Ferri, and Garofalo became known as "the glorious triad of the founders of that great movement for the reform of penal law" (Gibson, 2002, 35). Whether through scientific discovery or theoretical design, these scholars and family members provided Positivist "facts" or theorems for Lombroso to contemplate and put to use in the development of his revolutionary theories of criminal man and social defense.

CHAPTER 4
The Case for Positivism

"Anthropological and pathological features distinguish a criminal type within each race."
—Cesare Lombroso

O ut of the army in 1865, Lombroso was gravitating to several prominent themes in his research. While remaining centered on cretinism
and pellagra, Lombroso began looking at the broader topic of public
health, including criminal behavior, epilepsy, insanity and its variations in
relationship to race and the environment, even so far as meteorological influences (Gibson & Rafter, 2006; Lombroso-Ferrero, Chap. VI). In December
1865 Lombroso published his first attempt to explain the problems of public
health in relationship to the geographical regions of Italy and the influence
of race. He followed publication with a series of public lectures in Pavia on
the history of man and race at the invitation of Carlo Cantoni, who had suc-
ceeded Panizza as president of the University of Pavia (Lombroso-Ferrero,
Chap. V, 21).

In the spirit of Nationalism, Lombroso did not believe that a viable nation
could grow with a large portion of its population living in poverty, poor health
(both mental and physical), and under feudal institutions of governance and
land ownership (Gibson, 2002; Horn, 2003). Those problems were acute in
southern Italy, as he had learned in Calabria. In part, those questions composed a Southern Question. How can leaders unify a country so divided by
cultural, socio-economic, and life-style differences? Lombroso was most inter-

ested in the anthropological record documenting the impact of cretinism and pellagra on national health. At the core of his work, he connected the diseases with insanity. In his clinical studies and military observations, Lombroso also noted a link between mental illness and criminals.

Although Lombroso was very familiar with the threat of pellagra on public health, cretinism had been his primary concern during his university training and military service. That changed in 1868 when he made pellagra the center of his research interest without sacrificing his studies of insanity, race, and criminal behavior (Lombroso-Ferrero, Chap. VI, 9, 10, 11). He published a monograph entitled, "*Maniac Pellagra*" the same year, charging that pellagra could cause insanity (Lombroso-Ferrero, Chap. VI, 11). He noted that, since 1850 the number of cases of pellagra had steadily grown into an epidemic in northern Italy (Lombroso-Ferrero, Chap. VI, 11).

The Materialist understanding of the world informed much of Lombroso's study of health issues and crime. Regarding cretinism and pellagra, Materialism allowed him to consider that the diseases represented the influence of matter on matter — in this case, nature on humans. Materialism also informed Lombroso's research. He concurred with the contemporary belief that moldy or spoiled corn caused both cretinism and pellagra. Corn was the staple of most Italian farmers and peasants as well as poor people living in the cities. Also, cretinism and pellagra were common in both rural and urban environments. Most people had long assumed that avoidance of moldy corn prevented outbreaks of the diseases. That idea was so prevalent that the Venetian Senate had outlawed the sale of spoiled corn in 1776.

In 1868 and 1869 Lombroso conducted a series of human and animal experiments to determine the exact cause of pellagra. He determined that moldy or spoiled corn was indeed the culprit, but not specifically mold or fungi (Lombroso-Ferrero, Chaps. VI, 11; VII, 10-14). He concluded that, instead of the fungus itself, an alkaloid toxin that the fungus produced actually caused the diseases. He conclusions became part of the "maidic (corn) theory."

With further experimentation, Lombroso discovered that four milligrams of arsenic acid for adults and four milligrams of sodium "chlorur" [*sic*] for children would cure most cases of both pellagra and cretinism. He published his findings in hundreds of pamphlets and had them distributed to villages throughout Italy. In 1869, Lombroso presented his findings at an international conference in Florence. He encouraged government ministers in Rome to outlaw the sale of spoiled corn, but to no avail. Lombroso also reported his findings to an Italian commission studying the problem in 1870. The commission offered a cash prize for the most conclusive answer to the cause of the disease. While some observers acknowledged that Lombroso had earned the prize, the commission did not award it to him. Some members preferred, instead, the findings of other researchers' projects un-related to secondary toxins (Lombroso-Ferrero, Chap. VII, 10-12).

Other forces also conspired against Lombroso. Land barons and powerful members of parliament opposed him. Those power bases had various reasons to ignore Lombroso's discovery. They controlled corn production and distribution, and supported protectionist corn duties. Rather than waste spoiled corn and face an economic loss, the landed class and corn producers sold peasants the corn or bread made from it, thus perpetuating the health crisis. Lombroso was indignant about the practice and considered it nothing more than an act of slavery. Hinting at what would become a socialist bent in his politics, Lombroso observed that one could research whatever he liked as long as it did not interfere with economic interests (Kurella, 1911/2012, 154; Lombroso-Ferrero, Chaps. VI, 18; IX, 8-9; XI, 22, XII, 1).

The academic community saw in the upstart medical doctor and psychiatrist a threat to their favored position in society. They argued that Lombroso had no chemistry lab training and therefore his findings were suspect. Even when Lombroso secured supporting evidence from a chemist and numerous additional demonstrations that the alkaloid toxin existed and caused pellagra symptoms, the academic community rejected the findings. Fighting with the Italian establishment over the cause and potential cure for pellagra financially drained Lombroso. Adding to the rejection and hardship, the gentry and their wealthy friends boycotted Lombroso's medical services, causing further economic strain in the Lombroso household (Lombroso-Ferrero, Chaps. VII, 10-12; VIII, 4-13, 15; Wolfgang, 1961, 363; Kurella, 1911/2012, 150, 151).

Still determined, Lombroso made a major presentation of his research findings on pellagra and spoiled corn before the University of Turin's Medical Academy in 1872. He met with the same negative response. He and his scientific opponents conducted additional experiments in 1873-1874, but neither side swayed the other. In 1874 Lombroso called for a national conference of doctors in Pavia to discuss his findings. There he finally got a positive response as scientists agreed the treatment he had proposed in 1869 proved successful in reversing the disease in most patients.

More support came in 1875 when Lombroso's old friend and colleague, Alfred Maury, collected samples of the toxin extracted from spoiled corn and had two renowned chemists test them. They concurred that the toxin was an alkaloid. Lombroso had also concluded that the best way to avoid cretinism and pellagra was to keep corn dry to avoid spoilage.

In 1876, Lombroso accepted the Chair of Legal Medicine and Public Hygiene at the University of Turin. In the same year the provinces of Lombardy and Venetia, two of the hardest hit regions in northern Italy by the scourge of pellagra, followed Lombroso's advice and created large ovens to dry corn before distribution. In the 1880s Lombroso traveled to lecture and promote the use of ovens to dry corn. He also wrote extensively about pellagra, its cause and prevention in his *Archive of Psychiatry, Criminal Anthropology, and Penal Sciences*. Lombroso's interest and study of the disease and its prevention continued through the 1890s (Lombroso-Ferrero, Chaps. VII, 13; VIII, 5, 8-13, 14, 16-18; X, 6, 8, 12; XII, 1-3; XV, 13).

In 1892 the Italian government recognized Lombroso's efforts to combat cretinism and pellagra; however, a law banning the sale of spoiled corn remained elusive. Not until 1902 did the Italian Parliament act on Lombroso's research and begin a series of agrarian reforms in corn production, distribution, and taxation. Parliament also banned the sale of spoiled or rotten corn for human consumption. But in 1910, a new government commission mistakenly determined that it was not the corn but a parasitic microbe transmitted by mosquitoes or other blood-sucking insects that caused the diseases (Kurella, 1911/2012, 152; Gibson & Rafter, 2006; Lombroso-Ferrero, Chap. XIV, 13-14; Chap. XX, 9).

 Of course, later discoveries proved everyone wrong. In the 20th century scientists discovered that an iodine deficiency caused cretinism, which could result in physical growth impairment (for example, dwarfism) and mental deterioration. Plus, a deficiency of niacin and tryptophan, possible in a corn-based diet, can cause pellagra, which itself can result in physical deformity, dermatitis, digestive, nervous and mental disturbances, including a propensity to violence. If left untreated, pellagra can cause severe nerve damage, especially in the brain.

Lombroso was not wrong in sensing a link between cretinism, pellagra, and violent, criminal tendencies. But his observation was just that — a sense. As would be the case with so much of his research in criminal behavior, he was working beyond the reach of 19th century science. He thus relied on educated guesses and anecdotal evidence, coupled with statistical models that he himself had to create. As had his findings in the maidic cases, his later work in criminal anthropology would put him in foul odor with many of his colleagues.

Addressing the Southern Question

Just as Lombroso's studies of cretinism and pellagra dictated 40 years of his life, so did his military experience in southern Italy also drive much of his career. As noted, Calabria exposed Lombroso to the dichotomy between the relative prosperity and growing industrialization of northern Italy with widespread illiteracy, poverty, unemployment, crime, and feudal conditions of the south.

Northern Italians tended to perceive southern Italy as a backwater region occupied by amoral and infamous people (Morris, 1997; Horn, 2003). Relative to governance, "there were two different ways of life in Italy . . . in the north, people were citizens; in the south, they were subjects" (Schneider, 1998, 7).

Lombroso certainly recognized a virtual line separating northern Italy from the Peninsula. To him, Calabria exhibited a social dualism with racial overtones that could derail the social-economic development of Italy. It represented a clash between the acclaimed progressive European influence in the north, and a lamented Mediterranean heritage in the south (Melossi, 2000; Horn, 2003; Garland & Sparks, 2000).

During his military posting in Calabria, Lombroso had made rudimentary scholarly inroads into the idea of the social and anthropological dichotomy of Italy when he interviewed subjects and measured skulls. Lombroso returned to the subject in 1874 when he made it the center of research for publication of a medical, psychological, and physical geography of Italian races (Lombroso-Ferrero, Chap. VIII, 16). Lombroso and his colleagues clearly saw the influence of race in the Mediterranean settlement of southern Italy (Ferri, 1908/2017, 22), and Lombroso repeatedly referred to the North African and Arabian presence in southern Italy as the result of "invasions they had to undergo" over time (Lombroso-Ferrero, Chap. VI, 9).

The question of race energized any discussion of the Southern Question, and Lombroso did not avoid the taint of racism as he studied it. Southern Italians (Calabrians especially) and Sicilians had been historically racialized as inferior, and Lombroso thought the influence of North Africa and Arabia was a determining factor in that marginalization (D' Agostino, 2002, 339). As he would write in *In Calabria*, Lombroso noted the Greek imprint on physical characteristics of Calabrians, including their high forehead, straight nose, and black eyes (Lombroso-Ferrero, Chap. V, 10). Lombroso's study of insanity in the south bears the imprint of race — "insanity follows the tendencies of the time and race to which the sick person belongs only exaggerating its characteristics" (Lombroso-Ferrero, Chap. V, 6). Lombroso had studied races since he was 16 years old, so it was no stretch of imagination or logic for him to see in the Southern Question the effects of racial differences.

In 1871 Lombroso wrote in *White Man and Man of Color*, that white men and their civilization were at the top of the evolutionary chain, while men of color remained in arrested development at the bottom. His measurements of the craniums and research of the brains of both races were evidence enough to Lombroso of the inferiority of Africans (Lombroso-Ferrero, Chap. VI, 18; Gibson, 2002, 99-100; Lombroso-Ferrero, Chap. XVIII, 5). Criminologist and Lombroso biographer Mary Gibson relates that Lombroso's racial views were directly influenced by Lombroso's mentor Paolo Marzolo and his linguist studies on the link between language development and western civilization. In fact, Marzolo had encouraged Lombroso at age 16 to begin studying the differences between the white and black races (Lombroso-Ferrero, Chap. VI, 18).

Marked physical differences between northern and southern Italians, who were darker skinned and shorter in stature, made it easy for Lombroso to make connections between physical appearance, race, and inferiority. To the 19th-century anthropologist, both darker skin and short height equaled racial inferiority. Many of the physical and psychiatric characteristics that Lombroso would assign to criminal man were present in southern Italians. Lombroso claimed, "anthropological and pathological features distinguish a criminal type within each race," including southern Italians (Gibson & Rafter, 2006, 230). He attributed brigandage and criminality largely to the "Arabian imprint," which included darker skin and a "Semitic (Jewish) presence" on the Peninsula and in Sicily and Sardinia (Lombroso, 1911/2012, 25, 27). The Jewish imprint that Lombroso denoted was primarily cultural and historical. Lombroso placed larger blame for Calabrian degeneracy on Arabic influence:

> The blood of this people, at once conquerors and robbers, hospitable and cruel, intelligent and superstitious, inconstant, restless, and impatient of restraint, must have its influence in . . . fomenting the sudden and implacable revolts and in perpetuating brigandage (Lombroso, 1911/2012, 25).

Lombroso portrayed the Italian Peninsula as a troubled backward region over-run by a violent and inferior people, who were a threat to the race (Noyes, 2003, 42). In fact, the element of race gave Lombroso even greater impetus to identify the criminal elements in society so that he, and by extension the united Italian state, could defend against criminals. In his fifth edition (1896-1897) of *Criminal Man* Lombroso noted with caution that the mixing of races improved the indigenous people, but ultimately would lead to revolution (328).

Lombroso was not alone in his racial perceptions. Nineteenth-century European intellectuals used the term "scientific racism" to describe the "barbaric" peoples of North Africa, Africa, and the Middle East. The term held that those people were uncivilized and prone to violence and criminal activity. Geographically it held that the Mediterranean Sea brought mediocre people to the Italian Peninsula. Lombroso agreed that immigration was a source of criminality for Italy (Lombroso, 1911/2012, 63-67). He said flatly, "in our civilized world, to note the proof of the influence of race upon crime is both easier and more certain" (Lombroso, 1911/2012, 22).

Anti-Semitism, too, was historically widespread and deeply rooted in European culture. Lombroso was not immune to it, even though he had benefitted from toleration of Jews in northern Italy when he was a schoolboy. Despite a long history of Jewish assimilation and socio-economic influence in Italy, their faith clashed with the overriding Christianity of the nation. Jews were not only accused for the death of Christ, but were also labeled along with gypsies — or Romagna — as "thieves," guilty of usury and property crimes within the business community. And while Lombroso was Jewish, he did not hesitate to label the criminal elements within his own ethnicity. However, in *Crime: Its Causes and Remedies* published originally in 1911, Lombroso qualified his description of Jewish criminality in more favorable yet stereotypical terms:

> The statistics of many countries show a lower degree of criminality for the Jews than for their Gentile fellow-citizens. This is the more remarkable since, because of their usual occupations, they should in fairness be compared, not with the population in general, but with the merchants and petty tradespeople, who have . . . a high record for criminality (37).

While Lombroso may have categorized the types of crimes Jews as a "class" above the average criminal type, that did not, however, free them of another "disease" — insanity. Lombroso further qualified his remarks in *Crime* by adding that the "criminality of the Jews can be proved to be less than that of other races, a very different situation appears when we turn to the question of insanity, in which they have an unfortunate leadership" (Lombroso, 1911/2012, 39). Lombroso appears to have some ambiguity and personal conflict over the question of Jewish links to criminality and their place in the contemporary world.

Lombroso believed that anti-Semitism was largely the result of social status prejudice. In his statistical study of "race" in Italy and France, Lombroso reported that anti-Semitism was greatest when Jews were segregated. Lombroso noted that Jews were largely a part of the middle class, which caused both lower classes and elites to suspect them. He argued that the "Jewish race" could "transform" and "modify" itself to the larger society when given the opportunity. Conscious of his own place in society, Lombroso could also be a circumspect apologist for Jews (Lombroso-Ferrero, Chap. XV, 12).

In 1898, a group of Jewish Zionists approached Lombroso — for the second time. He had not taken an earlier visit seriously, but with the second visit he began to accept that his concept of Jewish assimilation was not the solution for Jews who wanted a homeland away from European persecution and humiliation. Lombroso did not become an overt Zionist, but he did agree with the necessity of the idealistic movement (Lombroso-Ferrero, Chap. XVIII, 10).

Criminality

Cesare Lombroso's earlier studies into disease and the Southern Question began to meld into something larger — the study of criminality. That the projects overlapped was not unusual. Lombroso had the ability to work on several divergent projects at once. His daughter Gina remembered her father as a man in constant motion between projects. She recalled that once, while on a train ride during his studies of cretinism and pellagra, Lombroso had a flash of insight that there was a close relationship between criminal and primitive man (Lombroso-Ferrero, Chap. XXIII, 7). The year 1871, however, became a turning point for Lombroso. That year he set aside his study of pellagra and cretinism (at least for the moment), to renew his research on insanity, the study of races, and "examination" of criminals (Lombroso-Ferrero, Chap. VII, 14).

Though he was no longer in the Italian army, nationalism — and the various other Enlightenment intellectual movements — still drove part of his research. Simply, unified Italy needed to define the elements of criminal behavior and how to treat them. The government needed to establish a national legal juris-prudence and penal code, and Lombroso believed the first priority should be the "direct analytical study of the criminal" (Lombroso, 1911/2012, 6):

> I began dimly to realize that the *a priori* studies on crime in the abstract, hitherto pursued by jurists, especially in Italy, with singular acumen, should be superseded by the direct analytical study of the criminal, compared with normal individuals and the insane (Lombroso, 1911/2012, 6).

Lombroso struggled with the idea that all men possessed reason or the power of choice. But what of criminals and the insane? Scientific inquiry, a gift of the Enlightenment, provided him the means of observation and logic to search the causes of criminality. Augmenting these skills with rudimentary statistics, Lombroso was able to calculate both real and perceived characteristics of normal and deviant members of society. He knew that the new Italian state would need to know what elements in society required control and suppression (Lombroso, 1911/2012, 361).

Lombroso also saw in the study of criminals an opportunity to address what he considered the fallacy of the Beccarian Model of jurisprudence with its interest centered on morality and legal structure rather than the origin of the criminal and his behavior (Lombroso, 1911/2012, 6). He began his work with the study of the anatomical conditions of the criminal, but expanded his studies to include the brain and other physiological conditions of criminals leading to the psychological nature of criminal man. Lombroso saw in science the promise to both study crime and address its social affects in a humane way for the benefit of the Italian people.

Lombroso's research into cretinism, pellagra, and the people of Calabria melded to become his life work on the nature of criminals. By 1871, he was convinced that criminal behavior was not the result of poor decisions and bad judgment, as the Classical School held, but was instead because of mental deficiencies in the criminals themselves. Those deficiencies, in turn, were the result of atavism — an anomaly linked to an earlier, primitive state of man and "the carnivores" (Lombroso-Ferrero, Chap. VII, 15, 16, 18). His results formed the nucleus of criminal anthropology.

CHAPTER 5
Criminal Man

> *"It will no longer be possible to deny the organicity of crime."*
> —Cesare Lombroso, 1893

C esare Lombroso effectively invented the scientific study of the causes of criminal behavior. From anthropological measurements to the use of mugshots, from the creation of statistical charts to the examination of the inside of skulls, Lombroso codified the methods of research. Unfortunately, he relied on anecdotal evidence as much as scientific, and his conclusions would later become doctrine among the fascist regimes of World War II. In all cases, Lombroso was reaching beyond what the science of his day could effectively underpin. Nevertheless, he was inventing criminal anthropology.

Part of Lombroso's interest in criminal behavior, undoubtedly, came from his work in asylums after he left the army. Lombroso began to see in the abnormal human condition a pattern of traits that could make for a diagnosis of the criminal type, but as yet there was no real clarity of structure to his observations. By his own admission, his early psychiatric research focused on the physical patient rather than the mental condition of insanity itself (Gibson & Rafter, 2006, 6; Lombroso-Ferrero, Chap. V, 11; VI, 1, 4-5). But all of his experiences, especially his time in Calabria pushed Lombroso to reframe his research (Lombroso-Ferrero, Chap. V, 5-6, 12). Working with the insane and mentally ill gave Lombroso the opportunity to compare his patients with what he perceived to be the criminal soldiers he had studied in the military. He concluded "most of the insane are not born so, but become mad, while criminals are born with evil inclinations" (Gibson & Rafter, 2006, 48).

Identification of the criminal type, the primitive savage, within society required careful and thorough study of physical and mental attributes of each subject in order to create a classification type. The "scientific" methodology that emerged in the 19th century, Positivism, provided Lombroso the framework to study both man and his environment. Positivism argued that authoritative knowledge is derived from the observation of natural phenomena and processed and determined to be true by the inductive process and empiricism based too often on supposed correlations.

By 1871 the basic elements for his nascent theory of criminality were beginning to gel while he was in charge of clinical psychology and anthropology at the mental hospital in Pavia. To date he had observed traits of criminality in soldiers of the lower social order and the declared dangerous classes, in brigands, and in those of poor physical and mental health. Following in the footsteps of Franz Joseph Gall, Lombroso made observations of criminals' craniums looking for clues to the origins of criminal behavior. He believed that cranial anomalies suggested that the criminal was "was closer to the savage than to the madman" (Gibson & Rafter, 2006, 304). He also measured and weighed the brain mass of deceased inmates. Positivist scientists of Lombroso's generation sought in vain to understand the functionality of the brain from their examination of its structure and shape.

From his study of psychiatry, Lombroso was familiar with the stages of mental deficiency and their impact on individual behavior. Lombroso already had the mechanism to explain physical changes in mankind. Evolution provided the instrument of change and regularity for both progress and degradation within a social context. It served for Lombroso as the framework on which all the traits of criminality coalesced into a pattern that revealed the criminal type and his place in the process of natural selection.

Integral to Lombroso's investigative paradigm were Darwinism and degeneration theory, which he applied to the study of 400 criminals in prisons and asylums. Lombroso believed a Positivist approach to science could unlock the secrets of the criminal mind and body. A Positivist researcher could glean "facts" from a variety of fields of inquiry. Lombroso, the polymath, moved comfortably within the scientific disciplines of medicine, psychiatry, biology, zoology, natural science, and anthropology, as well as the more humanities-based subjects of linguistics, literature, statistics, politics, history, criminal theory, law, sociology, theater, mythology, folklore, and philosophy.

Research Flaws

Scientists today, however, consider Lombroso's methodology to be sloppy. He had no compunction against plucking information from any one of fields that he enjoyed to illustrate and support his conclusions. He gave equal weight to all evidence regardless of its immediate validity or anecdotal nature, whether quantitative or qualitative. At times he confused the meaning of subjective and objective evidence, and he was comfortable working with conjecture. He made many assumptions about the nature of the criminal type that would later fuel scholarly criticism of his work. Even when Lombroso had limited data or facts to work with, he concluded that,

> However scant my data, I am confident that they support conclusions that are firmer than the superficial observations and *a priori* assumptions that have hitherto dominated this field without even being challenged (Gibson & Rafter, 2006, 99).

The process of collecting "facts" unfortunately too often superseded intellectual discretion as to what was truly pertinent and appropriate information for the question at hand. The preponderance of "facts" and associations that could be made thus became empirical evidence, the very root of knowledge. The lack of discrimination in choosing evidentiary material did not prevent the drawing of conclusions or making assumptions on perceived correlations for the Positivists. Lombroso's use of various assistants to conduct experiments lacked scientific controls for validity and dependability. Consistency of results were accepted at face value rather than subjected to a thorough and rigorous process of validation. When he compared groups or features of people, he never defined what constituted the "norm." In spite of his shortcomings in methodology or research values, he still deserves credit for opening a whole new field of criminal study, and biocriminality in particular.

Lombroso understood that, to develop a complete composite that distinguished criminal man from normal citizen, his evidence had to be quantified. Statistics had become a Positivist's primary tool to unlocking the mysterious relationship of nature with society, and criminal behavior was a "risk" behavior that could be better understood and mitigated through the use of statistics

(Horn, 2003). Lombroso also believed statistics could validate of his new theory of criminal anthropology. In 1878 he said:

> For many, progress is reduced to certain marvelous machines like the telegraph and the steamship. For me, instead, the true character that distinguishes our time from the ancient ages is the triumph of numbers over vague opinions, prejudices, vain theories. With their marvelous power, numbers have penetrated the mysterious world of life and of the intellect (Bianucci, Cilli, Giacobini, Malerba, & Montaldo, 2011, 20).

However rough it may have been, Lombroso delved into rudimentary statistics with his study of criminal behavior. At first he turned to a basic political tool. Beginning in the 19th century, many advanced European governments began to conduct a periodic census. Italy would begin a census as its various states unified. The resulting work created massive data sets of demographic and economic information for interpretation and analysis. Statistics, then, provided the means to analyze that data set (Porter, 1986). For Lombroso, statistics also provided a way to systematically explain the cause of crime and its effect on society in a systematic way (Wetzell, 2000).

Lambert Adolphe Jacques Quetelet (1796-1874) and Andre'-Michel Guerry (1802-1866) pioneered using statistics to explain crime. Quetelet was a Belgian astronomer who believed that the same natural laws that brought regularity to the universe also applied to society and crime. Natural laws, he thought, were the equivalent to statistical laws and could be applied to society. Guerry was a lawyer in the Royal Court of France who also had a great interest in statistical analysis and its ability to quantify large-scale social phenomena, crime in particular. The first publication of French crime statistics in 1827 provided Quetelet and Guerry, acting independently, their first large dataset to explore (Porter, 1986). They were struck by the regularity of crime over the years (Garland, 1985, 113). They concluded that the causal factors of crime were not poverty and education, but rather age and gender (Wetzell, 2000; Porter, 1986). Statistics appeared to support the use of empirical science to the natural environment of man. Quetelet called this new use of quantification "social mechanics," what is today called social statistics.

The Italian government did not systematically collect and publish criminal statistical data until 1879, and Lombroso would use the data extensively beginning with his third edition of *Criminal Man* in 1884. Before then, however, Lombroso used statistical charts and tabulations, which he created from his own observations, in virtually all his publications to illustrate the validity of his conclusions (Lombroso, 1911/2012). His primary use of statistics focused on the discovery of the mean, average, and frequency of crime. Lombroso made extensive use of the "law of averages" in both describing the psychical and physical anomalies of the criminal type and his or her place in society. His calculations and tabulations were often imperfect and imprecise, giving more emphasis to the collected totality of "facts" than to the science in the effort. Upon those surmised "facts" Lombroso made broad speculations and assertions that were often dubious at best and gave his detractors ammunition against him (Garland, 1985, 113).

The Discovery

Lombroso used a macabre collection of evidence he had begun amassing years earlier. Lombroso had 66 male criminal craniums that anatomical museums had donated to him (Gibson & Rafter, 2006). He always intended to use the craniums and skeletons to form a hypothesis regarding anthropological differences in populations and national health. Lombroso was first and foremost a social scientist. Now the skulls and skeletons would become the backbone, if you will, of a statistical system Lombroso invented to support his work.

Partial collection of skulls in the Cesare Lombroso Museum.

Borrowing from Gall the concept of skull or cranium measurement, Lombroso began to measure the skulls of the deceased and craniums of living patients with a craniometer.

He also conducted tests on sensitivity and recorded facial features (physiognomy) in the hope of discovering a link with degeneration and physical anomalies. The craniometer allowed researchers to measure the size and shape of the cranium and estimate the size of the brain in living individuals as well as the dead. Satisfied with this process, Lombroso decided to apply the same technique to his collection of criminal skulls. He was "anxious to apply the experimental method to the study of the diversity, rather than the analogy, between lunatics, criminals and normal individuals" (Lombroso, 1911/2012, 6).

To assist in his experimental research in comparing insane people and criminals to normal citizens, Lombroso used a variety of other instruments. Beyond the craniometer, he used a dynamometer to measure muscular force or strength; a plethysmograph (kymograph) to measure blood flow to the brain, a tachyanthropometer, which provided 11 measures to assist in identification of a person; and

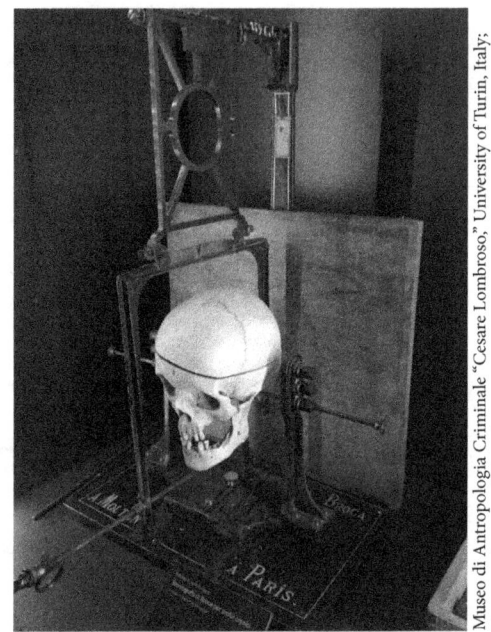

Craniometer

Plethysmograph (Kymograph)

Museo di Antropologia Criminale "Cesare Lombroso," University of Turin, Italy; Photographer: Randall Butler

Museo di Antropologia Criminale "Cesare Lombroso," University of Turin, Italy; Photographer: Randall Butler

an algometer to measure sensitivity to pain. Most of these instruments were available on the market, but Lombroso also created his own instruments, most notably an algometer. Initially, he built it using a Bunsen battery to provide electric shocks to fingers, soles of the feet, genitals, eyelids, and some 35 other locations. He later purchased a Ruhmkorff coil, which also used a Bunsen battery, to accomplish his sensitivity tests. This is only a partial list of the instruments Lombroso used, many are today housed in his museum collection in Turin, Italy (Lombroso-Ferrero, Chaps. VI, 9; X, 11; Bianucci and et al., 2011, 19-21; Horn, 2003, 84-92; Horn, 2006, 319-323; Lombroso-Ferrero, 1911/2012, 130, 133, 135, 137).

Lombroso's assessment of the original 66 skulls revealed that 39 were microcephalic (abnormally small craniums) and in only one-third were the cranial sutures (points where the sections of the skull were joined) normal. Lombroso concluded that the skulls with abnormally small craniums and open sutures had "many monkeylike anomalies" (Gibson & Rafter, 2006, 45).

In what was certainly an assumptive leap, Lombroso believed that he had found the link between the congenital criminal and primitive man in an arrested state. All that was missing in 1871 was a "tell" to bring clarity and unity to all of Lombroso's research and observations. He had already noted similarities between the crania of insane persons and criminals, but the anatomical "tell" he sought remained elusive.

That changed when Lombroso began study on a second group of 56 criminal crania also from his collection. Among this second group was the cranium of the alleged brigand, Giuseppe Villella from Calabria.

Although there are conflicting stories regarding the life, capture, and death of Villella, it appears that he was captured during the war on brigandage and imprisoned in Pavia where he died of natural causes in 1871. Lombroso conducted the postmortem of Villella and was given his skull to add to his

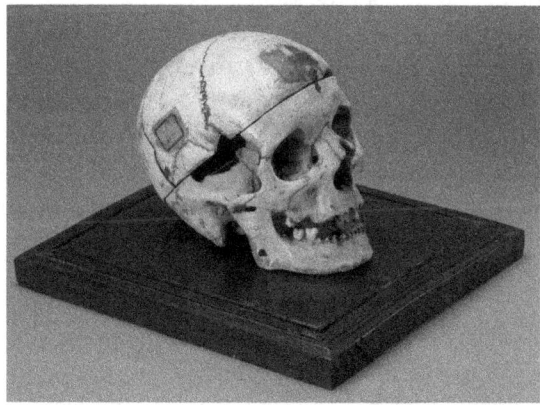

Villella's Skull

Museo di Antropologia Criminale "Cesare Lombroso," University of Turin, Italy

collection of criminal skulls. Villella's cranium was the most impressive in terms of anomalies within the group of skulls.

Lombroso often repeated his moment of discovery in his publications, with some variation in details and the date of occurrence. Nevertheless, it was truly a serendipitous moment for him:

> On his death [Villella] one cold grey November morning [1871], I was deputed to make the post-mortem, and on laying open the skull I found on the occipital part exactly on the spot where a spine is found in the normal skull, a distinct depression which I named *median occipital fossa,* because of its situation precisely in the middle of the occiput as in inferior animals, especially rodents. This depression, as in the case of animals, was correlated with the hypertrophy of the *vermis,* known in birds as the middle cerebellum. This was not merely an idea, but a revelation. At the sight of the skull, I seemed to see all of a sudden, lighted up as a vast plain under a flaming sky, the problem of the nature of the criminal — an atavistic being who reproduces in his person the ferocious instincts of primitive humanity and the inferior animals (Lombroso, 1911/ 2012, 6-7; for more details with slight variation can be found in, Lombroso-Ferrero. Chap. VII, 16-18).

Lombroso stated categorically, "it will no longer be possible to deny the organicity of crime, its anatomical nature and degenerative source" (Macdonald, 1893/2010, i). The discovery now provided Lombroso the physical "tell" or anomaly that distinguished the criminal from the normal person under the observation of a professional, the criminal anthropologist (Lombroso-Ferrero, Chap. VII, 15-17). He spent several years making cranial observations and creating a catalogue of anomalies from which a portrait of the criminal type emerged. The examples Lombroso collected and evaluated revealed in totality anomalies that he believed could only explain the origin and existence of a singular type, the congenital criminal. In 1876, the same year he was appointed full professor of Forensic and Public Hygiene at the University of Turin, Lombroso published his findings in the first edition of *Criminal Man*. With additions, modifications, and clarifications, *Criminal Man* would go through five editions.

Lombroso reported that close examination of Villella's cranium revealed one of the "most serious of all anomalies," an indentation at the base of the skull that Lombroso labeled the "median occipital fossetta," a feature which he found common in 13 other criminal skulls (Gibson & Rafter, 2006, 47).

Museo di Antropologia Criminale "Cesare Lombroso," University of Turin, Italy

Villella's skull with "median occipital fossetta" indentation at base of skull on either side of the hinge.

Lombroso found in Villella his "tell" or what he called his "totem, fetish of criminal anthropology" (Gibson, 2002, 20). From his years of anthropological study of man and the natural world, he knew the crania of apes, lemurs, and even birds had a similar characteristic (Gibson & Rafter, 2006). Lombroso believed they all shared a place in the evolutionary lineage linked to man, but in arrested stages of development. Further examination of Villella's skull revealed additional cranial abnormalities, but this one find provided Lombroso with the empirical evidence he needed to specify a type of human — criminal man. There are many questions about Villella that have been blurred by history and various accounts of his story, including variations of the spelling of his name. Lombroso and his daughter Gina believed that Villella was a brigand and murderer, but other accounts have him as only a thief, and it is very possible that as a simple peasant from Calabria, he was swept up as collateral damage in the military campaign in southern Italy during the war on brigandage.

Marks of Degeneration

In Villella, Lombroso not only found his "tell," but he also developed from his observations a typology of criminal man and an early — if primitive —

risk-assessment tool based on physical characteristics and features. He reported that, when compared to healthy men in the army, criminals in most regions were above the average Italian in weight and height. However, even within the criminal type,

> robbers and murderers are taller than rapists, forgers, and especially thieves. . . . Arsonists, and even more so thieves, tend to have gray irises; members of both groups are always shorter, lighter, weaker, and smaller in cranial capacity than pickpockets, who are in turn shorter, lighter, and weaker than murderers. . . . Female criminals are weaker than the insane and more often masculine looking (Gibson & Rafter, 2006, 50, 56).

From the use of a dynamometer to measure hand strength, Lombroso concluded that, "rapists, brigands, and arsonists are the strongest and thieves and forgers the weakest, based on measurement of traction. Murderers and pickpockets differ in strength only by a slight fraction" (Gibson & Rafter, 2006, 54). In later editions of *Criminal Man*, Lombroso added to the list of physical features of not only the "born criminal," but also other anomalies that were common to most criminals. Studies of the strength and agility of criminals by other researchers reported by Lombroso showed high marks for agility but lower levels of strength compared to "those of healthy, or rather free, individuals" (Gibson & Rafter, 2006, 209). In comparing tractive strength of criminals by their chosen professions, Lombroso found that: "If one considers only traction, murderers, robbers, and forgers show the greatest strength, while arsonists, rapists, [thieves], and brigands show the least" (Gibson & Rafter, 2006, 209). Lombroso made similar comparisons between the physical characteristics of criminals and their illegal activity throughout his works.

Preceding publication of the first edition of *Criminal Man* in 1876, Lombroso studied the cranial measurements of 832 criminals provided by fellow prison directors and physicians. He then selected a second group of soldiers for comparison and contrast. In addition to conducting craniological measurements of soldiers, he noticed that soldiers from lower social classes exhibited more antisocial behavior and intemperance. Some of these soldiers wore a variety of tattoos, often obscene, and some had a criminal record. He reported his findings in the opening pages of *Criminal Man*. From his earlier study of Piedmontese soldiers, Lombroso selected 868 whom he considered depraved, then he compared them with 390 of the "most notorious and depraved" male and female criminals and 90 lunatics (Gibson & Rafteer, 2006, 50). The physical comparison of the two groups and collected data revealed the born criminal to have, many of the characteristics found in savages, and among the coloured [sic] races, are also to be found in habitual delinquents [criminals]. They have in common, for example, thinning hair, lack of strength and weight, low cranial capacity, receding foreheads, highly developed frontal sinuses . . . darker skin, thicker, curly hair, large or handle-shaped ears, a great analogy . . . of the born criminal (Gibson & Rafter, 2006, 91).

One troubling point of comparison, in addition to the racist overtones, was that Lombroso did not differentiate between men and women, nor explain how many women were in the study.

Most congenital criminals, Lombroso noted, had thin beards, eyes of unequal size, black hair and brown eyes, broad check bones, smaller and asymmetrical or pointed craniums, protruding chins, a similarity between the sexes, insensitivity to pain, and muscular weakness (measured by a dynamometer). Additional features often found among born criminals included, "traumatic lesions of the head and oblique eyes," and "unequally sized pupils, distorted noses" (Gibson & Rafter, 2006, 56). By the fifth edition of *Criminal Man* (1889), Lombroso had discovered several additional physical features of criminals, including the lack of baldness and premature grayness, an over abundance of facial wrinkles compared to normal individuals, and overdeveloped canine teeth among murderers (310, 311). Lombroso also reported in the same edition the research of other scientists who had reported finding among criminals at large the anomaly of prehensile feet, "where the first two toes have a monkeylike ability to grasp objects," which also appeared in 31 epileptics out of 200 criminals (307).

Additional signature physical characteristics of criminals in general included the hypertrophy of male genitals, which Lombroso believed contributed to rape, murder, and arson. In fact, he concluded that, "All criminals, particularly thieves and murders, show precocious development of the genitals" (Gibson & Rafter, 2006, 132). Working with a small sample of prisoners and normal individuals, Lombroso discovered that sensitivity to pain was far less among criminals and even more so for the insane compared to the average normal person.

The invention of photography in 1839 promised a new method to visually identify individuals, and within a decade police agencies were photographing criminals. The early use of photography by police agencies lacked formal procedures or uniformity as a record, but that would soon change. Alphonse Bertillon (1853-1914), who worked in the Paris police department as director of its identification bureau, combined his interest in photography and biometrics in the 1880s to create the "mug shot." The criminal's photograph together with physical measurements of the body on a card provided a specific human record that could be used to differentiate between criminals and identify the alleged culprit. The new method was especially useful for identifying recidivist criminals. Bertillon also created the composite photograph of two or more criminals on a card, which aided identification by witnesses.

Bertillon is also credited with developing the fingerprint methodology. By the 20th century, the anthropometric method used by the police was replaced by the more reliable fingerprint record.

Lombroso was quick to adapt the use of individual and composite photographs of criminals as illustrations beginning with his second edition of *Criminal Man* in 1878. He often used photographs collected or sent to him to make visual criminal type classifications and judgments of dangerousness. Lombroso selected photos that prominently featured stigmata that he wanted to show. He also used facial drawings as illustrations and would deliberately alter features to accentuate them.

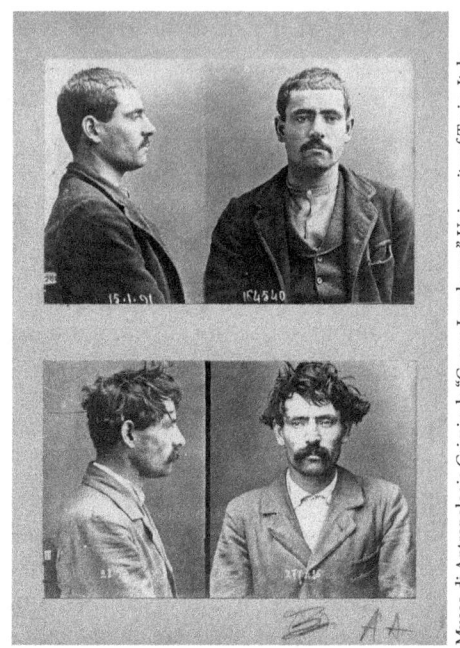

Bertillon type composite photo of two criminals (note the wire to hold the head straight during the photo process on the lower left figure).

Face of a "typical" criminal type.

On at least one occasion Lombroso and Bertillon met, in 1896 at a criminal anthropological conference in Geneva. While Lombroso admired Bertillon's work, their philosophies were diametrically opposed; Bertillon was an outspoken opponent of Positivism and instead championed the Classical School (Lombroso-Ferrero, Chap. XVII, 11).

Lombroso shared in the third edition of *Criminal Man* (1884) some findings of other researchers regarding criminals' functions of taste, smell, and sight. However, he was unusually reserved, and he avoided conjecture due to the small sample sizes of the studies and the need for additional research. Lombroso explored left-handedness and added it to the list of common anomalies found among criminals. "Compared to normal individuals, criminals show an almost twofold prevalence of left-handedness; in this they resemble children, primitives, and idiots" (Gibson & Rafter, 2006, 211). According to his own research, Lombroso found that left-handedness was most prevalent among swindlers (33 percent) compared to other types of criminals (Gibson & Rafter, 2006, 211). Left-handedness was to Lombroso just one more regressive trait to add to his growing list of atavistic characteristics (Kushner, 2011).

In general, criminals were also lazy, vain, and loved gambling and alcohol. Furthermore, Lombroso argued in the first edition of *Criminal Man* (1876) that primitive men and criminals shared a,

> lack of moral sense, revulsion for work, absence of remorse, lack of foresight, vanity, superstitiousness, self-importance, and, finally, an under developed concept of divinity and morality (Gibson & Rafter, 2006, 91).

Lombroso often mixed psychical and physical characteristics within the same context revealing his tendency to make physiognomic conclusions. Vanity, he emphasized, was common to both male and female criminals (Gibson & Rafter, 2006, 65-66).

Lombroso noted that criminals might not look "fierce" or threatening, but "there is nearly always something strange about their appearance" (Gibson & Rafter, 2006, 51). Physical appearance and mental illness were also defining features of cretinism and pellagra, the study of which, of course, provided the foundation of his work. Physical anomalies were the signs of disease and depravity, which in itself was an extension of degeneracy or atavism, and arrested development (Horn, 2003). Lombroso explained in the fourth edition of *Criminal Man* (1889) that cretinism, atavism, and pathology explained arrested development of the congenital criminal.

Criminal man was a savage anomaly, an "atavistic phenomenon" harkening to the past, a product of arrested development, and not adaptable to contemporary society (Lombroso, 1911/2012, xiv). Lombroso was keenly aware of the danger criminals presented to the social fabric of the recently unified Italy. He believed that physical abnormalities visible as stigmata, were the very anomalies that identified the criminal type who, in turn, formed a dangerous class. The term "dangerous class" was common in 19th-century Europe, used to describe not only criminals but also the working class, unemployed, and the underprivileged in general (Pick, 1989; Merriman, 2004).

Primitive Savages

In his publications, Lombroso often compared the natural world to the human experience. He found it "natural" for him "to make zoology the foundation of the new school of criminal anthropology" (Gibson & Rafter, 2006, 167). There was violence in the plant, insect, and animal world so it was reasonable to see the same in man. Lombroso believed that the violent actions of animals, insects, and plants could not be called criminal since they were systemic to the species, so also with savages. Of course, those actions were not criminal since moral standards were not applied to them (Gibson & Rafter, 2006; Lombroso, 1911/2015). He also found startling similarities between animals, carnivorous plants, and insects with the congenital criminal:

> The most ferocious animals are physiognomically close to the born criminal; tigers and hyenas have bloodshot gray eyes identical to those of assassins. . . . 'birds of prey, including hawks, have a short curving beak with a sharp tooth on the upper jaw and *eye socket filled with blood.*' . . . It is impossible to study the physiognomy of insects because of the immobility of their faces; however, the strength of their jaws shows that they are carnivorous predators (Gibson & Rafter, 2006, 172-173).

Following the same evolutionary based frame of thought, Lombroso relayed that the palm of the hand of monkeys and apes most closely resembled the palm of the born criminal, thieves in particular: "The monkey is a true pickpocket. While being petted or stroked, it reaches into pockets, steals without being noticed, and hides the booty in curtains or bedclothes, much as servants do" (Gibson & Rafter, 2006, 172). Biological anomalies in Lombroso research linked the congenital criminal with the evolutionary process. Even criminals' eyesight was considered more acute than the average person and closely linked to the "savage" (Lombroso-Ferrero, 1911/2015, 26). Perhaps more startling than his believed discovery of an evolutionary link between the world of animals and man was the lack of solid comparative evidence beyond the realm of conjecture and a few illustrations.

The process of biological determinism marked the congenital criminal as a throwback to a more primitive man in the evolutionary progress, what he called the "atavistic" man, a "distinct anthropological type" (Lombroso, 1911/2012, xxi). The atavistic criminal harkened to a more primitive time when his actions were no more criminal or immoral than the violence in the natural world. However, in a modern society, there was no place for this throwback to another time. Criminal man was inclined to criminality by birth and unable to change, he represented an immoral regressive and degenerate presence in the modern world of 19th century Europe. Lombroso did not coin the term "born criminal," that distinction goes to his former student, fellow researcher and jurist, Enrico Ferri, but he fully embraced the term by his third edition of *Criminal Man* in 1880. Within Lombroso's ultimate criminal classification schematic, Ferri, Raffaele Garofalo, and Sergio Sergi contributed two additional types to the born criminal, the occasional criminal, and the criminal by passion.

Lombroso's study of the "primitive savage," or the "congenital criminal," was the founding of Italian criminal anthropology, "the natural history of the criminal" (Ferri, 1908/2017, 7). In addition to using the term, criminal anthropology, Lombroso also called his new approach to the understanding of criminal man the "Modern, or Positive, School of Penal Jurisprudence" (Lombroso, 1911/2012, 16). During the 1905 Congress of Psychology in Rome, Lombroso affectionately referred to his school of criminal anthropology as the "Cinderella of modern science" (Lombroso-Ferrero, Chap. XXI, 7). In Europe the new criminology was also called The New Italian School. Lombroso's fellow researcher, Enrico Ferri, labeled the new movement with the broader and more inclusive title of the "Positivist School of Criminology" (Ferri, 1908/2017, 5).

By the use of all these terms at various times, Lombroso and others sought to distinguish between their research of the mentally deficient criminal man as an anomaly and the Beccarian emphasis on the moral responsibility of the actor and the legal response of the state to offenses (Gibson, 2006; Rafter, 2006). The new school of criminology owed its existence to the eclectic mind of Lombroso, a ready population for study in Italian prisons and asylums where he worked, advances in data collection and analysis, and the popular explanatory power of psychiatry.

Criminal Man and Subsequent Editions

Lombroso's life work was an extended ever-expanding project. In books, articles, and presentations he continued to define the nature and world of criminal man, his research was a perpetual work in progress. He also learned to accept and modify some of his positions in accord with changing science and poignant criticism or helpful insights and suggestions of associates and other scholars. In his first edition of *Criminal Man* (1876), Lombroso originally generalized that all criminals represented a single type, a congenital or atavistic criminal. Lombroso recognized in his later years that one should be cautious in labeling a "type" of criminal, because "the idea of type . . . [cannot be] carried out in its complete universality," advice he did not heed earlier in his career (MacDonald, 1893/2010, i). He argued that a "type" was determined by an "ensemble of the most prominent traits, and those repeating themselves the most often" (ii).

By the fourth edition of *Criminal Man* in 1889, Lombroso explained that a group of characteristics, including a minimum of five or six anomalies, were necessary to identify the criminal man (Gibson & Rafter, 2006, 271). Most likely he had grown tired of arguments made over how many anomalies were required to identify a criminal. In addition Lombroso faced questions whether normal people were free of atavistic characteristics or anomalies. In the same edition, Lombroso explained that it was not uncommon for normal individuals to show one or two anomalies.

Over a period of 20 years, *Criminal Man* went through five editions. The first four built in succession on the previous editions and introduced a classification scheme along with additional physical characteristics and mental maladies. The fifth edition was a summary work in four volumes. The first edition however, would always remain his seminal work.

The first use of a formal criminal classification appeared in Lombroso's second edition of *Criminal Man* (1878). Lombroso ultimately through the remaining editions designed a classification scheme that included six specific types of criminals and a variety of subcategories. In addition to the born criminal, Lombroso in the second edition introduced the criminal by passion, a contribution from Ferri, Garofalo, and Sergi. The third (1884) and fourth (1889) editions expanded Lombroso classification of the above types to include the epileptic, and Ferri and associates' second contribution, the occasional criminal. These same two editions also revealed the classifications of the insane and morally insane.

The place of criminal women in Lombroso's typology of criminals was incomplete until the publication of *Criminal Women, the Prostitute, and the Normal Woman* in 1893, and *The Female Offender* in 1909. References to women by Lombroso in the five editions of *Criminal Man* are sketchy and do not appear central to his study of the criminal type. Lombroso admits in the first edition of *Criminal Man* that, "I do not have enough information on normal women to make a comparison with criminal women" (Gibson & Rafter, 2006, 54). This statement, however, does not prohibit him from making inferences based on minimal observations throughout the five editions of *Criminal Man* and other publications.

The fact that Lombroso included women at all in his editions of *Criminal Man* is likely due to growing interest and criticism in the scholarly community to explain the applicability of atavism to female criminals. Another major influence was much closer to home. In addition to his wife Nina, Lombroso's two main assistants were his daughters, Gina and Paola. Gina in particular worked with her father during his entire lifetime and carried on the propagation of his work following his death in 1909. She was also a medical doctor, which contributed to her understanding of her father's work.

Paola and her doctor husband, Mario Carrara, also worked closely with Lombroso on his many projects. Mario was especially interested in the legal aspects of penal reform while Paola had a special interest in music. She worked with Lombroso in the early 1890s on a project to determine the relationship of music and sound to the deafness of musicians and their ability to play professionally. They also encouraged Lombroso to broaden his criminal research to include women (Lombroso-Ferrero. Chap. XV). Gina's husband, Guglielmo Ferrero, was also a voice for inclusion and served as the co-author with Lombroso of *Criminal Woman, the Prostitutes, and the Normal Woman* (1893) and *The Female Offender* (1909). The topic of criminal woman as a type forms the content of chapter 6.

The first edition of *Criminal Man* (1876) focused on the descriptive physical characteristics or features of the atavistic criminal, a biologically determined specimen. Lombroso introduced atavism as the principle cause of criminality in this landmark edition. This edition did not yet reveal a formal classification scheme, although the congenital criminal he described was a specific criminal type. The first edition is primarily an investigation into the atavistic origins of crime. Lombroso followed a topical arrangement beginning with his Villella discovery and continuing through organized crime and punishment. Of special interest to Lombroso was the slang used by criminals and their literature. Undoubtedly, his interest in linguistics from his association with Marzolo made language and its expression of great import. Another element of interest was tattooing, which appeared to be common among both soldiers and criminals. During his military tours of duty, he observed and rendered on paper drawings hundreds of tattoos worn by soldiers. Lombroso also made a significant but confusing, even contradictory, argument regarding the role of education and criminality.

With the publication of the second edition of *Criminal Man* in 1878, Lombroso added to his congenital criminal of the first edition a new classification, the criminal by passion, a major contribution of Ferri, Garofalo, and Sergi. He also introduced with minimal detail the morally insane criminal. Lombroso's description of the impulsive nature and anti-social behavior of the passionate criminal is strikingly similar to the present-day theory of impulsivity. He proceeded in the second edition to make a more thorough investigation into the etiology of crime noting causal social conditions in addition to the inherent atavistic characteristics of criminal man. Psychical conditions of the criminal mind are also a new focus for Lombroso in this edition. Lombroso acknowledged, perhaps for the first time in print that, "crime has complex causes" (Gibson & Rafter, 2006, 118). Punishment is a re-occurring topic, but Lombroso also added a discussion of recidivism, most certainly a reflection on his years of service in prisons and asylums. The second edition of *Criminal Man* marks the transition away from atavism and the congenital criminal as the sole explanation or classification for criminality.

The third (1884) and fourth (1889) editions of *Criminal Man* included new classifications including, the occasional, and epileptic criminal types. His classifications of moral insanity and insanity are also given more descriptive attention and comparison. His comments regarding the female criminal are limited primarily to a comparison of crime statistics with males. Lombroso began the third edition with a description and analysis of the universality of crime in the natural world and among primitive peoples and children. The issue of moral insanity runs thematically through the third edition. He defined moral insanity as essentially a natural phenomenon common to all children, but good parenting and education could ameliorate the condition and train a person to respond to stimuli in a normal or acceptable fashion. Crime prevention virtually started Lombroso stressed with the children. The third edition continues the addition of criminal types begun with the second edition and continued discussion of the psychical nature of criminal.

Lombroso recognized that atavism was an insufficient explanation for multiple anomalies found in criminals and also the presence of anomalies in normal persons. The role of degeneracy through hereditary disease in place of atavism alone as a cause for criminality is explored in both the third and fourth editions of *Criminal Man*. In the fourth edition (1889), which was published in two volumes, Lombroso made the case for the "fusion" of the born criminal with the morally insane and epileptic criminals, and introduces the occasional criminal type. Several subcategories of criminals are also discussed, including hysterical, mattoid, habitual, and latent criminals.

The fifth and final edition of *Criminal Man* (1896-1897) was published in four volumes, which are mainly a synthesis of earlier editions. The fourth volume of the edition consists primarily of the tables and illustrations from the previous editions and is entitled the *Atlas*. Several new physical characteristics of criminal men are described, including prehensile feet and wrinkles. Also new are the discussions on "scientific policing" and early strategies for crime prevention. The fifth edition also reflects a socialists' perspective, the result of Lombroso's recent "conversion" to the Socialists Party in 1893. He found the parliamentary form of government wanting and admired the democratic institutions of the United States (S. Montaldo, interview, September 20, 2016).

The Italian government seemed to Lombroso to be either unwilling or unable, or both, to meet the needs of the Italian people (S. Montaldo, interview, September 20, 2016). Some solutions he offered were taxing the rich to redistribute wealth, expropriation of church lands, greater equity in wages, make jobs more accessible, promoting the "social welfare" via the state, and philanthropic initiatives leading "ultimately" to "collectivism" (Gibson & Rafter, 2006,334). In a telling remark in his first edition (1876) of *Criminal Man*, Lombroso addressed the political class:

> I know that many politicians, even if they are convinced of the truth of the truth of the positivist school, seek to stifle its teachings. They fear that positivism encourages communistic ideas and, even worse, criminal behavior. In fact, if one looks at the evidence, the opposite is true (71).

Through all five editions of *Criminal Man* there was a progression from the singular explanation for criminal man to the more complex identity of criminal types. Atavism following the first edition no longer had sole relevance for explaining a criminal type. This process reflected Lombroso's conceptual maturation from the original idea due to the influence of close family and associates and criticism from fellow scholars that his perspective of the criminal type was too inclusive and perhaps even prejudiced. Lombroso deflected criticism and skepticism of his work, which "always follow in the train of audacious innovations" (Lombroso, 1911/2012, 8). In his second edition of *Criminal Man* (1878), in defense, Lombroso acknowledged that: "From a scientific point of view, it [first edition] was marred by defects that can be excused only by those who have followed lonely paths into little-known field of research" (Gibson & Rafter, 2006, 99). His remarks may be indeed self-serving, but they reflect the convictions of a theoretical pioneer.

The process of recognizing new criminal types and determinate factors or characteristics required Lombroso to modify the percentage of atavistic characteristics found in each new criminal type. Starting from a range of 100% in the congenital criminal, Lombroso reduced the percentage of atavistic features in other types to 60% in the fourth edition, 35% in the fifth, and 33% in *Crime: Its Causes and Remedies*. His daughter, Gina Lombroso-Ferrero, also determined that the number of atavistic characteristics found in non-congenital criminal types was 33% in the summary of her father's work, *Criminal Man,* first published posthumously two years after his death, in 1911.

Criminal Typology

While impulsivity (lack of impulse control) emerged in the late 20th century as a formal causal theory for criminal behavior, Lombroso provided in the first edition of *Criminal Man* (1876) perhaps the first articulation of the concept. Criminals he noted gave little thought to the consequences of their actions, they "are generally very illogical and always imprudent. However able they may be, they bring to their crimes the lack of foresight. . . . Powerful and violent passions cloud their judgment" (Gibson & Rafter, 2006, 72). This definition for crimes of passion evolved into the second classification for "criminals of passion," found in the second edition of *Criminal Man* (1878). Crimes of passion according to Lombroso "might be better labeled crimes of impulse" (Gibson & Rafter, 2006, 105).

Lombroso described passionate criminals as "almost insanely emotional," who "display exaggerated sensitivity and excessive affections" often triggered by "rage, love, or offended honor" (Gibson & Rafter, 2006, 106-107). In the explosion of emotion "even murder assumes the character of a crime of passion because it is nearly always carried out in broad daylight; without ambush, accomplices, or a plan" (107). Lombroso explained that physical anomalies were rare among criminals of passion, because their appearance could be quite normal thus masking their identity in society. These individuals could be almost anyone and appeared for the most part quite normal until emotionally triggered. To Lombroso, "all criminals share the important traits of impulsiveness, cortical irritation, insensitivity [moral and tactile], and immorality" (Gibson & Rafter, 2006, 231; Lombroso-Ferrero. Chap. XII, 6).

Closely associated with impulsiveness and the rarity of physical anomalies was the criminal who suffered from epilepsy. Crime and epilepsy were indelibly linked in Lombroso's mind: "the anthropological character of epileptics is marked by moral degeneration and a tendency to evil" (Gibson & Rafter, 2006, 251). The question of criminal responsibility for those who suffered from epileptic seizures was a current topic in Europe. Based on the review of several high profile murder cases familiar to Lombroso, he concluded in 1884 that the epileptic criminal suffered from a form of moral insanity (Lombroso-Ferrero. Chap. XII, 6-7, 8).

Lombroso explained in the fourth edition of *Criminal Man* (1889) that epilepsy was another characteristic of criminal man, which also signified a new classification of criminal, the epileptic criminal. He explored this further in his books, *Man of Genius* (1891), and *Crime: Its Causes and Remedies* (1911) published posthumously. In the mind of Lombroso there was no distinction between criminals and epileptics,

> the greatest criminals showed themselves to be epileptics, and, on the other hand, epileptics manifested the same anomalies as criminals. Finally, it was shown that epilepsy frequently reproduced atavistic characteristics, including even those common to lower animals (Lombroso, 1911/2012, 7).

Lombroso described epilepsy and epileptics as both atavistic and pathological. On a linear scale of atavism and psychological, the similarity of born criminals and the morally insane was unmistakable to Lombroso,

> what I call the epileptic type includes not only obvious epiphenomena but also secondary characteristics, bringing together all the traits of the morally insane and the born criminal in a pronounced way . . . . the epileptic's impulsivity, fleeting sentiments, and tendency to inflict hard for harm's sake are also characteristics of the born criminal and the morally insane (Gibson & Rafter, 2006, 247, 251).

The term "moral insanity" was first proposed in 1835 by the British psychiatrist James Prichard. He described moral insanity as affecting the emotions and the will, in contrast to insanity, which was an intellectual dysfunction (Wetzell, 2000, 19). Moral insanity and organic insanity vary in origin and degree, relayed Lombroso, but he believed they shared common psychological and physiognomic traits and characteristics. To Lombroso's thinking there was a very close correlation between insanity and crime. He found it nearly "impossible to neatly distinguish between . . . madness and crime" (Gibson & Rafter, 2006, 43). Lombroso initially labeled the born criminal as insane; however, by 1880 he had decided that because they sometimes exhibited intelligence, they were more closely aligned with the morally insane who lacked a moral sense of right and wrong and compassion (Lombroso-Ferrero. Chap. XII, 5).

Morality or the moral nature of the criminal was a familiar theme in Lombroso's editions of *Criminal Man*. Following the first edition, Lombroso gave greater coverage to psychological elements of criminality after he received criticism that the first edition overplayed the causal role of biology at the expense of criminal psychology. The new emphasis on psychology reflected the scholarly interest of Ferri, Garofalo, and Sergi, among others. In his second edition (1878), he provided an inclusive categorical definition of criminal psychology as perhaps a defense for his broad interpretation and use of the term:

> Criminal psychology involves the study of the passions, writings, jargon, religion, morality, education, and mental illnesses of offenders, as well as the influences of history, climate, hereditary, and nutrition on crime (Gibson & Rafter, 2006, 100).

In each succeeding edition of *Criminal Man*, Lombroso addressed these issues in varying degree of detail, but often blended them together interchangeably between causal factors and actual attributes or characteristics of the criminal. His most complete etiology of crime, following summaries found in the fifth edition (1889), is found in *Crime: Its Causes and Remedies* (1911).

Lombroso believed that criminals exhibited moral insensitivity, especially an insensitivity to the suffering of others, essentially, a lack of conscience. In addition to insensitivity to pain, moral insensitivity combined with "infantile impetuousness" or "precipitous passions," Lombroso argued, explained the criminal's "lack of logic and recognition of the gravity of their deeds" (Gibson & Rafter, 2006, 64). Incapable of regulating their own emotions or actions, criminals acted impulsively, making them oblivious to the pain and suffering of their victims. Once again Lombroso found a link between criminals and savages in the lack of moral sensitivity or moral sanity. To Lombroso, moral insanity was an endogenous moral defect. Moral insanity was not a new concept in 19th century Europe; however, Lombroso assigned it a leading role in determining an individual's life-course (Wetzell, 2000, 30).

The use of the term moral insensitivity by Lombroso closely aligns with his use of the term, moral insanity, which first appeared in the third edition of *Criminal Man* (1884). Lombroso believed that moral insanity or insensitivity was primarily a congenital pathology, but he did not rule out the possibility of its origin as a disease. He often associated moral insanity with "cerebral afflictions." Lombroso explained that there were really only two different conditions of mental illness, insanity and moral insanity, which shared many physical and psychical abnormalities and anomalies. Physically both groups of insane shared common characteristics. In addition to the congenital criminal and criminal by passion, Lombroso in the fourth edition of *Criminal Man* (1889) recognized insanity and moral insanity as the fourth and fifth classifications of the criminal type.

Moral insanity allowed a person to commit depraved acts while remaining rational and logical, but unsympathetic, it stemmed from a lack of self-control. Lombroso explained that moral insanity was a congenital condition. He claimed a direct link existed in the etiology of both crime and moral insanity, "both born criminals and the morally insane manifest their tendencies from infancy or puberty" (Gibson & Rafter, 2006, 218). Lombroso described children, like savages, as morally insane within their first few months or even their first year of life. This state of moral ambiguity was spontaneous with birth.

Children, Lombroso argued, had no moral compass to guide their actions, "good or evil for them is that which is permitted or prohibited by their parents" (Gibson & Rafter, 2006, 189). Proper parenting, nourishment, and education, Lombroso asserted, could ameliorate the condition resulting in a normal person who would respond to stimuli appropriately. However, without such positive attention to changing behavior, moral insanity would "take its place beside atavism as a major determinant of criminal behavior" (Gibson & Rafter, 2006, 162). Moral insensitivity and moral insanity were descriptive terms used by Lombroso to describe the same malady of criminal indifference to humanity.

In early 19th century Italy, criminality was generally equated with insanity or moral insanity, resulting in criminals and the insane being incarcerated together. The movement to separate the insane and criminals into different institutions gained greater traction following the unification of Italy. Lombroso contributed to this movement by taking the position for separation of common criminals from the criminally insane, even though he equated criminality with insanity (Lombroso-Ferrero. Chaps. V, 12; VII, 14, 18; VIII, 1-2; X, 1). Contradictory conclusions were not uncommon for Lombroso, they appear to reflect a mind and thought process in constant motion and not necessarily on a linear progressive line. Lombroso followed first and foremost an eclectic system of thought. To the charge that Lombroso simply determined morality from physiognomy and cranial measurements, he responded to those who challenged his theory and methodology:

> The ability to ascertain moral temperament from physiognomy and the cranium is not equivalent to solving a riddle or telling fortunes, as ordinary people believe, and with them, undiscerning critics. Instead, it is a scientific method of discerning character and is made all the easier because we are not limited to the face but can also take account of handwriting, gestures, and sensitivity (Gibson & Rafter, 2006, 233).

The pathological condition of insanity was equated by Lombroso with madness or criminal insanity; he used these terms interchangeably. He found that the origin of insanity in contrast to moral insanity was a different matter, "few of the insane are born wicked or immoral; rather, they become so after an illness changes or modifies their character. Like the criminal, the mad rarely feel remorse or pity" (Gibson & Rafter, 2006, 82). In some cases, Lombroso stated that madness could, "simply [be] a criminal tendency, a lack of any sense of morality" (Gibson & Rafter, 2006, 83). He never swayed from his conviction that insanity or madness and criminal behavior were virtually two sides of the same coin. However, if there was a "line between crime and madness," Lombroso explained, it was a "subtle division that is often not perceived until it is too late" (Gibson & Rafter, 2006, 83).

Lombroso associated all criminals with "cerebral afflictions" and "above all, madness" (Gibson & Rafter, 2006, 83). He concluded, "nearly every type of mental abnormality contributes in some way to criminality" (Gibson & Rafter, 2006, 84). Insanity was sometimes, Lombroso admitted, a hereditary mental disorder that rendered responsibility for actions irrelevant to the criminal mind. But the onset of insanity or "madness," according to Lombroso in his first edition of Criminal Man (1876) could also be "provoked" by physical "trauma" or other "anomalies of the head, and liquor" (81). Lombroso added the subcategories of alcoholic, hysterical, and mattoid criminals to the broader insane type. While hysteria was most frequent among young females, he determined that among men though it was less prevalent but more serious. He believed that the condition was largely hereditary and most closely associated with epilepsy (Gibson & Rafter, 2006, 281). Lombroso also called attention to the similarities between hysteria and epilepsy. He claimed that:

> Hysterical convulsions are almost always indistinguishable from epileptic seizures. . . . Aside from . . . minor difference, however, the hysteric offers many parallels with epileptics — and with children, born criminals, and the morally insane as well (283).

Also related to epileptics, was the alcoholic criminal, who Lombroso believed could be cured in contrast to the epileptic. Lombroso noted that alcoholism was a historical factor in the history of man, furthermore it was both a rural as well as urban problem, although more pronounced in cities. In Lombroso's opinion, alcohol and in fact all "stimulants have the capacity to drive us to crime, suicide or insanity" (Gibson & Rafter, 2006, 277). Lombroso gave mention to alcohol in all five editions of *Criminal Man* in addition to other publications, but it was in the fourth edition (1889) that he discussed alcoholism specifically in the context of insanity. In *The Man of Genius* (1891) and *Crime: Its Causes and Remedies* (1911). Lombroso linked alcoholism and other drugs with genius, remarking that "great and powerful brains" require stimulants in greater quantity (Lombroso, 1891/2015, 101; Lombroso, 1911/2012, 316).

In many ways, the alcoholic criminal easily crosses boundaries between moral insanity and insanity. As early as his published monograph on the "Medical Geography of Italy" in 1865, Lombroso had described the deleterious effects of alcohol use (Lombroso-Ferrero. Chap. V, 20). Based on his studies, Lombroso believed that alcoholism had two primary manifestations, it was heritable and it tended to be chronic. He described the psycho-somatic effects of continued use of alcohol, including tremors, hallucinations, incipient paralysis, blurred vision, and fits of delirium. Lombroso himself did not drink alcoholic beverages out of his concern for perceived links to insanity (S. Montaldo, interview, September 20, 2016; Gibson & Rafter, 2006).

Mattoids were defined by Lombroso as a degenerate offshoot of the insane type of criminal, however unlike born criminals they rarely displayed any physical signs of degeneracy. Under Lombroso's classification of insane, mattoids could be surprisingly rational, affectionate, even to an "excess" with men (perhaps this is a nod to homosexual tendencies), and intelligent, but impulsive. According to Lombroso, mattoids tended to exaggerate their attributes including a belief in order and sobriety. They tended to be verbose and producers of writings in abundance all to feign their prowess. All these characteristics he explains were but a mask for their own sense of self worth. These individuals were vain and completely self-absorbed. They tended to be "crafty" and manipulative in their dealings with others. The characteristics that Lombroso describes are a close match to the DSM-5 definition of a sociopath in modern parlance. He argued that these individuals were often bureaucrats but typically professionals, including doctors, professors, theologians, and politicians. Lombroso added that while mattoids were generally "innocuous," their impulsive tendencies made them dangerous (Gibson & Rafter, 2006, 284-287; Lombroso, 1891/2015, 242; Lombroso-Ferrero. Chap. XI, 20, 26, 27).

The sixth criminal type classification, the occasional criminal, was introduced by Lombroso in the third edition (1884) of *Criminal Man*, but fully described in the fourth edition (1889). The occasional criminal type was the creation of Ferri, Garofalo, and Sergi. Unlike the born criminal, the insane, epileptic, or criminal by passion, which were explained by either atavism or disease, the occasional criminal was a victim of neither cause. The occasional criminal committed his crimes as a result of extraneous circumstances, including self-defense, support of family, and exceptional opportunity (Lombroso, 1911/2012, 414). Ferri further explained that the primary difference between the occasional criminal and the born criminal,

> is that the former simply has weak resistance to external incentives to commit crime, while the latter is driven by an internal compulsion to find a crime and commit it (Gibson & Rafter, 2006, 294).

The rationale for the occasional criminal was that his acts were minor offenses, the bulk of crime statistics, and he did not represent a dangerous class of criminal.

The new criminal type recognized the role of the physical and social environment as a perpetrating factor for criminal behavior. Ferri ascribed to crime the label of "social phenomenon," and defined the occasional criminal as one who was "led astray by his conditions of life . . . [more than] the aggressive energy of a degenerate personality" (Ferri, 1908/2017, 31). The occasional criminal was another attempt, like the criminal of passion, which was also developed by Ferri, Garofalo, and Sergi, to explain a broader range of criminals who did not fit the physical or psychiatric profile of the born, epileptic, or insane criminal. Lombroso had earlier proclaimed atavism and disease as the primary causes of crime but the occasional criminal and criminal by passion opened a new area of research and diagnosis. But even the category of occasional criminal was too broad and needed further delineation, and so several subcategories were created to explain either specific types of crimes or criminal status.

With his colleagues, Ferri and Garofalo, Lombroso identified four subcategories of the occasional criminal: pseudocriminals, criminaloids, habitual criminals, and latent criminals. All four subtypes of criminals exhibited too few anomalies to be classified as born criminals, yet they were responsible for a fair amount of crime. Pseudocriminals consisted of two groups, the individual who commits crimes involuntarily, and the individual who commits crimes voluntarily, but poses no danger to society. An example of the first would include the act of manslaughter, and the second included acts like theft to support a family that were illegal but not necessarily immoral by social standards.

In contrast to pseudocriminals, criminaloids were predisposed to crime, but acted only when circumstances pushed them over the edge. The criminaloid was described by Lombroso as caught in the middle between being a criminal and an honest citizen, but showed degenerative characteristics. Degenerative anomalies, included large jaws, swollen sinuses, jug ears, microcephaly, crooked noses, prognathism, head trauma, epilepsy, alcoholism, left-handedness, and tactile insensitivity. Lombroso concluded that the criminaloid shared some abnormalities with the born criminal but at lower rates (Gibson & Rafter, 2006, 293; Lombroso, 1911\2012, 374). Lombroso's daughter, Gina, noted that the real difference between the criminaloid and the born criminal was psychological rather than physical (Lombroso-Ferrero, 1911/2015, 62).

Children who were not the product of good parenting and education, Lombroso relayed, could become in later life a habitual criminal due to latent tendencies left unchecked. Habitual criminals were minor offenders who in their life-course resembled born criminals in their pattern of offending and recidivism. Lombroso did not assign to the habitual criminal any specific abnormalities other than their repetitive habit of offending. They were motivated according to Lombroso by a moral deadness and vanity aggravated by the abuse of alcohol and anger toward society. Crime for the habitual criminal, Lombroso explained, "for them becomes an organic phenomenon" (Gibson & Rafter, 2006, 295). He suggested that habitual criminals should "be treated like born criminals but subjected to a less severe discipline" (Lombroso, 1911/2012, 419).

The final subcategory of the occasional criminal was the latent criminal. By definition, Lombroso stated that latent criminals, do not reveal their criminalistic tendencies, either because they lack an opportunity or because wealth or power gives them means to satisfy their depraved instincts without breaking the law (Lombroso, 1911/2012, 419).

Wealth and privilege masked latent criminals' propensity to crime and shielded them typically from prosecution for their crimes. Examples of criminal behavior included soliciting prostitution, embezzlement, and bribery.

Lombroso proceeded to identify other characteristics or traits that fused the born criminal and morally insane into one type with similar small size and asymmetrical cranium, sensitivity [tactile, and to pain], left-handedness, agility, range psychologically from genius to imbecile, obscene behavior, tattooing, and recuperative power (Gibson & Rafter, 2006, 247-256). In order to further clarify the connection between the congenital criminal and morally insane, Lombroso explained:

> I am not arguing that moral insanity is the same thing as epilepsy or that all epileptics are morally insane. Rather, I am interested in a type of epilepsy that is becoming more common and has been little studied. It takes many forms . . . all of which also constitute acute forms of moral insanity and congenital criminality. Essentially, the difference among epilepsy, moral insanity, and born criminality is only a matter of degree (Gibson & Rafter, 2006, 263).

In regard to physical anomalies, Lombroso argued that it only took one to identify a morally insane person: "Although regressive anomalies tend to appear in clusters, experience has shown that individuals with even a single anomaly may display profound moral maladjustment" (Gibson & Rafter, 2006, 164).

The use of alcohol was a common binding element between epileptics, born criminals, and the morally insane. Lombroso explained, "alcoholic intoxication is added to the effect of atavism and still more to that of epilepsy" (Lombroso, 1911/2012, 370). The born criminal, Lombroso noted, was less prone to epileptic fits because they were latent in nature, but could flare with the use of alcohol. He believed epilepsy was a "degenerative psychosis" with a strong family generational history and afflicted the group of morally insane and genius, whether altruistic or evil in intent (Lombroso, 1891/2015, 333, 334). Lombroso associated alcohol with criminal behavior as an aggravating factor. Alcohol was a precursor stimulant to criminal activity.

Not only was epilepsy linked to the criminal type and the insane, along with moral insanity, it was endemic, he claimed, to men of genius throughout history (Lombroso, 1911/2012, 38, 336-337). Lombroso concluded, "Genius, like insanity, has its basis in epilepsy. It is not absurd, then, to see moral insanity united with genius, and by that very union made not only harmless but sometimes even useful to society" (Lombroso, 1911/2012, 449). Examples of this, he explained, could be found among some of the great men in history, including leaders, conquerors, and even saints. Lombroso considered criminality, insanity, and epilepsy in totality to be regressive traits. Although Lombroso did not label "genius" as a separate criminal type or classification, it was the focus of an entire book (1891), *The Man of Genius*. He described genius as a neurosis resulting from an inherited degeneration. The genius had a unique personality: impulsive, inquisitive, precocious, melancholy, and megalomania. The genius was often short in stature, bald, pale, and with cerebral convolutions that were numerous. These men (seldom women) were given to misoneism and meditation. Their originality was "usually of an aimless kind" (Lombroso, 1891/2015, 36). In conclusion, Lombroso summarizes:

> Taking all this into consideration, we may confidently affirm that genius is a true degenerative psychosis belonging to the group of moral insanity, and may temporarily spring out of other psychoses, assuming their forms, though keeping its own special peculiarities, which distinguish it from all others (333).

Another regressive trait, left-handedness, Lombroso determined was commonly shared among epileptics, the morally insane, and men of genius. In an historical context, left-handedness is described by the Anthropologist David G. Horn in *The Criminal Body* (2003) as culturally and linguistically linked with "danger, dishonesty, and fraud" (71). Lombroso made a similar link with Italian folklore, which referred to a left-handed person as "sinister" (Gibson & Rafter, 2006, 211). Left-handedness was part of the larger anomaly of left-sidedness, which Lombroso associated with criminality and regarded as a "character of atavism and degeneration" (Lombroso, 1911/2012, 13). Because left-handedness resulted from dominance of the brain's right hemisphere over the left, Lombroso jumped to the conclusion that criminals tended to think with the right brain (Gibson & Rafter, 2006, 211). Criminals, Lombroso explained, showed "an almost twofold prevalence of left-handedness; in this they resemble children, primitives, and idiots (Gibson & Rafter, 2006, 211). The atavistic state of nature, Lombroso continued, bound both criminal man and the animals, including crustaceans, parrots, lions, and monkeys, with the common trait of left-handedness (Gibson & Rafter, 2006, 167-173, 211).

Also common to criminals in general and epileptics in particular was a status of religiosity, which alternated with cynicism and served as a pretext for impulsive acts (Gibson & Rafter, 2006, 252). Other psychological traits common to epileptics Lombroso considered, while not sufficiently researched, he believed to be "obvious enough to give what artists call local color," included a tendency to vagabondage, love of animals, somnambulism, obscenity, recuperative power, suicide, tattoos, and fraternization (Gibson & Rafter, 2006, 253-256).

Lombroso ascribed to excessive vanity the "most common motive" for crime; criminals, he explained, had an "excessive sense of self-worth" (Gibson & Rafter, 2006, 65) and emotional intensity (69). In their emotional intensity, Lombroso stated, "criminals closely resemble not the insane but savages" (69). Murder, mayhem, cruelty, and revenge, according to Lombroso, were the consequences of this sense of self-worth; criminal activity was the natural result of the depraved criminal mind.

At the apex of Italian criminality was organized crime. Lombroso was interested in organized crime because of the "powerful effects of association" (Gibson & Rafter, 2006, 85). The power of group identity could "revive savage tendencies and, reinforce them with group discipline" with terrible results (85). Lombroso also identified race with Italian organized crime, arguing that the Mafia and Camorra were the offspring of the "rapacious Arab conquerors of Sicily who were related to the Bedouins, a "race" he had already labeled a criminal type (Gibson & Rafter, 2006, 91). During his years in the military, Lombroso had encountered elements of the Mafia and Camorra in Southern Italy. Perhaps this experience and the fact that little research had been conducted on organized crime prior to 1876, appealed to his intellectual curiosity.

The Mafia and Camorra date back centuries and during the struggle for Italian unification, they had been associated with resistance and brigandage, in fact Lombroso labeled them as "nothing but variations on the old theme of brigandage" (Gibson & Rafter, 2006, 88). The Mafia was primarily located on the island of Sicily and the city of Palmero, while the Camorra were principally found in the city and region of Naples. Both groups had strong prison cadres, but the Camorra in particular. Lombroso found the hierarchical structure of the organizations and the centralization of dictatorial power of great interest. Even in this, Lombroso saw the similarities with savage tribes. He described gang members as generally illiterate, young males, unmarried, commonly orphans, and often, former soldiers. As such, they were a serious impediment to law and order in the new Italy. All the other physical and psychical traits of the criminal type applied to gang members. The same traits of the gang member were also common to all criminals.

Criminal Behavioral Traits — Self-Expression

Over years of observation, Lombroso took special interest in the habits of criminals including their pleasure seeking as identifying characteristics. He recognized that habits and intelligence differed among criminals similar to a person's status in society, but the common criminal of whom Lombroso writes, was exceptional in his pursuit of pleasure. In particular was the desire of criminals to engage in orgies (Gibson & Rafter, 2006, 68). Drinking, eating, gambling, and cavorting with prostitutes were part of the social life of criminals. But "the pleasures of gambling, eating, sex, and even revenge are nothing but intermediate steps to criminals' predominate passion, that of the orgy" (Gibson & Rafter, 2006, 68). Another characteristic of criminals was the desire for self-expression.

The general criminal type according to Lombroso exhibited several social or cultural behaviors in addition to the physiognomy and physiological characteristics noted above. For Criminal Man, Lombroso continued the study of tattoos that he had begun in Calabria. He added studies of criminals and insane people to his studies of soldiers during the war. He found tattooing to be a "common occurrence" and a "most singular characteristic of primitive men and those who still live in a state of nature" (Gibson & Rafter, 2006, 58). Tattoos, Lombroso concluded "function as pictographs for criminals as they do for savages" (Gibson & Rafter, 2006, 239). For the criminal anthropologist, "Tattooing often reveals the psychology, habits, and vices of the individual" (Lombroso-Ferrero, 1911/2015, 127). In Lombroso's mind there were two main reasons for tattooing, "among Europeans, the most important reason for tattooing is atavism and that other form of atavism called traditionalism" (Gibson & Rafter, 2006, 61).

The use of the terms, "state of nature" and "atavism" are analogous to Lombroso's references to the "savage" state of primitive man. The fact that many of the criminals Lombroso encountered were from southern Italy, a region already identified as primitive and backward, simply furthered the racial stereotype. The processing of tattooing was painful, but its common practice on a large scale on the body of criminals in particular was another indicator to Lombroso of criminals' insensitivity to pain.

Lombroso divided the symbols and meanings of tattoos into the categories of love, religion, war, and profession. He reasoned that the criminal's insensitivity to pain facilitated tattooing even on the genitals of males. For each category, Lombroso provided a hypothesis, for example, in the case of religion it was historically common to inscribe the name of a saint or the sign of the cross in the flesh. Inscribing the name of one's lover or expressing erotic sentiments was also widely observed. Lombroso hypothesized that the common practice of inscribing a symbol among soldiers of the same unit was an expression of camaraderie. And for professional criminals, like the Mafia and Camorra, Lombroso surmised that tattoos were used to signify membership and loyalty. In general, Lombroso believed that tattooing was an act of vanity and even laziness among prisoners with time on their hands.

Tattoos were not the only form of visual art practiced by criminals. Lombroso started collecting literary and artistic expressions of inmates while director of the Pesaro Asylum. Drawings or pictographs in beautiful and even exquisite stylistic forms and floral or geometric patterns were made with ink and sharpened sticks or quills on paper. Multiple colors and colored filled in areas are also characteristic of the pictographs. These works were, according to Lombroso, often the product of the insane or mentally afflicted who were limited by inadequate language skills, yet sought to express themselves in their art. Lombroso believed that this work re-

flected a "primitivism" linked to an older and lost time in the history of mankind (Bianucci and et al, 2011, 41). Tattoos and pictographs were to Lombroso further evidence of a direct connection or lineage to "savages" and perhaps their cave drawings (Gibson & Rafter, 2006, 239).

Regardless of psychical origin, the drawings or pictograph representations reveal a single-mindedness to detail, rather than mental chaos. Savage connections or not, Lombroso came to believe that the artistic and literary works of asylum patients demonstrated that insanity, contrary to popular wisdom, revealed an "extraordinary lucidity" (Lombroso-Ferrero. Chap. X, 10).

An asylum inmate's hand-drawn pictograph.

Museo di Antroplogia Criminale "Cesare Lombroso," University of Turin, Italy

Prisoners also crafted clay water jugs, and other art pieces often made from bread crumbs. Water jugs were usually decorated by hieroglyphics or other drawings and phrases.

Prisoner's courtroom scene on clay water jug.

Clay water jug expressing Viva Liberty!

Museo di Antropologia Criminale "Cesare Lombroso," University of Turin, Italy

A prisoner's courtroom scene.

Museo di Antropologia Criminale "Cesare Lombroso," University of Turin, Italy;
Photographer: Randall Butler

The use of hieroglyphics was described by Lombroso as basically the expression of words in pictures, a primitive art. Courtroom scenes and even depictions of murders were not uncommon to both bread-crumb and clay art pieces. Prisoners in addition to the utility of water jugs and canteens also crafted smoking pipes from wood or clay.

Museo di Antropologia Criminale "Cesare Lombroso," University of Turin, Italy

Clay pipes

Altogether, prisoner art and the making of usable products, including clocks often reveal exceptional craftsmanship and previously underutilized talent within a prison environment based on the principle of deprivation.

Their art also ventured into the field of pornography, or as Lombroso expressed in the fourth edition of *Criminal Man* (1889): "The obscenity of certain bread sculptures confiscated in prison is extraordinary and seems to provide a safety valve for repressed sexual desire" (245).

Lombroso was also intrigued by criminal handwriting, signatures in particular, "man's handwriting can provide clues to his psychological state" (Gibson & Rafter,

Museo di Antropologia Criminale "Cesare Lombroso," University of Turin, Italy

Prisoner's homemade clock made from wood.

2006, 111). However, Lombroso also found in criminal's handwriting associations or correlations with different types of offenses, and their afflictions, which he explained in the second (1878) and fourth (1889) editions of *Criminal Man*. Out of a collection of 407 signatures Lombroso divided them into two specific groups:

> Only the signatures of semi-illiterate criminals, who include some of our most famous brigands, retain a childish character and are not easy to categorize. The first group is made up of signatures of murderers, highway robbers, and brigands, who generally elongate their letters, adding curves to the upper and lower extensions . . . many . . . murderers show traces of a trembling hand, which is perhaps a sign of alcoholism or nervous disease. . . . The second group of signatures, belonging mostly to thieves, is distinct from that of highway robbers and lacks emphatic verticals. In general, the letters are soft and ill-formed, and the signatures are clear and easy to read. This kind of writing is similar to that of women and indeed to normal handwriting (Gibson & Rafter, 2006, 111-113).

In the fourth edition Lombroso shared an experiment he conducted with a criminal under hypnosis that revealed handwriting changes from normal to brigand and infantile. Lombroso concluded that the experiment "stupendously confirmed the atavistic nature of the handwriting of criminals" (Gibson & Rafter, 2006, 241). By the 1880s the use of hypnosis for psychical studies and entertainment was very popular on both sides of the Atlantic Ocean.

Another form of criminal expression that interested Lombroso was jail and prison poetry or prose along with graffiti often found on cell walls. Perhaps Lombroso's curiosity in criminal writings and marks reflect his interest in psycholinguistics. Even in their crudeness and rudimentary cadence, Lombroso found the poetry "powerful and rich," examples of a "special literature" produced from interminable and lonely hours of confinement (Gibson & Rafter, 2006, 79). Prisoners, Lombroso stated, "love the poetic form, which responds to their boiling passions and enables them to depict themselves and their suffering with extraordinary eloquence" (80). Several selections from his first edition of *Criminal Man* (1876) illustrate the reality of prison life, maternal grief, and desire:

> Prison, my life, sweet, happy!
> How I love being inside you!
> Only crazy heads speak ill of it,
> Or think it causes loss of peace.
> Here you only find brothers and friends,

Money, food and serene peace;
Outside one is always among enemies,
And if you can't work, you die of hunger (79).

From the flats of the Vicaria prison,
She signals with little hands;
I see that she is my mama
And that her eyes are two little fountains.
Mother, only you think of me,
I am in the midst of evil Christians . . .
We are condemned to hell
And you, mother, are outside crying (79).

In another example, Lombroso saw the work of "exquisite delicacy . . . of a troubadour:"

When I saw you and heard you speak
The blood froze in my veins
And my heart wanted to escape from my breast. . .
Every word when she speaks
Attracts, ties, pierces, nay, wounds (79-80).

Either satirically or in honesty, the poems in all their simplicity reveal the comfort yet anxiety of separation from society. Lombroso called the authors of such poetry "the unfortunates" who still could express their feelings, "truly a surprise from such pens" (Gibson & Rafter, 2006, 79-80).

One way to escape long days of solitude and loneliness in prison was the act of suicide. Lombroso on the topic of suicide among criminals was heavily influenced by the work of his fellow colleague at the University of Turin, Enrico Morselli (1852-1929) a physician and psychical researcher. From his own investigations and discussions with Morselli, Lombroso concluded that suicide served as a,

safety valve against the prospect of long-term deprivation. For others, it is part of the same tendency that led them to crime. And for yet others, it is a sort instrument of 'rehabilitation' after the crime, a way of requesting pardon from others and from oneself (Gibson & Rafter, 2006, 103). Suicide was most frequent, based on Lombroso's statistics, among criminals of passion and the insane (103).

Another form of expression that intrigued Lombroso was a special "private" form of language used especially among recidivist criminals "when they form organizations in big cities" (Gibson & Rafter, 2006, 77). Lombroso described criminal jargon or slang as similar yet very different from normal discourse:

> Its general sounds, grammar, syntax, and idiom remain standard, but its lexicon differs completely. . . . The most curious innovation, one that suggests a relationship between criminal jargon and primitive tongues, is that of naming something according to its attributes (Gibson & Rafter, 2006, 77).

Lombroso provided in *Criminal Man* (first edition) examples to illustrate this criminal idiomatic innovation:

> For example, a goat becomes a *jumper*, while death is called the *thin, raw,* or *certain one*. Like savages, criminals create many words by onomatopoeia, as in *tap* for stamp, *tuff* for pistol, and *tic* for watch. The strangest aspect of criminal jargon is its retention of archaic words that have been completely lost from living speech. Examples include *arton* for bread, *lenza* for water, *strocca* for prostitute (in Calabria), and *marcone* for pimp (Gibson & Rafter, 2006, 77).

Sometimes reflected in their poetry but often used in speech, criminal slang was a convenient means for criminals to fool surveillance by the police on the street, not that far from contemporary usage among criminals and gang members.

The Role of the Church and Education

Other criminal attributes that interested Lombroso included their relationship to religion and education. While most criminals Lombroso reported on where Catholics, a few were atheists. The criminals with a Catholic background were well aware of God and the "immortality of the soul" according to Lombroso, as one criminal said to him in prison, "what do you take us for — unbelievers" (Gibson & Rafter, 2006, 70). In his study of brigandage and the Camorra in southern Italy, Lombroso found a unique relationship between the church and criminals with everyone else in between:

> The religion taught by the priests was nothing but the fear of the devil; the prevailing politics consisted of nothing but fear of the king, who held the middle class in subjection through their fear of the proletariat; while both classes were kept in order through

the fear of a brutal military and police force. Fear took the place of conscience and devotion to duty. Order was kept not by elevation [of] man, but by degrading him. And what happened? Fear became a ready weapon in the hands of the most violent (Lombroso, 1911/2012, 215).

These remarks revealed not only the relationship of faith and crime but also the role of the state. By the time of this writing shortly before his death Lombroso was already a well-known and outspoken Socialist. It is not difficult to read his political beliefs and frustrations with the church in this paragraph. In short, Lombroso did not believe that outside of southern Italy religion or atheism either inhibited or condoned criminal activity (Gibson & Rafter, 2006, 71).

Regarding education and intelligence, Lombroso found that most criminals were below the average and "generally very illogical and always imprudent" (Gibson & Rafter, 2006, 79). For many criminals the repetition of criminal acts was their sole mastery of a skill set, not necessarily a triumph for public education. However, Lombroso did distinguish between three specific types of criminals on the intelligence scale, including criminals of genius, learned criminals, and illiterate criminals. Lombroso declared that many of the great men of history were little more than criminal men of genius. He published a complete treatise on the topic, *The Man of Genius* in 1891. Learned criminals included for Lombroso men of letters, poetry, philosophy (e.g., Rousseau), writers, and especially artists who were more "inclined than writers to crime, especially crimes of blood inspired by love and professional jealousy" (Gibson & Rafter, 2006, 74). A review of educational statistics revealed to Lombroso that while,

> illiteracy rates fell as education spread in Italy . . . the illiteracy rates of criminals increased. . . . This implies that lawbreaking is becoming less frequent in the middle classes. In sum, it is not possible to say that education decreases crime, nor can it be said that it increases it. When education is spread through all classes, it is in fact beneficial, reducing crimes among those with middling education (Gibson & Rafter, 2006, 76).

Nevertheless, the spread of education was a two-edged sword, "where education is widespread, the number of educated criminals increases, but the number of illiterate criminals rises even more" (Gibson & Rafter, 2006, 76). While not a rousing endorsement for public education, Lombroso realized that education was both a boon to those who had strong families and healthier lifestyles than the larger portion of the population who lived in poverty and often came from broken homes or were simply incorrigible. Lombroso was a firm believer in the need for moral education at the earliest age to help thwart the inclinations to evil deeds.

The Utility of Crime

Lombroso's desire that the Italian judicial system be the equal of any in Europe always predicated his study of criminal behavior. The study of the criminal type was an extension of Lombroso's nationalistic interest in improving the quality of Italian life, as well as the identification and reform or removal of criminals. He believed that crime was a "natural phenomenon" of society, but governments had to defend against it with what he called a preventive "social defense." Lombroso described in the fifth edition (1896-1897) of *Criminal Man* the utility of crime, or precisely, the symbiosis of crime in relation to society:

> Just as brilliance of intellect in geniuses is counterbalanced by their energy and lack of moral sensibility, so, too, are the abnormal emotions of criminals accompanied by energy and openness to change. . . . Therefore criminals see more clearly than average men the defects of current governments (Gibson & Rafter, 2006, 352).

The trick for society Lombroso believed was to harness that energy for managed, not revolutionary, change. His concept of utility is similar to that of Emile Durkheim, also considered with Comte' a founder of sociology.

Lombroso concluded that: "Crime is necessary, but so is defense against it, and thus punishment, when we justify punishment in terms of social defense, it becomes more logical and effective," something of an odd statement (Lombroso-Ferrero, Chap. VIII, 1). His phrase "crime is necessary" reflects his belief that crime was a natural element in the progress of civilization and the increase of criminal opportunities, it also served as a motivating force for progressive change to maintain social order for the "fatherland" — Italy (Lombroso-Ferrero, Chap. XI, 6). Positive criminal anthropologists held faith in Darwinian evolutionary progress, but at the same time feared the presence in society of degenerates who represented generations of regressive heredity or arrested development in the evolutionary process.

A contemporary of Lombroso, William Noyes (1857-1941), explained the phenomenon of crime as, "the mark of an atavistic tendency, and that, in the process of evolution, crime has been one of the necessary accompaniments of the struggle for existence" (Noyes, 2003, 34). Crime was the natural result of a savage past relived through the evolutionary process into modern times. The criminal was a degenerate with traits of savagery, who "wages a persistent war against civilization. They are in the world but not of the world, and they are a twin relic of barbarism," and therefore an "enemy of the race" (Noyes, 2002, 42). Lombroso argued that "it is no longer enough to repress crime: we must try to prevent it" (Gibson & Rafter, 2006, 135).

Prevention of crime was the cornerstone of Lombroso's research into the medical-biological causes of criminal behavior. Lombroso pioneered the theory of a public defense against physical and social pathology, and suggested practices for its implementation. He recognized that crime was a social problem that required a "scientific" solution. Lombroso was not the first individual in the 19th century to propose a medical-biological explanation for criminal behavior (Wetzell, 2000); however, his melding of psychological, physiological, physiognomy, and social factors was unique and served as the precedent for the Positive School of Criminology — the scientific study of the origins of crime.

As for crime itself, Lombroso argued that there was no cure. "Instead of trying to cure crime, we must try to prevent it by neutralizing its causes," he said (Gibson & Rafter, 2006, 135). The principal cause of crime, in Lombroso's view, was the biological nature of the criminal himself. His objective was the "curing instead of punishing" of criminals (Lombroso-Ferrero, 1911/2015, 16). Lombroso suggested that society should,

> think of criminals as overgrown children. Morally ill, they must be cured with care rather than with severity. Endowed with vengeful and prickly natures, they view even a light punishment as unjust torture (Gibson & Rafter, 2006, 143).

The "curing" of a congenital criminal is a conundrum that Lombroso never successfully addressed. The only real solutions he offered was the neutralizing affect of incarceration or isolation, or, for the incorrigible, execution. In fact, Lombroso said in the first edition of *Criminal Man* (1876) that the "concept of atavism helps us understand the inefficacy of punishment," a contradictory statement to a desirable "curing" of the criminal. For these "true criminals" he held little faith in successful reform since recidivism was the rule (Gibson & Rafter, 2006, 93). As Lombroso expanded his classification of criminal types following the first edition of *Criminal Man* beyond the congenital criminal, other forms of punishment and treatment became both plausible and possible.

In time, social defense would become the social prevention of crime by abolishing the causes and thus its effects (Ferri, 1905/2014). Fellow students of crime with Lombroso, Raffaele Garofalo and Enrico Ferri both believed that the prevention of crime could be found within "human and social life itself" (Ferri, 1908/2017, 5). Although they accepted the general proposition of the born criminal, they believed that the social environment was a key determinant for many other types of criminals. In response to crime, Ferri argued that,

> The teaching of science tells us plainly that in such a case of endemic criminality, social remedies must be applied to social evils. Unless the remedy of social reforms accompanies the development and protection of labor; unless justice is assured to every member of the collectivity, the courage of this or that citizen is pent in vain, and the evil plant will continue to thrive in the jungle (Ferri, 1908/2017, 41).

The Lombrosian approach to criminality and defensive measures was essentially threefold, prevention, reformation, and ultimately extinction. The actions taken required an informed public committed to its defense and survival.

The Born Criminal

Even though Lombroso came to recognize other types of criminals, he firmly believed that the initial criminal type was born, not made, and seldom deterred from his life-course.

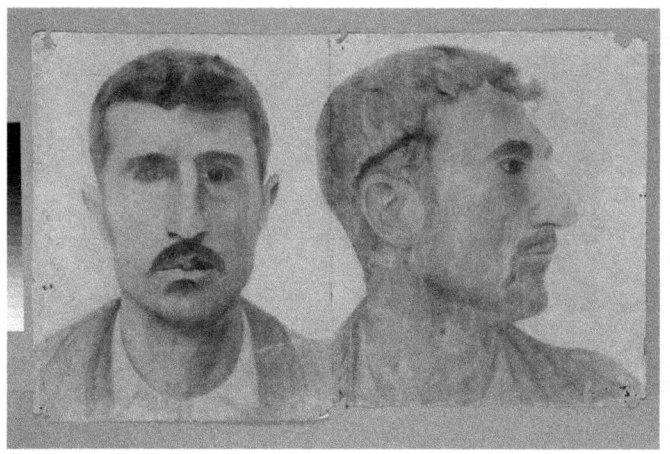

Museo di Antropologia Criminale "Cesare Lombroso," University of Turin, Italy

Criminal Man

Congenital criminals were biologically determined to be criminal and certainly had no mental capacity to consider choice of action. "Most criminals really do lack free will," Lombroso said (Gibson & Rafter, 2006, 43; Lombroso-Ferrero, Chap. VII, 12). Lombroso emphasized that congenital criminals were evil by nature and thus unable to exercise free will; criminal man was an inherently immoral creature, "a distinct and highly individualized class" (Noyes, 2003, 32). That was a major break with Beccaria's Classical School and its emphasis on offender responsibility and using the criminal justice system as a deterrent to crime.

Lombroso postulated that "anthropological and psychical [sic] marks of degeneracy [are] signs of criminal tendency" (Lombroso, 1911/2012, 274). That short phrase sums up the Positivist criminologist's central point that exterior physical defects reflected an internal lack of moral sensitivity. Degeneracy was the natural conclusion to the passing of inheritable negative traits. Criminal man was not capable of rational thought because he had a diseased mind, an inherited savagery. Nor was criminal man subject to moral dictates or standards of behavior. Lombroso argued that insanity and criminality were simply stages on an evolutionary continuum; both were atavistic and only differed in intensity. In essence, criminals represented a variety of insanity on a linear evolutionary scale (Lombroso-Ferrero, Chaps. 7, 16; 8, 2; X, 1).

The argument that criminality was the product of medical-biological determined behavior was inconsistent with Beccarian classicism and its narrow focus on the exercise of free will. Lombroso saw in the complexity of disease the seat of the pathological. He said in the third edition of *Criminal Man* (1884), that "disease [insanity] and atavism are the two main causes of criminality" (Gibson & Rafter, 2006, 221). The terms of diagnosis and prevention from Lombroso's medical training defined the challenges for criminal anthropologists who studied criminals and proposed social defenses to the commission of crime.

Crime, in Lombroso's mind, had a natural cause: "every crime is above all a natural and social phenomenon" (Ferri, 1908/2017, 19). He explained the nature of criminals and his break with Beccaria in his introduction to Gina Lombroso-Ferrero's summary of her father's work in *Criminal Man*, published in 1911. The essential point of study to Lombroso was,

> [not] the study of crime in the abstract, but of the criminal himself, in order adequately to deal with the evil effects of his wrong-doing, and that which classifies the congenital criminal as an anomaly,

partly pathological and partly atavistic, a revival of the primitive savage (Lombroso, 1911/2015, 2).

He took the same approach to the study of the relationship of crime and psychiatry:

> "I realized how inadequate were the methods hitherto held in esteem, and how necessary it was, in studying the insane, to make the patient, not the disease, the object of attention" (Lombroso, 1911/2015, 6).

Criminal man, Lombroso concluded, was not capable of making rational decisions and could be easily persuaded by "passions" and "vanity" to commit offenses (Gibson & Rafter, 2006, 65, 68).

Choice was not an option for criminal man, who was predisposed to criminality. Lombroso's theory of the congenital criminal was an expression of the deterministic tradition of monomania. Criminals, Lombroso wrote in the first edition of *Criminal Man* (1876), exhibited "a certain moral insensitivity" (Gibson & Rafter, 2006, 63). Lombroso believed that the predisposed depraved nature of the criminal lessened his responsibility for his actions. The offender still had to be held accountable for his actions but Lombroso argued that punishment should match the degree of culpability.

Lombroso believed that there was a difference in scale between the criminally insane and the ordinary offender. As early as 1863, Lombroso sought to "differentiate with fairness the guilty from the insane," which should result in the separation of the two between prison and the asylum (Lombroso-Ferrero, Chaps. V, 12; VIII, 1). The shift from Beccarian "choice" to the Lombrosian "predisposition" for crime provided enhanced opportunities for individual and "class" intervention. Lombroso's idea represented a paradigm shift from a "rational man" approach to a "predatory man of nature" approach. That required a new — and for the judicial and penal establishment — a radical approach to intervention and prevention.

Lombroso believed that "the first object of punishment should be the protection of society, and the second the improvement of the criminal" (Kurella, 1911/2012, 144); the "danger to society . . . should form the basis of punishment" (Gibson & Rafter, 2006, 345). The element of danger to society included for Lombroso the unacceptable rates of recidivism, which he claimed reached rates from 30-80 percent (Gibson & Rafter, 2006). Punishment was not a deterrent to an offender who was already a biological and psychical degenerate predisposed to criminality. Lombroso outlined in several editions of *Criminal Man* different measures of punishment, including indeterminate sentences, probation, exile, house arrest, and training in a useful trade. The level of dangerousness with its corresponding variable degree of mental pathology for Lombroso determined the appropriate measure of punishment.

A preventive defense to criminals required determination of the level of dangerousness posed by individuals within society. Taking exception to Beccaria's emphasis on the criminal act, Lombroso stressed the importance of studying the criminal and his environment. Lombroso and the Positivists sought to shift the discussion from the offender's responsibility to his level of dangerousness and the appropriate response of the state. The proposed shift from the act to the actor, from responsibility to dangerousness was a significant development in Italian jurisprudence. The shift in response could put the criminal anthropologist community into the judicial mix of determining the degree of dangerousness and give them a proactive role in helping to control aberrant members of society.

Lombroso started with the hypothesis that criminal behavior was inherent and defined in anatomical anomalies of the offender. Physical stigmata often revealed anomalies. But more than mere physical manifestations, the physical stigmata were only the outward appearance of a morally depraved individual. The congenital criminal was both physically "marked" and internally lacking of moral checks and balances. As Lombroso expanded his classification of criminal types, he assigned for each type of criminal, based on their criminal activity, unique distinguishing physical characteristics.

Criminals, Lombroso proposed, needed an assessment to determine their level of dangerousness. While judges could weigh the offender's recidivism record and the nature of the crime with the merit of justice, only Positivist criminologists could inform the court of the atavistic traits of the offender and therefore his probable recidivism. According to Lombroso, only qualified criminal anthropologists, such as members of the Positivist Modern School, could recommend an appropriate sentence (Gibson & Rafter, 2006). To Lombroso's thinking, "only a small number of specialists can discern the organic and congenital causes of crime," including himself (Gibson & Rafter, 2006, 289).

The Challenge to the Italian Judicial System

Only the "expert" could discern the true nature of the criminal. His stated goal was to provide judges with "experts" who had the physical and the psychiatric diagnostic tools to differentiate between the insane, insane criminals, ordinary offenders, and normal citizens. Armed with this expert assistance, judges could be helped to separate the insane who were recidivistic by nature from ordinary offenders and place them in asylums. Lombroso was dismayed by the high rates of recidivism and hoped that the separation of the insane from prison would help reduce the problem of recidivism (Lombroso-Ferrero, Chaps. VIII, 1-2, XIII, 2. Gibson & Rafter, 2006, 147-148, 346-148).

Interjecting the criminal anthropologist into the adjudication process would be a significant shift in power from the judge and jury to the "expert." Lombroso denied that this was his motive. He was not trying to revolutionize the court or usurp it, but rather provide expert testimony as a witness. That is something along the lines of a pre-sentence report in modern courts. Nevertheless, what he proposed was a dramatic change to a long established "liberal" system of justice (Lombroso-Ferrero, Chaps. VII, 18; VIII, 8; XIII, 3; X, 4).

Scientific methods of psychical and anatomical analysis aided by instrumentation, statistical tabulations, and professional testimony welded by the Positivist criminologist held the key to appropriate sentencing in a court of law. Those skills were non-existent in the contemporary judicial system, nor did there seem to Lombroso a desire to utilize them (Lombroso-Ferrero, Chap. X, 2).

Lombroso expressed disdain for this class of criminal, who was often a politician. He believed that the Italian Parliamentary system was flawed for several reasons, but not limited to hosting too many latent criminals, including political geniuses who, like Napoleon, disguised their deeds "by the prestige of success" (Gibson & Rafter, 2006, 296). Lombroso mistrusted the Italian Parliament and its members to willingly serve the interests of the people. His lack of trust in the parliamentary form of government is found scattered in the various editions of *Criminal Man,* and elsewhere in his writings. More than musings, Lombroso's conviction that a democratic system was tied more closely to the people and more responsive to social needs, presaged his eventual joining the Italian Socialist Party in 1893.

Lombroso had little faith in Italian jurors and judges "corrupted" by potential bribery and misguided views of defendant's rights. Jurors, he argued in the fifth edition of *Criminal Man* (1896-1897) "can be easily corrupted because they are answerable to no one and have nothing to lose through an acquittal" (Gibson & Rafter, 2006, 335). The jury system in his view was "another institution that is atavistic in its ineffectiveness and corruptibility" (Gibson & Rafter, 2006, 187). Lombroso complained that the existing system was capricious, inept and dwelt in abstractions raised by the question of free will (Lombroso-Ferrero, Chap. XVII, 12). He noted that the rich largely avoided prison while the poor did not. Rhetorically, Lombroso questioned the justice of such a system. In a more conciliatory mood (perhaps hoping to persuade the judiciary) following the success of his earlier editions of *Criminal Man,* Lombroso wrote that judges are born,

> with the reluctance to do bad and so they think the [*sic*] others are too and they do not want and probably cannot come down from the wonderful word of metaphysic to the humble one of prisons. The judge . . . is easily drawn by that momentous preoccupation common to all of us in all vents of life, the interest in the moment being so great that one does not easily see the connection with the general laws of nature (Lombroso-Ferrero, Chap. X, 4).

More than corrupted juries or judges, the existing legal system dealt in "legal abstractions" rather than the "realities of experience" and "facts" (Ferri, 1905/2014, 4). These "abstractions" according to Lombroso represented the Beccarian belief that criminal activity was episodic in the offender's life and should be responded to individually with prison sentences. The result, Lombroso noted, was recidivism and a "primitive form . . . of social vengeance" (Lombroso-Ferrero, Chap. X, 2). Classical jurisprudence sought to separate the crime from the offender, which for Lombroso and criminal anthropologists was a contradiction of purpose and outcome.

Because crime was so closely linked to mental pathology for Lombroso, he believed that the better solution for sentencing was placement of insane offenders in asylums. The "system" failed to differentiate between the criminally insane and other offenders. Rehabilitation was not an option for the criminally insane.

Lombroso had little patience or regard for the Italian legal system and participated in the Positivists efforts to reform Italian jurisprudence (Gibson, 2002). Virtually all other Positivists agreed with his attitude toward the Italian legal system (Garland, 1985, 117; Ferri, 1908/2017, 4). Lombroso hoped that his research would lead to judicial and penal reform (Lombroso-Ferrero. Chap. X, 1). Reform would largely follow in his footsteps.

Only by identifying the criminal within society could appropriate defensive prevention be undertaken. Lombroso described the struggle against criminality as a "war on crime" (Lombroso, 1911/2012, xxxvi, 93). Perhaps the first in modern history to coin the term "war on crime," Lombroso recognized the value to society of identifying the criminal type. If anatomical characteristics and mental illness could identify a criminal, then incarceration or isolation upon conviction in order to protect society would serve as the ultimate defensive measure (Lombroso, 1911/2012, 93).

In an era of limited civil and criminal rights, Lombroso never satisfactorily addressed the question of pre-emptive arrest based on physical appearance, but it seems logical to assume that could be an unintended consequence. The stigmata he identified could become markers or signs that the government could use in a misguided prevention program, something even Lombroso recommended (Gibson & Rafter, 2006; Lombroso, 1911/2012). By virtue of their own physical and psychical anomalies, criminals were known to society and thus open to control and regulation. Without realizing it, Lombroso created an early context for profiling.

Only after criticism over the potential use of physical anomalies for arrest did Lombroso qualify his position by stating that he intended their use only for suspected or convicted criminals. However, waiting for conviction would seem to greatly reduce the efficacy and practically of his theory for identifying criminals in society. Lombroso could not foresee the consequences of his claims if a state, like those under Fascism some sixty years in the future, abused his theories in the quest of ethnic cleansing.

CHAPTER 6
Criminal Woman

"Rarely is a woman wicked, but when she is she surpasses the man."

—Italian Proverb

I n the 19th and early 20th centuries, men expected women to take care of the household and supervise children. In fact, Victorian-era prudery toward gender roles and the "appropriate place" for women governed Western European society. Women were not to challenge the domain of men due to an alleged inferior intellect and lack of appropriate discernment for politics and legal matters. Men expected the "weaker sex" to be a helpmate but not an equal. The status of a woman was closely linked to that of her father and husband. Men were believed to be better fit in every manner for the rigors of the work place and civic responsibilities that required governance and due diligence. In Darwinian terminology, the adult male in all species ruled over the female.

The New European Woman

A feminist movement in the 19th century was the product of the Enlightenment in the previous century with its tenets of equality and rationality. The Enlightenment held the promise of possible improvement for women in the new century. The overthrow of traditional European absolutism generated the rise of a new middle class based on the principle of capitalism. The new order favored the role of men in building a new society associated with industrialization and modernization, continuing the marginalization of women. Darwin and Spencer argued that men had the greatest potential for development, much superior to women who were bound by nature to the primary role of reproduction.

The dramatic economic and social changes threatened to leave women in the backwash of history. Paternal despotism substituted for the old absolutism with the aim for the protection and exclusion of women from the upheavals of the new socio-economic and political sphere of power carved out of the old order by newly empowered middle class men. Men of the 19th and early 20th century viewed the subjection of women as necessary for female happiness.

The democratic movement for women's civil and political rights and liberties threatened to upend this social construct. For men like Lombroso and Ferrero, who turned their study of criminality to the subject of women in the larger scheme of crime, it is not surprising that they theorized women's roles through an anthropological-biological lens rather than a historical one. They based their functional deterministic framework on presumed constant factors that were anthropological in nature. Their work reflected a certain mistrust and misunderstanding of the rise of the "new woman" and her challenge to man's created social order. Maternity and child bearing gave women a specified status in society, but that did not extend to the realm of politics and the marketplace (Pomata, 1993, 158, 159, 162).

A feminist movement began in the West, more slowly in western Europe than in America, with the exception of England. In 1851 Harriet Taylor Mill (1807-1858) published anonymously *The Enfranchisement of Women*, which called for an end to the inferior status of women and the right to vote. Her husband, John Stuart Mill (1806-1873) in 1869 published *The Subjection of Women* in which he argued that in a society defined by market relations, women should be allowed to compete as equals. Their arguments echoed across Europe and certainly charged the discussion and the movement for change.

The movement for women's rights and equality found fertile ground among middle class women. As nations industrialized and urbanization brought people into greater proximity, a variety of social movements found ready advocates and audiences. The role of women also began to incrementally change from keeper of the home only to embracing opportunities for participation in the national discourse over the role of women in a modern society. Women's call for equality included in addition to the right to vote, equal opportunity for education and the opening of the professions and the marketplace.

The right of franchise was at the core of women's demands for equality. But opposition was formidable, particularly with the queen of the British Empire. Queen Victoria called such demands "on which her poor feeble sex is bent . . . a mad, wicked folly . . . forgetting every sense of womanly feeling and propriety" (Merriman, 2004, 873). This same opposition to women's suffrage prevailed in the political institutions of Europe. With the exception of Socialists, who for the most part stood on the principle of gender equality, conservative and moderate politicians stood firm against the principle of equality between the sexes.

The Italian Positivists, including Lombroso, Ferri, Ferrero, and Garofalo, found their beliefs in penal and social reforms compatible with the Italian Socialist Party (PSI). Lombroso joined the PSI in 1893 primarily because of shared concern for reform of the penal laws and practices. While sympathetic to economic reforms, his advocacy was tempered by criminal justice concerns, a point of view that at times put his ties to the PSI to question. However, in spite of PSI reform principles, including gender equality, Positivists were firm in their belief that women were physically and psychologically inferior. Their claimed scientific findings clearly conflicted with socialist tenets. Men like Lombroso and Ferrero who studied and wrote on female criminality wrestled with internal conflicts between socialist idealism and Positivist biological determinism.

The Positivists' contradictions in principle made opposition to suffrage ideologically difficult, at best, if not outright untenable (Kurella, 124-126). Ferrero, Lombroso's co-author with interests in the PSI, had his own opinion on female suffrage, which he opposed in Italy on grounds that it was not necessary because of protections provided through marriage. However, he conceded that it might be appropriate in other more politically progressive countries (Gibson, 2002, 80, 82). Lombroso offered his own best case for women's voting rights cast within a socialist framework, but with a caution attached:

> In the general view, universal suffrage works for the abolition of class distinctions, but in the hands of the corrupt and the uncultured it may be directly subversive of freedom. Let us therefore advocate everything that can be for the advantage of the common people, but let us at the same time give these latter only so much power as may be necessary to wring from the upper classes the concessions needful for the good of the community (Kurella, 126).

Clearly, in the hands of "corrupt" and "uncultured" people, women's suffrage could be transformed into a bludgeon for more radical change. Lombroso usually used the term "corrupt" in his writings for criminals and politicians, for whom he had little regard. His use of "uncultured" reflects specific class elitism, as well as to describe geniuses and criminals of passion, who often achieved success in the political and business world in spite of a lack of cultural acumen.

In Italy as elsewhere in Europe, the feminist "new woman" movement had its proponents and defenders. The idea that women were biologically and psychologically determined to be inferior to men was subject to the sharpened pens of Irene de Bonis de Nobili, Maria Marselli-Valli, Dr. Anna Kuliscioff, and F.P. Diana. Maria Marselli-Valli, as an example, challenged the Positivist proposition that intelligence was correlated to brain weight, a view espoused by Ernst Bischoff and other Positivists including Lombroso. In her book, *Women and Feminism* (1908), Marselli-Valli wrote with a sense of irony and humor that following the death of Bischoff, his autopsy revealed that his brain weighed "less than that which he himself had established as the average for women" (Gibson, 2002, 83). The question of intelligence also pertained to the importance of education.

******

In the Victorian era very few doors were open to women who sought higher education. Lombroso's daughters Gina and Paola were among the fortunate ones. Gina Lombroso-Ferrero successfully completed her medical degree. Although Paola did not complete her baccalaureate, she had a broad range of interests, including childhood education, pedagogy, psychology, literature, and music. The sisters shared a common interest in children's education and a program called School and Family that Gina visited in Milan on a return trip from Paris with her father. Although the School and Family program was not a program to house orphans, it shared the same health and educational goals of the English Ragged School movement for children.

In 1896, with the Milan school as a model, Gina and Paola worked with Lombroso to establish in Turin an after-school program for youths of all social classes. Here children could mingle freely with each other, receive meals, read and play with donated books and toys, and get encouragement in their studies. Within a year the program was so successful that there were four centers supervising over 500 children seven days a week. In time the municipality of Turin took over the "after school clubs" (Lombroso-Ferrero, Chap. XVII, 5). This educational method was very similar to the English Ragged Schools and the more famous Montessori schools established by educational reformer Maria Montessori in Rome in 1907. There is no direct connection between the two schools, but Montessori certainly did know of Lombroso and was reportedly influenced by his theories in her own studies (Gutek, *Montessori Method*, 13; Stewart-Steinberg, *Pinocchio Effect*, 311).

It is very possible that at some point in time the sisters met Dr. Maria Montessori (1870-1952). Montessori, Gina Lombroso-Ferrero, and Anna Kuliscioff were among the first female medical doctors graduated in Italy. Montessori was most interested in the psychology and pedagogy of childhood education, and was an advocate for the rights of women. Her first school for children was established in Rome in 1907. The School and Family program and Montessori schools shared similar concepts of childhood education. Montessori was an Italian medical doctor like Gina Lombroso-Ferrero and an innovator in education. The Montessori Schools today are her legacy (C. Cilli, personal communication, March 21, 2017; Lombroso-Ferrero, Chaps. XV, 9; XVII, 5).

The Lombroso Parlor

Some historians have argued that the development of feminism in Western Europe contributed to a perceived crisis in men's masculinity. Women's challenge to the mores of western society behind the façade of Victorianism put great pressure on men's sense of place and contributed to a fear of weakness in their position. Although Lombroso never expressed that fear in print, its shadow hangs over much of his writing on the questions of women's morality, evolutionary history, atavism, and social status (Buttavuoco, 1993, 180-182; Merriman, 856).

As the leading Positivist criminal anthropologist, Lombroso found himself in the midst of the debate over gender equality. His position on the nature of criminal woman remained firm, but on the larger issue of feminism he waivered. Both of Lombroso's daughters were accomplished women with strong social consciousness. With their father, they believed that social class distinctions were detrimental and arbitrary. Nina Lombroso, Cesare's wife, also added another layer of interest to the family dynamic. Lombroso had picked a woman who could be both a helpmate and a partner in his research work. He spoke of Nina as a source of strength and advice. Raised by an incredibly strong mother and surrounded by strong and competent women, Lombroso likely found the strictures of society on women difficult to reconcile.

The Lombroso family habit of entertaining open parlor discussions with imminent leaders, writers, and thinkers of Italy and beyond often included female scholars as well. One of those was Anna Kuliscioff, a doctor of Jewish-Russian descent who was a co-editor and writer for the PSI weekly, *Critica Sociale*. Kuliscioff often had dinner with the family while Lombroso and Ferrero were researching female criminality and writing *Criminal Woman*. Kuliscioff also quietly gave a copy of J.S. Mill's *The Subjugation of Women* to Gina and Paola (Gibson, 2002, 82; Rafter & Gibson, 2004, 13). Gina and Paola were in their early twenties at the time; what exact influence or impression the book and Kuliscioff had is not known, but they both married prominent Positivists who embraced socialism and worked closely with Lombroso.

Kuliscioff's militant advocacy of Marxism and championing social factors as the cause of crime and women's lower status most likely created intellectual discord for Lombroso. While not always in agreement, Lombroso paid reference to her published lecture, "The Monopoly of Men" in *The Female Offender*. One area of mutual interest in her lecture was the education of women and the right to vote, but the Positivist belief that science proved female intelligence (size of brain) inferior created a disjunction between the worlds of politics and changing social norms, and science. There is no evidence that Lombroso ever totally reconciled the man of science with the man of politics and social custom (Gibson, 2002, 82, 84, 85).

All the conflicting attitudes and beliefs over female equality and their potential criminality within a society of change created a dilemma for Lombroso. He was proud of the success of his daughters but at the same time reluctant to admit that his Positivist views of women's moral and intellectual inferiority was entirely wrong. To do so would have challenged his belief in the immutability of science. Lombroso apparently believed that some women could arise to success in spite of their deficits. He could point to his immediate family and Kulisciff as examples.

In the preface to *Criminal Woman, the Prostitute, and the Normal Woman* (1893), Lombroso recognized and honored the success of five women, including Kulisciff. For "normal women" — that is, not criminal — he probably had to look no further than these and his own family. While Lombroso supported the education of women, he also saw a danger in the outcome:

> A factor that drags honest women into crime with increasing frequency is the way society is starting to give them access to higher education while at the same time, bizarrely, refusing to allow them

to practice their profession or earn a living (Rafter & Gibson, 2004, 197).

That refusal could force women to crime and prostitution. Rejection, combined with inferior social status and physical abilities due to the fate of nature was a serious concern for Lombroso. He just happened to have two very talented daughters in their early twenties about to enter the world dominated by men.

In Defense of Women

The fact that Lombroso and Ferrero considered women to be inferior to men, did not license their abuse or exploitation. In their first book, *Criminal Woman, the Prostitute, and the Normal Woman* (1893). Lombroso makes the point in defense of women that:

> Not one line of this work justifies the great tyranny that continues to victimize women, from the taboo, which forbids them to eat meat or touch a coconut, to that which impedes them from studying, and worse, from practicing a profession once they are educated. These ridiculous and cruel constraints, still widely accepted, are used to maintain or (sadder still), increase women's inferiority, exploiting them to our advantage. The same happens when we shower a docile victim with hypocritical elegies and, while pretending that she is an ornament, ready her for new sacrifices (Rafter & Gibson, 2004, 37).

Lombroso followed this testament with a tribute to his daughter and Ferrero's future wife, Gina, who was "my steadfast collaborator and inspiration" (37). This affectionate expression and the above statement reveal the dichotomy and dilemma of male bias in a century of transition and flux. While celebrating the need for greater opportunity and respect for their intelligence, Lombroso and Ferrero still declared almost apologetically that women were victims of their own inferiority. They perpetuated the role of the male as protector of the "weaker sex," women needed male support and protection. Lombroso's understanding of science and its limitations did not preclude him from making assumptions that today would be characterized as expressions of racist and sexist ideology. The world that Lombroso and co-author Ferrero along with Positivists in general lived was far different than today. Their beliefs reflected the contemporary understanding of gender relations, male superiority, and social structure. These underlying beliefs and attitudes influenced their scientific perspective and findings, and colored their attempt to define and describe the origin of deviance, and the normalization of deviance as a construct of evolutionary regression.

Female Criminality

With the growing interest and debate over woman's status in late 19th century European society, Lombroso embarked in 1890 on a thorough study of female criminality. Lombroso embarked on the study of women and sexual practices at a time when sex was a taboo subject. In his first book (1893) *Criminal Woman*, he covered such sensitive topics as adultery, frigidity, lesbianism, masturbation, premarital sex, sexual psychopathy, and anomalies in female genitals. Lombroso was perhaps the first professional sexologist. His interest in criminal woman as a type developed slowly over previous decades as a logical extension of his concept of the born criminal and the growing social interest in female deviance. It is also probable that his circle of female scholars and family members in addition to other Positivists influenced his decision to study the etiology of female criminality. Lombroso's first three editions of *Criminal Man* (1876-1884) made bare reference to the criminal nature of women. By the fourth edition, in 1890, he began to make inferences and draw parallels between the biological and psychical characteristics of criminal man and woman.

Lombroso was convinced that female criminality would increase with the "march of civilization" (Rafter & Gibson, 2004, 148; Lombroso & Ferrero, 1909, 111). He borrowed the conventional idea that equated women with nature and men with society, a common distinction of gender roles that was not seriously challenged until the 1970s. Lombroso had already made a study of revolution and what he called "inertia" as the motivating force. His study of the French Revolution revealed the prominent role played by women. Lombroso no doubt saw in the female a propensity toward passion, the potentially empowered sentiment for revolution. He likely saw in the feminist movement the elements of a revolution and found himself in a quandary over how to address the onslaught of change. If women were indeed to rise to equality with men, Lombroso certainly wanted to understand the implications to criminality that would also rise to greater prominence. A subjugated woman by social and legal custom was one thing, but a free woman with criminal tendencies raised a whole other set of factors linked to her criminality, and required thorough study.

The growth of cities and urban life, which accompanied the progress of civilization would also provide ample opportunities for the criminally inclined, whether male or female. Lombroso tabulated the difference in the level of female crime
in the more "civilized" northern regions of Italy to the rural and more backward southern regions. While the number of female crimes in the north rose in
pace with modernity, the more backward southern regions had in some types of
crimes like murder and assault doubled their rate. Cultural and geographic bias
aside, Lombroso sought to make the point that "more serious crimes regularly
increase as civilization decreases" (Lombroso, 1911/2012, 187, 188).

Lombroso and his future son-in-law Guglielmo Ferrero, a lawyer, published
Criminal Woman, the Prostitute, and the Normal Woman in 1893, then *The
Female Offender* in 1909. The latter work was largely a compilation and extension of the first book rather than original; however, more anthropometric
measurements and discussion of pathological anomalies were provided the
reader. The principal author in both books was Lombroso. Those were the first
studies of their kind on the subject of female criminality ever published and
remained classic referrals until the early 1970s and the rise of the women's
liberation movement.

******

In their attempt to explain the nature of women's inferiority, Lombroso and
Ferrero could not escape the perceived constraints of biology and society in
the process of defining women's specified place in the social order. On the
measure of intelligence the authors concluded:

> It is indisputable that the inferior development of women's intel-
> ligence is partially caused by the physical inertia that men have
> imposed on her. But it would be an error to label this a man-made
> cause because the inferiority is also natural and because it reflects
> a general tendency among all animals on the evolutionary scale for
> males to participate more fully in the struggle for existence (Rafter
> & Gibson, 2004, 87).

The authors explained that the intellectual advantage for men in the modern
"struggle for existence" was the result of men "continually chang[ing] their
'types of activities and life circumstances' in the attempt to be successful professionally" (Rafter & Gibson, 2004, 87). Men were upwardly mobile compared to women, who because of motherhood, were bound to the home and
had fewer opportunities to "awaken and nurture the intelligence" (Rafter &
Gibson, 2004, 87).

For Lombroso, the problem for women was akin to that of lower animals and uncivilized women, a lack of cerebral activity compared to men that resulted from her degenerative status in the natural world. Once again the limitations placed upon women by nature confined their role in society. These same constraints of home and nature had the positive effect of reducing women's potential for criminal behavior. Neither Lombroso nor Ferrero ventured to suggest that the average woman could readily advance above her evolutionary status through education or professional employment. Such a suggestion would have brought to question their own belief system in the superior evolutionary status of men and challenged conventional Victorian norms.

According to Lombroso and Ferrero, women's primary intellectual deficiency was in "creative power." Women did not compare well with men on the scale of genius. The common form of female intelligence was only intuition. The greater development of the male cerebral cortex explained for Lombroso why more men exhibited genius than women. Lombroso was fascinated with the quality of genius in the human species, but in regards to gender frequency, he noted that "man's superiority is widely recognized as immense" (Rafter & Gibson, 2004, 83, 148). Furthermore, Lombroso and Ferrero determined that women in general fell behind even the average male in intellectual and creative power:

> While woman is barred from creating great things by her lack of genius, she is also less adapted than man to the minor productions at which average men succeed. This is due to her lack of originality, which is overdeveloped in the man of genius and found in more modest proportions in the average man. In fact, women have no particular talent for any art, science, or profession . . . but only rarely do they carry the stamp of true originality in any branch of work (Rafter & Gibson, 2004, 83, 85).

Perhaps the last reference to "occasional originality" among women is a veiled acknowledgment of the achievements of the women in Lombroso's home and intellectual life.

While women's intelligence was in question, Lombroso and Ferrero did credit women with having greater patience then men. In contrast, men had greater perseverance. Their belief that women were more patient than men seemed to contradict Darwin who had it reversed. In responding to this perceived contradiction, Lombroso and Ferrero explained that, "women's patience is an effect of her lesser sensibility and lower degree of cortical excitability, which lower her need for stimulation . . . her patience is more that of the camel than of the man of genius" (Rafter & Gibson, 2004, 86). Regardless, the authors considered women to be handicapped by nature in the development of their psychical ability, and even lacked the potential for much improvement.

Women's Biological and Social Inferiority

They considered biology the greater restraint on female intelligence compared to men. In summary, Lombroso drove the point home:

> Underlying all . . . other causes is a biological one that serves as the foundation. The intelligence of the male, like his organic structure, has a primitive potentiality greater than that of the female thanks to his lessor role in the preproduction of the species. As I have demonstrated, intelligence varies inversely to fecundity in the entire animal kingdom; there is an antagonism between the reproductive and intellectual functions. Today, the work of reproduction has for the most part devolved onto the woman, and for this biological reason she has been left behind in intellectual development (Rafter & Gibson, 2004, 87).

Seemingly, women were trapped in their own paradox imposed more by nature than man. The role of the sexes was determined biologically, while the boundaries of men were near limitless, those of women were limited by nature.

Neither Lombroso, Ferrero, nor the Positivists had a reasonable solution for the advancement of women constrained as they were by nature. They could only offer a hopeful belief that somehow civilization and the evolutionary process would raise them above their existing moral and psychical deficiencies. It would be easy to see this stalemate with nature as an excuse for women's lesser role. But in recognizing the success of their own female family members and friends, the authors must have realized that a change in social norms was in the making. They did note that "greater participation in the collective life of society would raise woman's intelligence," but how that was to be accomplished with biological and social constraints was left unexplained (Rafter & Gibson, 2004, 88).

Even in recognizing the changing role of women in society and perhaps even within the male sphere of power over the home, Lombroso and Ferrero were still faced with the dilemma of reconciling their own points of view with the social reality and biological determinism of their time. They were themselves caught in their own unresolved hypocritical view of women as degenerate by nature yet somehow entitled to greater respect for their achievements and release from the "ridiculous and cruel constraints" placed upon them. Lombroso and Ferrero defended their position on female inferiority on the vagaries and constraints of evolutionary biology, the arrested development and degeneration arguments.

Lombroso and Ferrero admitted that, "the criminal type is a rarity in the female compared to male" (Rafter & Gibson, 2004, 144; Lombroso, 1911/2012, 181). Women in the authors' view committed less crime because they were "less essentially criminal." Women were less involved in crime according to Lombroso because they consumed less alcohol and were less engaged in commerce (Gibson & Rafter, 2006, 327). In so much that criminal behavior among women might be less, this did not infer a moral superiority (Gibson & Rafter, 2006, 127; Lombroso & Ferrero, 1909, 111; Lombroso, 1911/2012, 181). In fact the authors believed that women were "always fundamentally immoral," their moral sense was "deficient," and "wickedness [is] latent [even] in normal women" (Rafter & Gibson, 2004, 80, 207; Lombroso & Ferrero, 1909, 151). The authors argued that in general "the moral physiognomy of the born female criminal is close to that of the male" (Rafter & Gibson, 2004, 192). Moral degeneracy was common to both born criminal types. They believed that all women were to some degree deviant. Lombroso and Ferrero stated that moral sensitivity in women was weaker than in men, therefore, "woman . . . feels less, just as she thinks less" (Rafter & Gibson, 2004, 64).

Only the normal female in Lombroso and Ferrero's conviction, could overcome the latent nature of immorality inherent to the gender by focusing on her positive attributes, her maternal instincts, and capacity for compassion. Nevertheless, even normal woman's potential to overcome her latent immorality was tempered the authors reasoned by the fact that:

> Normal woman has many characteristics that bring her close to the level of the savage, the child, and therefore the criminal (anger, revenge, jealousy, and vanity) and others, diametrically opposed, which neutralize the former. Yet her positive traits hinder her formal rising to the level of man, whose behavior balances rights and duties, egotism and altruism, and represents the peak of moral evolution" (Rafter & Gibson, 2004, 81).

Lombroso and Ferrero recognized and admitted that the social-economic environment could trigger a woman's immorality, "often just women in whom dreadful living conditions have brought out the basic immorality that exists in all women, even the normal ones" could result in their criminal behavior (Rafter & Gibson, 2004, 225). Regardless of a normal woman's positive qualities and her avoidance of deviance, the authors stood firmly on their belief that immorality was an underlying female trait and that women would never rise to the level of man. Women were literally handicapped by their assumed immorality, which placed them closer in the evolutionary stage to the savage.

******

Lombroso and Ferrero saw a very fine line between the normal and criminal woman, between compassion and savage cruelty:

> Her weakness makes her cruel and compassionate at the same time. It makes her cruel because cruelty is the only offense and defensive weapon that a weak being can use against one that is stronger. . . . The savage woman is more cruel than compassionate; vindictive, oppressed, and relatively strong, she has the motive and means from time to time, to discharge her hatred in cruelty. The civilized woman, in contrast, becomes progressively compassionate (Rafter & Gibson, 2004, 71).

Women's propensity to cruelty reflected her own "weaknesses:" "Because she is unable to destroy her enemies, woman torments them, pricking them with needles of pain and immobilizing them with misery" (Rafter & Gibson, 2004, 68). Lombroso and Ferrero painted a rather bleak picture of women's character and vindictive nature, which they assumed was woman's natural state. Apparently, a woman's "savage" nature could be easily triggered by her own vanity, jealousy, anger, and vindictive sense of revenge, and her oppressed status in society. When a woman's jealousy and vengeance involved sexuality, her evil traits "manifest themselves under a more terrible aspect than usual" (Lombroso & Ferrero, 1909, 157). It is therefore no surprise that Lombroso in particular spoke so highly of the female's maternal instincts, encouraged respect for her accomplishments and her value in the context of society as a counterweight to her impulsive potential for vile disruption of order.

Woman's biological and social inferiority, her "lesser sensibility, greater impulsivity, and lesser degree of control over wicked impulses" made her virtually unpredictable (Rafter & Gibson, 2004, 71). The disjunction and contradiction between cruelty and compassion as corresponding female traits and her psychological state of mind were difficult for Lombroso and Ferrero to explain. They found it easier to simply conclude, "evolution will resolve [the contradiction] in favor of grace and pity" (Rafter & Gibson, 2004, 72). In the positive forces of progressive civilization and evolution, the authors found their comfort. The forces of civilization would however in their own belief system never provide an equal level of achievement since women had a much greater degree of separation from men in the evolutionary process.

Civilization in Lombroso and Ferrero's estimation could serve to help women rise above their defensive cruel nature, but civilization also held dangers:

> "Because cruelty in women is becoming a disadvantage and compassion an attraction, women repress their wicked impulses and stimulate compassion, as one sees all too frequently today in the hypocrites who behave charitably in order to seduce a man" (Rafter & Gibson, 2004, 72).

The power of female seduction was a millennia held male construct used to help explain or justify their sexual desires as natural needs complimentary to women's maternal instincts. While sex was to males about gratification and copulation, Lombroso and Ferrero explained that love was the most important thing to women, but "that trait flows not from eroticism but their need to satisfy the maternal instinct and be protected, without which women's existence is incomplete" (Rafter & Gibson, 2004, 60). Maternal love was considered to be women's strongest feeling.

Women's Immorality

Lombroso and Ferrero admitted like Darwin that men had greater sexual needs or drives, but making the woman the seducer (another Victorian conviction) perhaps helped to assuage man's own moral weakness and justify his actions. But regardless of morality, procreation was a human necessity in the evolutionary process of both nature and civilization. But to Lombroso and Ferrero, women would always find their fulfillment and protection from men. The woman's movement for equality in status challenged their belief system and would shift the paradigm to greater gender balance in the next century. The authors along with positivism in general were caught in the dilemma of a changing world where science was losing its preeminent explanatory power for female subjugation and inferior status.

Female immorality stemmed in Lombroso and Ferrero's estimation from excessive egoism or vanity, a desire for revenge, impulsive fits of anger, greed, a pathological habit of lying, and a propensity to jealousy. Furthermore, women according to Lombroso were "notorious" for their "intensity and tenacity" when committing crimes, and "perversity" when it existed usually "expressed itself more strongly than in men" (Rafter & Gibson, 2006, 128). All of these traits were evidence of an evolutionary arrested moral development in contrast to woman's male counterpart (Lombroso & Ferrero, 1909, 154-163; Rafter & Gibson, 2004, 64, 77-79, 80, 81).

One defining feature of woman's moral deficiency was her "instinct for lying." Lombroso and Ferrero described in *Criminal Woman* (Rafter & Gibson, 2004) a series of causes that contributed to the "development of women's ability to lie:"

- Because women are weak and servile, "having no power" they need to use "cunning and lies"
- Because men are "disgusted" by female menstruation, women have learned to hide it
- Because women "must hide feelings of love" (at the risk of her reputation) and "bodily functions have forced her into a state of lying"
- Because of maternal-reproductive needs, women have learned to hide her defects, age, illnesses, and "anything that could harm her in men's eyes"
- "Woman, like the child, is weak and thus has an instinctive need to be protected; in man's protection she finds her pride"
- "Women are extremely suggestible"
- "Maternity obliges women to dissimulate because child raising depends on a series of clever or stupid lies designed to hide information about sex, to camouflage mothers' own ignorance of things, to guide children on the paths of morality through fear of God and the devil, and so on"
- In sum, "in women as in children, the moral sense is inferior" (77-79).

In addition, Lombroso made the point in *Criminal Man* that since women "perceive truth much less clearly than men" they can more "easily deny it" (Gibson & Rafter, 2006, 283). Ranging from biology to conventional custom and mores to conjecture, Lombroso and Ferrero's attempt to explain why women instinctively lie leaves the reader with more questions than answers. One unsatisfied question is the lack of recognition for man's culpability for the cause of women's negative attributes and sense of necessity to lie, or commit a host of other offenses.

However, it was more than a moral deficit that afflicted women, Lombroso and Ferrero (Rafter & Gibson, 2004) claimed that, "woman is a male of arrested development, the fact that she is somewhat less criminal than he, and a little more pitiful, can compensate a thousandfold for her deficiency in the realm of intellect" (37). In fact, "during the first and last stages of men, in the lower classes and above all in the many savage races the correspondence with the male is very strong; the woman's face becomes virile" (Rafter & Gibson, 2004, 52). Somehow the underdeveloped intellect, race, social status, and her state of atavistic misfortune equated to a woman's law-abiding accomplishment. The triple insult is that women were considered biologically, physically, morally, and intellectually inferior to men. The fact that women committed fewer crimes was considered another sign that they had not evolved at the same pace as men. The illogic of this argument seems to have escaped the authors.

The male gender as a whole was considered to have progressed to a higher evolutionary status and thus better able to control their temperament and balance duties with a greater sense of responsibility and altruism, which placed the male at the "peak of moral evolution." Of course the born criminal and other criminal types, were the exception to man's moral achievement. There were other moral failings among men as well including homosexuality, which Lombroso labeled as "found only among the degenerate classes" (Rafter & Gibson, 2004, 60). He argued that homosexuals were born not "nurtured" and should be confined from youth to avoid their "contagion" as a source of a "great number of occasional criminals" (Lombroso, 1911/2012, 418). This conclusion reflected the social and moral taboo of Victorian Europe on expressions of sexuality and even the public discussion of sex.

******

The perception of sexual deviance whether by male or female prostitution or homosexuality was considered predominately to be a lower class phenomenon and subject to the same Victorian censure. The upper class could more easily hide their own indiscretions while labeling the lower class as degenerate and their indiscretions the result of sexual pathology. This labeling process reinforced the perceived evolutionary separation of degree between the lower classes and members of high society, and thus perpetuated the myth of natural selection and survival of the fittest.

The physical, moral, and intellectual status of women was considered not much higher than the primates who were at the seat of human origin:

For example, in the lowest zoological series, the female is superior to the male in size and organic complication, almost the mistress of the species; but then she becomes a humble slave, diminished in power, variability, and so on. In the human race she appears equal or superior to the male before puberty — equal in strength and stature, even in intelligence; but gradually she falls behind, leaving proof of that precocity that is standard among the inferior races (Rafter & Gibson, 2004, 35-36).

The argument is similar to what Darwin and Spencer postulated that in the early evolutionary process size, strength, and hereditary tendencies were greater in the female, but in going up the evolutionary scale man soon surpassed the woman.

The biological, psychical, and moral development of women was considered by Lombroso and the Positivists to be inferior to men, a condition of gender separation that would not appreciatively decrease with the pace of civilization and modernity. Marks of female physical inferiority were also pronounced, in height, weight, fewer number of red corpuscles, and smaller size of skull and brain (more childlike than like men), women were "always inferior and always offer less variation than . . . the male" (Rafter & Gibson, 2004, 50). Not only anatomically inferior, the authors reasoned that women showed less variability than men. Variation within the human species or gender in the case of women was considered important on the evolution scale of advancement. Furthermore, external differences were fewer "between female criminals and normal women (Rafter & Gibson, 2004, 125).

******

Lombroso and Ferrero considered the female's infantile physical differences as degenerative characteristics, which extended to woman's "weaker strength, more frequent left-handedness, and lesser frequency of white-headedness and baldness" (Rafter & Gibson, 2004, 57). They explained further that: "In the male, the bone and muscular systems predominate; in the female, on the other hand, it is fat and connective tissue, which explains the greater rotundity of her form" (Rafter & Gibson, 2004, 48). While the authors' general description in this last statement of the female physique was unflattering but essentially anatomically accurate, their classification of these same features as degenerate in origin raises serious questions rather their conclusions were the product of science or an inherent contemporary male bias, or just a "scientific" bias postulated by the authors.

There was also a strong racial overtone to their description of the differences between the European woman and her "Negro and Asiatic" sisters for whom,

> "fat and connective tissue become even more developed through sexual selection and artificial means (immobility, special diet of beer and milk, and tight clothing). In these races fat appears at a younger age than with us" (Rafter & Gibson, 2004, 48).

Lombroso and Ferrero considered the "Negro and Asiatic" races, Arabs and the "Hottentot" people of Southern Africa to be inferior to the white man of Europe. This attitude was universal on either side of the Atlantic. The late 19th and early 20th centuries saw the rapid colonization of the Third World by the Great Powers of Europe and America for raw materials, new markets, and prestige under the guise of the "White Man's Burden" to Christianize the world. This misogynist and racist sentiment was the norm and reflected both Darwinism and the influence of Victorian social and political standards. A similar bias extended to women who were seen as mere children, like the undeveloped world, who also needed the protection and moral influence of men.

The Inner Child in Women

Lombroso often compared women to children and both to savages who in their formative years lacked a moral sense; in sum, they were morally insane. While Lombroso lauded the role of good parenting and moral education to engrain morality in children, he was more circumspect about similar success for women. According to Haeckel's recapitulation theory, which Lombroso and Ferrero subscribed to, the human embryo passed through the same stages as animals in the natural world, from the simple to the complex. In the earliest months from the womb, children continued to mimic early animal biological and psychological characteristics, thus the primate and human child shared common traits, there was continuity between animal and human behavior. Lombroso was especially interested in the criminal traits of children. He and Ferrero theorized that some women and children never fully matured biologically or psychologically, their development was arrested and recapitulation to full maturation was never completed. Women remained more childlike with their moral sense inferior to men according to Lombroso and Ferrero.

Lombroso and Ferrero in *The Female Offender* (1909) described a latent tendency to criminality shared by women and children alike:

What terrific criminals would children be if they had strong passions, muscular strength, and sufficient intelligence; and if, moreover, their evil tendencies were exasperated by a morbid psychical activity! And women are big children; their evil tendencies are more numerous and more varied than men's, but generally remain latent. When they are awakened and excited they produce results proportionately greater (151).

The authors saw many of the same traits in women and children, a deficient moral sense, jealousy, vengefulness, and an inclination to "refined cruelty when they take revenge" (Rafter & Gibson, 2004, 183; Lombroso & Ferrero, 1909, 151, 158). They added that the "passion for evil" in women need not spring from external causes, rather it was inherent and sprang from a "morbid irritation of the psychical centers" (Lombroso & Ferrero, 1909, 158). The crimes of women in the authors' view were "almost always deliberate" (Lombroso & Ferrero, 1909, 171).

In short, immorality was an inherent feature in every female and when aroused they could be a formidable force for evil (Lombroso & Ferrero, 1909, 216, 265). Lombroso expanded on this thought by explaining that women "have no fondness for evil's sake . . . she develops a taste for evil only under exceptional circumstances. . . . But woman is always fundamentally immoral, and oftentimes her immorality is even a by-product of her compassion" (Rafter & Gibson, 2004, 800). Perhaps not only in crime, but an impassioned woman seeking equality might also be deemed by men as a threat to be feared. In the guise of explaining female criminality, Lombroso and Ferrero may also be revealing a bias in the struggle of the "new woman" to gain equality and inclusiveness. The "morbid psychical activity" they address might just also be flexed to advance woman's parity in society.

******

Because of their underlying pathological traits, women in Lombroso's estimation were en class morally insane. The females' protected status in society helped to augment their more favorable attributes such as compassion and maternal feelings and desires: "Maternity, together with women's lesser intelligence, strength, and variability, explains why women are not only less moral but also less criminal than men" (Rafter & Gibson, 2004, 36). If the logic of this conclusion seems to defy the reader, Lombroso cautioned that nature is not logical. It was the same maternal instincts and "intensity of feelings" that Lombroso and Ferrero claimed made up for women's "deficiency of intellect"

(Rafter & Gibson, 2004, 37). Maternity, they explained also "worked as a sort of moral vaccine against evil" (204).

In addition, the normal woman was "kept on the path of virtue" due to her "weakness and piety," and "undeveloped intelligence," but when these influences failed and she turned to crime, she was a "monster" (Lombroso & Ferrero, 1909, 151, 152). Lombroso and Ferrero noted further, "when muscular strength and intellectual power come together in the same individual, we have a female criminal of an indeed terrible type" (Rafter & Gibson, 2004, 192). By nurturing their positive traits women could potentially rise above their criminal tendencies. The defining line for Lombroso and Ferrero between the normal and criminal woman was sexual pathology, which they claimed was prevalent in primitive societies and determined the psychological nature of women. The tendency to equate women with sexual pathology is an ancient conflation of female deviance and sexuality. Primitive women, the authors claimed, were more likely to become prostitutes than criminals.

Female Dangerousness

Considered en total intellectually and morally handicapped, the latent condition for potential criminality in women made them especially dangerous to society. In *Criminal Man* Lombroso outlined strategies for a social defense against criminal activity with the standard of measure being the level of dangerousness posed by an individual or a class of people, such as the born criminal. The born criminal, male or female, posed the greatest threat to society.

On a linear scale of regression, Lombroso and Ferrero defined three types of criminal females in the title of their first book, *Criminal Woman, the Prostitute, and the*

Ladra   Tedesca

Museo di Antropologia Criminale "Cesare Lombroso," University of Turin, Italy

Criminal Woman

Normal Woman. The three types reflected a range with some variations within from the born criminal on the lower end of the evolutionary scale to the normal woman at the higher end of the scale. While one was incorrigible due to atavism, the other was able to supersede her latent immorality primarily by accepting her maternal instincts. The atavistic criminal woman was individualistic and self-aware, therefore most dangerous, while the normal woman was communal and law-abiding. To the Positivists, biology was the determinant in both cases, in the first case for self-preservation, and in the second case for nurture and protection. The authors made a distinction between the born female criminal and other female criminals, and between born criminal prostitutes and the more common professional prostitute. Feminists rejected biological distinctions for criminality as an explanation for gender inequality.

According to Lombroso and Ferrero, criminal woman was the equivalent to criminal man who were both born to criminality due to their atavistic heritage, they represented a new human subspecies:

> There is a perfect correspondence between the anthropology and the psychology of the female criminal. In the majority, degenerative traits are but few or weak, but there is a subgroup in which such traits are almost more marked and numerous than in male criminals . . . whose criminal propensities are more intense and perverse than even those of their male counterparts. These are the female born criminals, whose evil is inversely proportionate to their numbers. . . . In short, while female born criminals are fewer in number than male born criminals, they are often much more savage (Rafter & Gibson, 2004, 182, 183).

Deviations in the born criminal woman were more significant than similar deviations found in criminal man. The lineage of born criminal woman and man were similar due to biological determinism, which relegated them to the lower primitive ranks of arrested development. However, "the born female criminal is . . . doubly exceptional, as a woman and as a criminal. For criminals are an exception among civilized people, and women are an exception among criminals" (Lombroso & Ferrero, 1909, 147, 151).

For Lombroso and Ferrero, "as a double exception" criminal woman was a "monster," a "rare and monstrous exception," not even beauty could hide her "virile nature" (Lombroso & Ferrero, 1909, 152; Rafter & Gibson, 2004, 225, 143). But even the normal woman, according to the authors, could become a savage when, a morbid activity of the psychical centers intensifies their bad qualities, women seek relief in evil deeds. When piety and maternal feelings are replaced by strong passions and intense eroticism, muscular strength and superior intelligence, then the innocuous semi-criminal who is always present in the normal woman is transformed into a born criminal more terrible than any male counterpart (Rafter & Gibson, 2004, 183).

The evil tendencies in normal woman according to the authors could be mitigated or "neutralized" by her "piety, maternity, sexual coldness, physical weakness, and underdeveloped intelligence" (Rafter & Gibson, 2004, 183). Lombroso often attributed normal women's "sexual coldness" as due to maternal and reproductive exigent circumstances rather than any erotic drive for sexual fulfillment. To his psychologist mind, men were driven to copulate while women were motivated to give birth and nurture offspring.

Lombroso estimated that only between 11-20 percent of all female offenders "have inborn criminal tendencies" (Rafter & Gibson, 2004, 344). The born female criminal was "inclined to dissipation, and both astute and audacious," but this too could describe a normal woman under unmitigated circumstances (Rafter & Gibson, 2004, 192). Atavism explained the nature of the born criminal woman, but it also explained for Lombroso the rarity of the criminal type in women and the potential danger waiting in even normal women (Lombroso & Ferrero, 1909, 112).

******

Lombroso and Ferrero emphasized that the born criminal woman lacked maternal affection to help moderate her behavior, which was another "strong proof" of degeneration. In their study of criminal woman as a type, they observed that rejection of maternal feelings frequently resulted in infanticide. Lombroso also made a distinction between women in a primitive culture who were immoral but not criminal and the born criminal woman. On the scale of atavism, the born female criminals were even lower than primitive women (Lombroso & Ferrero, 1909, 152).

Regardless of the environment or circumstances, no born criminal female of any degree could escape her biological determinants, including her sexual pathology. Lombroso and Ferrero reminded readers that the "female equivalent of the male born criminal is the prostitute and . . . she shares the same atavistic origin" (Rafter & Gibson, 2004, 37). Prostitution was the "natural" and "masculine" retrogressive state of women, in fact Lombroso noted, "female born criminality hardly exists except in the form of prostitution" (Rafter & Gibson, 2004, 137, 221; Lombroso & Ferrero, 1909, 111). The authors emphasized that among young females, prostitution "completely takes the place of crime" (Lombroso, 1911/2012, 185). While prostitution was an assumed lower class trait in Victorian Europe, Lombroso and Ferrero made a bold assertion for their time, "it would be foolish to believe that the phenomenon explaining innate prostitution in the lower classes does not manifest itself as well in the upper classes" (Rafter & Gibson, 2004, 220).

The authors also found a close link between female criminals' sexual promiscuity and moral insanity, a similar discovery was reported by Lombroso in his research of the male born criminal. Lombroso and Ferrero concluded in *Criminal Woman* that lacking "maternal and family feeling" the "born prostitute . . . unscrupulous in the pursuit of her desires, and mildly criminalistics — presents the complete type of moral insanity" (Rafter & Gibson, 2004, 216). In moral insanity the authors found an explanation for female prostitution:

> Prostitutes are both sexually frigid and sexually precocious. They represent us with a real tangle of contradictions: an eminently sexual profession, practiced by women in whom sexuality has almost been extinguished; and women who, despite their weak sexual drive, devote themselves to vice at an age at [sic] when they are barely physically ready for sexual intercourse (Rafter & Gibson, 2004, 213).

They concluded that moral insanity rather than lust explained the contradictions inherent in the choices made to practice the world's oldest profession. Among professional prostitutes, the authors concluded that true love was rare. In the born male criminal and born female prostitute, Lombroso and Ferrero deduced that "according to logic" the "psychological and anatomical similarity . . . could not be more complete: both resemble the moral lunatic" (Rafter & Gibson, 2004, 221). Insanity perhaps also helped to explain the fact that religiosity in the born male and female criminal was "neither weak or rare" (Rafter & Gibson, 2004, 188).

Lombroso and Ferrero deduced that atavism was the very attribution of prostitutes' precocity and apparent beauty. As an occasional offender, the prostitute differed "little from the normal" woman "in whom circumstances have developed the fund of immorality which is latent in every female" (Lombroso & Ferrero, 1909, 216). The authors considered moral and biological deficits as determents for female sexual pathology. They did not entertain the question of how the social environment might affect the matter of choice in becoming a prostitute. The prostitute in their judgment was truly the "milder" born criminal among women, yet still an example of regression.

The authors wrestled with exactly what frequency of degenerative characteristics or anomalies constituted a born female criminal type. Lombroso had pondered the same question in his early editions of *Criminal Man*. He and Ferrero came to a similar conclusion that Lombroso had settled on earlier:

> The mere frequency of degenerative traits is insufficient to give us an exact idea of the criminal type among women; that type emerges clearly only when we study various characteristics in combination. We can refer to a complete type when we find four or more degenerative traits; a half-type when at least three such traits are present; and zero type when the offender exhibits only one or two physical anomalies or none whatsoever (Rafter & Gibson, 2004, 145; Lombroso & Ferrero, 1909, 103).

Prostitutes exhibited a more complete type than other female criminals according to Lombroso and Ferrero. They also concluded that, "almost all anomalies occur more frequently in prostitutes than in female criminals, and both classes have more degenerative characteristics than do normal women" (Rafter & Gibson, 2004, 134). Yet, the authors calculated that about 63 percent of prostitutes had few or almost no degenerative traits (Rafter & Gibson, 2004, 222). This meant that only 37 percent of prostitutes exhibited the complete type of the born criminal woman. The percentage is strikingly close to Lombroso's last calculation for born male criminals reported in *Criminal Man*.

The Born Criminal Woman

Regardless of the number of degenerative anomalies or stigmata present in the female criminal type, she remained an evolutionary throwback like her male counterpart. Born criminals of both genders carried upon them the marks of degenerative stigma, however woman's,

> "relative scarcity of degenerative stigmata, which at first seems to be evidence of superiority, pertains nonetheless to her lesser variability, an inferior characteristic. At the lower levels of evolution, as for example in monsters, the sexes are equal in degenerative stig-

mata, but this is a condition that, curiously enough, human sexual selection removes" (Rafter & Gibson, 2004, 36).

Criminal woman might exhibit fewer stigmata, but she was nevertheless a deplorable and depraved being. Left unexplained was how in the evolutionary process degenerative anomalies or stigmata were reduced or less pronounced in the female of the species.

Differences in the "prevalence of the complete criminal type among female criminals" was discovered by Lombroso and Ferrero to correspond to the type of offense committed. For example, female thieves in Turin showed 15.3-16% of the complete type, murderers 13.2%, swindlers 11%, and procurers 18.7% (Rafter & Gibson, 2004, 146). It is interesting that the percentage of anomalies and examples of a "complete type" of female born criminal are relatively low, forcing the authors to concluded that: "The surprising rarity of anomalies in the female criminal does not contradict the incontestable fact that like other female animals, atavistically she is nearer to her primitive origin than the male and thus ought to be richer in abnormalities" (Rafter & Gibson, 2004, 146). Perhaps the anomalies "ought" to be more pronounced, but in fact their research did not apparently find that connection to be statistically relevant enough to report. The authors attempted to answer this quandary with this puzzling response:

> Truly atavistic abnormalities that more strictly define the degenerative character or type, and as in cretinism, madness, and (much more import to us) epilepsy, they manifest themselves less markedly and less frequently in women. Moreover, anomalies are rare even in normal women, compared to normal men (Rafter & Gibson, 2004, 147).

Perhaps unable to answer their own unspoken question of why the presence of degenerative anomalies were so few among female criminals, excluding prostitutes, they shifted the emphasis to the lesser frequency of "truly atavistic" traits. The authors wish us to believe that regardless of the number of anomalies, women were still closer to their atavistic origin than men. A few pages later in *Criminal Woman* Lombroso and Ferrero again attempted to respond to the discrepancies in logic and evidence regarding the presence of anomalies by noting that the female criminal was,

> less typical physiognomically than the male criminals because she is less essentially criminal; because in all forms of degeneration she deviates to a lesser degree; because, being organically conservative,

she retains the characteristics of her type even when she deviates from it; and finally because beauty, being for her a supreme necessity, resists the assaults of degeneracy (Rafter & Gibson, 2004, 149).

Whether resisting degeneracy or not the authors added that women could artificially hide their anomalies or stigmata with their hair, makeup, and clothing.

******

The physical anomalies of the born criminal woman, and on a sliding scale to a lesser degree the normal female, were less pronounced than in criminal man. Prevalent physical anomalies exhibited by criminal women included a variety of degenerative stigmata. These included in part deep wrinkles (with exception of prostitutes), an "exaggerated jaw and cheekbones," grey or white hair, prehensile feet (especially among prostitutes), shortness in height, anomalous ears, anomalies of the forehead, moles, cephalic craniums, cranial asymmetry, and small brains in comparison to "honest women." Lombroso and Ferrero noted that normal women of the "better class" had a cranial capacity "five or six times" greater than criminals, prostitutes, and lunatics. Criminal women in general also had an early appearance of facial hair and "downiness" (Lombroso & Ferrero, 1909, 21, 71, 72, 73, 76, 80, 82, 102, 187; Rafter & Gibson, 2004, 124, 125, 126, 130-133; Lombroso, C. (1892, March 1). [Letter to Felix Alcan (S. Lapini-Lozzi, Trans.)]

Additional physical abnormalities of the born female criminal included the hymen and labia, which resembled "that of Negroes and Moors and Hottentots" but "less distinctly" in European women. Lombroso went to great length to explain the differences. The authors used conventional anthropological and Darwinian racial references to differentiate the white women of Europe from the darker skinned women of Africa and the Middle East, and even southern Italy. Lombroso described how the darker skinned female criminals of Sardinia resembled males, "and males of ancient days." Lombroso and Ferrero in summary concluded that prostitutes and other female offenders particularly of color had a larger number and greater frequency of characteristics of degeneration and male masculinity than normal women (Rafter & Gibson, 2004, 53, 240; Lombroso & Ferrero, 1909, 23-24).

Sensory anomalies described by Lombroso and Ferrero included dullness in touch, and a duller sense of taste, smell, hearing, and field of vision compared to normal women. Using his algometer, Lombroso determined that normal women were more sensitive to pain than the prostitute or other female criminals, in fact the prostitutes' insensitivity to pain corresponded to the male born criminal. However, in "all types of sensitivity" women are "inferior to men." Closely related to sensitivity to pain was the atavistic trait of tattooing. Lombroso described in *Criminal Man* how tattooing in the military had initiated his interest in the atavistic nature deviant behavior. In his study of criminal women, he noted that tattooing was less common compared to men with the exception of lower class prostitutes who showed less sensitivity to pain in general (Rafter & Gibson, 2004, 75, 151, 165-168; Lombroso & Ferrero, 1909, 116, 134, 140-141, 145, 146). In every physical and sensory category, the born prostitute exhibited the most anomalies.

Lombroso's research found that, "female born criminals and prostitutes had more sexual sensitivity than normal women, just as they menstruate and lose their virginity at a younger age" (Rafter & Gibson, 2004, 171). Another major area of research interest to Lombroso was the link between criminality and epilepsy; however, unlike the born criminal man, he found that in criminal women hysterics was more common than epilepsy, especially among prostitutes. In contrast to the born criminal man or woman, Lombroso estimated that epilepsy was found in only one percent of prostitutes (Rafter & Gibson, 2004, 232, 240).

As with Lombroso's description of the born male criminal, there were degrees of variation in the born criminal woman's classification. The more vile criminal women were in a class by themselves; they were the murderers (especially by poison) and assassins who shared with their male counterparts "the same passion for evil," which springs from a "morbid irritation of the psychical centers" (Lombroso & Ferrero, 1909, 158). Such women Lombroso claimed exhibited masculine moral traits and a "love of firearms" (Rafter & Gibson, 2004, 202). The average female criminal however was more involved with petty theft (shoplifting), prostitution, receiving stolen goods, abortion, fraud, and domestic theft (Gibson & Rafter, 2006, 128, Lombroso, 1911/2012, 184, 192).

Female Criminal Types

Lombroso and Ferrero determined that most criminal women were occasional offenders. Within the ranks of the "occasional criminal" were two female types, one who exhibited a "milder" form of the born criminal woman, and the occasional offenders who were closer to normal but to whom circumstances triggered their inherent latent immorality. Female prostitutes exemplified the "occasional criminal" type who Lombroso described as most often driven by circumstances outside their control, including poverty and poor education or the lack thereof. The authors predicted that the numbers of occasional women offenders would grow as "opportunities for evildoing increase." The impact of civilization for both good and evil was a common theme in Lombroso's work. On a moral scale, Lombroso equated the prostitute with primitive women, who were immoral but not criminal by nature. Lombroso and Ferrero described the key characteristic of occasional female criminals to be their lack of prominent degenerative traits (Rafter & Gibson, 2004, 148, 193, 199, 220; Lombroso & Ferrero, 1909, 187, 192, 216).

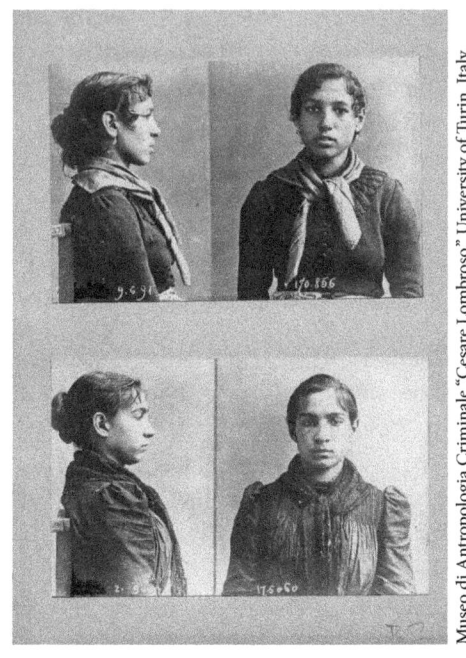

Bertillon Female Criminal Composite Photo

Museo di Antropologia Criminale "Cesare Lombroso," University of Turin, Italy

Another category common to women was the "criminal of passion," which reflected women's "greater excitability and lesser inhibition," and were more "ardent in their affections than normal women" (Lombroso & Ferrero, 1909, 36; Rafter & Gibson, 2004, 202). Crimes of passion were "predominately" committed by young female offenders; youth also defined crimes committed by males. The authors determined that love and egoism were common motivations for crimes of passion. Out of love a woman might follow her lover into crime or because of his infidelities turn on him.

Lombroso and Ferrero coined the term *passionate-egotistical* to describe a seemingly normal woman who was "impelled by self-centered jealousy." Such women allowed latent "wickedness," vanity and an "inordinate sense of self" to overcome their better self, too often resulting in an attack on their victim without provocation (Rafter & Gibson, 2004, 207; Gibson & Rafter, 2006, 66). In terms of the passionate female criminal's resemblance to the criminal type, Lombroso and Ferrero (Rafter & Gibson, 2004). explained that:

> In crimes of passion woman proves herself inferior to man, not so much numerically as in her tendency to resemble first the born criminal, then the occasional criminal, while the male offender in

this category is truer to type. Moreover, premeditation and savagery play a greater part in women's than men's crimes of passion. Otherwise, however, men's and women's crimes of passion parallel one another (201).

The authors described the most common crime of passion committed by women as deadly assaults on their lovers or their male partner's mistress. Lombroso and Ferrero commonly associated passionate induced violence with female jealousy, desire for a new lover, greed, or male infidelity. In most cases the female carefully plotted her attack and in some cases used an "immodest" proposal to lure her victim into an opportune moment to attack. The inference to seduction used by women to lure their victim or apparent tendency to violence reflects the male bias and sexist perspective on the unpredictable volatility of women. Female passionate "savagery" was clearly to the authors an expression of women's degenerative nature.

Cases of domestic violence used as examples by the authors generally portrayed the female acting out in violence against her male partner. There is very little discussion in Lombroso's writings or the two books written with Ferrero depicting or describing male instigated violence within the domicile. In virtually every case the female was the aggressor. While not excusing the authors, this incomplete picture of domestic violence reflected a Victorian sensibility prohibiting discussion of home affairs in public, or empowering the police to violate the sanctity of the home and the male prerogative to "discipline" their spouse, significant other, or escort. In a culture that tended to demonize or marginalize women, it was too easy to make their violent acts a retrogressive aberration. Crimes against prostitutes were also seldom discussed openly for the same reasons, and data was also limited to the most flagrant acts of assault or murder. Prostitutes were considered the lowest of all women, an evolutionary degenerate that was all too easy to dismiss as unworthy of serious consideration or rehabilitation.

Not only were passionate women subject to latent criminality and violence, but they also lacked good judgment in the choice of men according to Lombroso and Ferrero:

> While the woman whom passion leads to crime is very different from the born criminal, who violates the laws of chastity from lust and love of idle pleasure, nonetheless such good, passionate women are fatally inclined to love bad men. They fall into the hands of frivolous, fickle, and sometimes depraved lovers who later aban-

don them, often adding to betrayal the even greater cruelties of scorn and slander (Rafter & Gibson, 2004, 203).

In Victorian Europe there was no greater disgrace for a woman than to lose her virginity and be the subject of social disgrace. Female "honor" was one of the most important Victorian principles.

Woman's Sexual Pathology

For Lombroso and Ferrero, sexual pathology was the underlying link between the born criminal woman, the prostitute, and normal woman. While prostitution was a scourge on the sensibilities of modern society, it also had value within the social context. The authors recognized that prostitution had a social utility as a "safety valve" for young men:

> In any case, [prostitution] would not exist without male vice, for which it is a useful, if shameful, outlet. One might say that the more women degrade themselves and the more they sin, the more they are helping society (Lombroso & Ferrero, 1909, 37).

Prostitution was considered to serve as a male crime prevention measure, a virtual "dyke against the irresistible flood of male sexuality that would otherwise scandalize and threaten honest society" (Gibson & Rafter, 2006, 344). Prostitution and young men's "rapacious" sexual appetite were in a symbiotic relationship that benefited society. Regulated prostitution was not classified by the newly unified Italian government as a crime, only the independent prostitute risked arrest. In the mind of Lombroso and Ferrero prostitution did not rise to a degree of dangerousness requiring criminalization. Serving the greater good of men, the authors did not consider "the occasional criminal" female prostitute a dangerous threat to society.

Lombroso outlined a number of measures to help regulate the oldest profession including regular medical checks and police registration for women who committed more than two or three offenses. In regards to punitive measures, Lombroso recommended probation, judicial warnings, and in an interesting observation he offered that:

> Given female vanity and the importance women place on clothes, knickknacks, and furniture, prison sentences for female offenders can often be replaced by penalties such as cutting their hair or con-

fiscating their ornaments and furniture (Gibson & Rafter, 2006, 344).

One suggestion made by Lombroso (Gibson & Rafter, 2006) to re-educate or reform prostitutes was offered in good faith but perhaps with a slightly wishful thinking. He recommended that not only female prostitutes but even female murderers and swindlers be placed in a convent:

> Nuns can train them to replace sexual love — the most frequent cause of female crime — with religiosity. Honest and religious fanaticism will eventually become substitutes for criminal tendencies (344).

Lombroso claimed to have seen this proposal actually work to the reform of inmates.

Lombroso and Ferrero reasoned that the born female criminal was in a minority compared to her normal sisters, but her criminal nature was revealed in her sexual pathology. While admittedly women committed fewer crimes than men, if prostitution and abortion were included in the statistics, their rates of crime were nearly identical if not larger, the authors determined. The authors deduced from statistics that as civilization progressed and urbanization became more prominent, women's crimes including prostitution and lesser offenses like petty theft, abortion, trafficking in stolen goods, and poisoning of male partners would noticeably increase. A reason or motive for the increased use of poison was left unexplained, perhaps this was a subliminal response to either an anticipated rise or simple recognition of domestic violence (Lombroso, 1911/2012, 185, 192; Rafter & Gibson, 2004, 98, 128).

While young men stole to prove their virility, women's "lesser criminality, their atavism, and men's rapacious sexual desire help us understand why women are less likely to be born criminals than prostitutes. Logic alone could not lead one to this conclusion. . . . [but] nature is never logical" (Rafter & Gibson, 2004, 36; Gibson & Rafter, 2006, 127-128). Supposedly atavism condemned some to a life of crime while others escaped the curse. The position taken by Lombroso and Ferrero is counterintuitive since the point of Positivism was to discover through a scientific methodology the uniformity of natural laws. The seeming randomness of some humans being born criminals and others normal posed a serious problem of logic. Their only real explanation hinged on the concept of hereditary degeneration and retrogression.

In addition to prostitution, Lombroso and Ferrero described two other prominent female offenses, abortion and infanticide. The authors explained that all three offenses were closely associated with primitive cultures. They were common practices among savage peoples, but found relevance in contemporary society. Abortion and infanticide were punishable under the Italian criminal code. In a predominately Catholic nation, abortion and infanticide were much more than violations of the law, they were violations of God's gift of life. Lombroso provided the most detailed descriptions of abortion and infanticide in his fifth edition (1896-1897) of *Criminal Man* and his suggestions for legal reform.

The Ultimate Crimes

Prostitution was the necessary "safety valve" for perceived male sexual needs and also served as a diversion from the commission of other crimes, particularly by young men. Abortion served the greater social interest by reducing the number of orphans and unwanted children that would require the intervention of the state at a cost. Both acts were described by Lombroso as common practices in primitive cultures and were by inference residual influences in the degenerate nature of women. With the exception of "professionals performing abortions for profit," or a woman being forced without her consent to undergo an abortion, Lombroso argued that women who aborted their fetus should not be charged with a crime. In opposition to the penalization of abortion, Lombroso echoed the reasoning of the prominent Italian jurist, Raffaello Balestrini:

> First . . . abortion does not undermine family order because most cases involve young, single women who are trying to avoid the creation of an illegal family. Second, abortion does not violate the legal protection of bodily integrity because the law punishes any abortion committed against a mother's will as a violent crime. Third, society derives no advantage from the birth of illegitimate children. Finally, it is contestable whether the fetus is a social being because the fetus is still at an animalian stage of evolution and not yet human (Gibson & Rafter, 2006, 345; Lombroso, 1911/2012, 407, 408).

For these reasons, Lombroso believed that an abortion performed by a woman on herself should not be prohibited or punished under the law. He believed that in most cases the male was guilty for suggesting abortion and should be held accountable before the law. Women on the other-hand should be held to the lower standard of probation or a judicial warning. Lombroso does not mention the health risk of a self-inflicted abortion. He also made the claim that only a trained embryologist during the first few months could identify a fetus as a "future human." This latter point begs the question left unanswered by Lombroso as to when in terms of months does a fetus become human, obviously he did not believe it was at the moment of inception.

Lombroso believed that the same logic regarding abortions also applied to infanticide. In both cases he argued that the birth of an illegitimate child brought "no advantage to society" and only "infamy" on its mother. Furthermore, he claimed that the state's support of unwanted illegitimate children in "foundling homes" resulted in the high mortality rates. He calculated the rate of mortality in Italy's orphanages at 50 percent due to the lack of sufficient care:

> We must, then, deduct from the theoretical evil caused by the murder of the new-born child, the amount of certain or probable evil which would come from the preservation of a life which exposes the father and mother to an irreparable loss of honor, compromises the peace of one family and sometimes of several, or, at least, in case the child is deserted, puts society in a perplexing situation . . . by constantly accepting the bringing up of these children as an obligation, it incurs the risk of encouraging desertion and makes charity degenerate into a reward of immorality (Lombroso, 1911/2012, 408).

In his mind, Lombroso rationalized that abortion or infanticide was a positive outcome for both the mother and the state. Lombroso argued that prison sentences for infanticide "leave women completely depraved by removing them from their homes, denying them their habits of housework, and thereby ruining their prospects for rehabilitation" (Gibson & Rafter, 2006, 345). While the act of infanticide was immoral, Lombroso argued it should not be criminalized, to do so was an injustice. To allow unwanted children to populate the streets and promote criminal activity was both a disservice to them and to society (Gibson & Rafter, 2006, 131).

Women who committed infanticide or abortion in Lombroso's reasoning were not a serious danger to society. Because infanticide was primarily a "crime" of passion or occasion, and thus rarely repeated, Lombroso believed that a judicial admonition was sufficient punishment. Lombroso's public stance against criminalization of professional prostitution, or the commission of abortion or infanticide was pragmatic and rather bold within the confines of a Catholic state. His position was based on what he perceived to be a progressive necessity in building a modern nation, which based its criminal law and punishments on the principle of dangerousness to society (Gibson & Rafter, 2006, 106, 345).

"Every crime has its origin in a multiplicity of causes."

—Cesare Lombroso

The author of *Criminal Man; Criminal Woman, the Prostitute, and the Normal Woman; The Female Offender* and *Crime: Its Causes and Remedies* took a rather broad and sweeping approach to the study of the origin of crime and criminal behavior. Lombroso found the seat of criminality in a range of causal factors, including biology, physiology, neuropathology, alcohol, education, religion, weather (what he called meteorology), geography, orography, the march of progress, poverty, race and hereditary, and the fact of simply being young. His exploration and scope of research was truly phenomenal and a first in the study of crime and its origins. The complexity of causal factors for crime did not escape Lombroso; in fact, he seems to have relished the challenge.

The Youth Factor

Lombroso made an insightful forecast from his study of crime statistics that young men between 15-25 years of age were responsible for the majority of crime. He also noted that female offenders, especially prostitutes, were in the same age bracket. Designating youths and young adults between the ages of

15-25 as the potential criminal pool is nearly identical to the common bracket of 16-25 used today. On another occasion Lombroso used the age bracket of 20-30 as containing the most criminals. What is important is that Lombroso recognized that age was a co-relational factor for crime. Young men and women were still morally immature, impressionable, and adventurers (Gibson & Rafter, 2006, 127; Lombroso, 1911/2012, 175).

Related to youth was the problem of abandonment. Lombroso warned that abandonment of children and the corresponding lack of education resulted in a "great number of orphans and step-children found in the prisons" (Lombroso, 1911/2012, 147). Orphanages and the streets were potential breeding grounds for criminality. He also noted that a large number of criminals came from broken homes, "sprung from unsound parents" (Lombroso, 1911/2012, 148). The idleness of youth, Lombroso explained, was another cause of criminal activity. Idleness not only affected youths. Lombroso claimed that idleness was also associated with priests and monks who participated in brigandage, and of course the Mafia and Camorra in rural southern Italy (Lombroso, 1911//2012, 218, 219).

Determinants to Crime

Throughout the five editions of *Criminal Man,* and *Crime: Its Causes and Remedies* among other publications, Lombroso drew upon his extensive research to describe a number of biological determinant factors to criminal behavior. First was his belief that male and female born criminals were inherently evil due to "savage" traits that represented their arrested development in the evolutionary process. Born criminals made up about 40 percent of all criminals and were considered the most dangerous class of criminal to the social order. Because of their atavistic nature, born criminals could not successfully adjust to civil society and the rigors of honest labor. The born criminal was biologically and psychologically determined to deviant behavior. Congenital criminality reflected the evolutionary struggle for survival, which doomed them to a life of crime. This group of individuals could not be rehabilitated to social norms; they were hereditary throwbacks and unfit for modern society. In the new Italian state there was simply no reconciliation possible with the born criminal type. In essence their crime was being born.

In *Criminal Man* Lombroso provided additional criminal types or classifications that were ancillary to criminal man, including the occasional, passionate, epileptic, insane, morally insane, hysterical, criminaloid, and mattoid criminal. Lombroso deduced that there was a close association between the born criminal and epilepsy, moral insanity and insanity; the difference was in fact only a matter of degree between all three pathologies (Gibson & Rafter, 2006, 263, 264). Epilepsy, moral insanity, and insanity were to Lombroso atavistic characteristics. These conditions could also be found independently or in the "milder" forms of the born criminal.

Moral insanity was the natural condition of humans at birth and exemplified children's lack of understanding about what is right or wrong and the tendency to throw tantrums when they did not get their way. The lack of moral judgment mimicked the natural world and reflected an early state of evolution. Lombroso held that appropriate education and parenting could ameliorate the congenital condition and lead to productive citizenship, morality was a learned behavior. Insanity according to Lombroso could be inherited (most common), induced by alcohol and an immoral or deviant life-style, or onset by other physical or psychical conditions at some later point in life. He deduced that 30% of Italian offenders suffered from insanity (Gibson & Rafter, 2006, 268). He also claimed that hereditary traits for either honest individuals or criminals were primarily paternal rather than maternal in origin (Gibson & Rafter, 2006, 327).

In a confusion of characteristics and conditions, physical, mental and environmental, Lombroso identified factors that create a predisposition to both crime and madness or mental illness:

> civilization, celibacy, a hot climate, being male, living in an urban area, and working at certain jobs (shoemaker, cook, domestic servant, and, perhaps, soldier). Many criminals have insane relatives; and in many the tendency to crime or madness is provoked by trauma, anomalies of the head, and liquor.

> Meteorological conditions, especially heat, influence both murderers and the mad . . . Moreover, many of the insane present the same physical deformities as criminals: abnormal ears, scanty beards, filmy and wandering eyes, darkened skin, headaches, and arrested physical development. Like the insane, some criminals are completely insensitive to pain; and members of both group[s] exhibit emotional imbalance . . . Criminals and the mad frequently lack affection entirely, showing neither pity nor benevolence nor remorse . . . If there is a line between crime and madness, it is a subtle divi-

sion that is often not perceived until it is too late" (Gibson & Rafter, 2006, 81-83).

The references to epilepsy, urbanization, celibacy, the influence of civilization, and climate marked new research interests for Lombroso.

******

Lombroso found abnormal cranial similarities between the insane and criminals, few "doubts remain about the frequency of pathological anomalies in the brain tissues of criminals, for these appear every time a criminal is autopsied" (Gibson & Rafter, 2006, 198). In reviewing the medical research of other scholars, Lombroso concluded that a "long list of anomalies shows that criminals equal the insane in diseases of the brain" (Gibson & Rafter, 2006, 199). Anomalies discovered in autopsies of criminals included not only those found in the brain, but also the internal organs, blood vessels, and genitals.

The smaller cranial capacity Lombroso found among criminals was another sign of arrested development in the evolutionary process. Lombroso was quick to compare cranial size to the inability to make sound moral judgments and conduct cognitive processes. A smaller brain "suggests not a sublimity of the primate, but the lower level of the rodent or lemur, or the brain of a human fetus of three or four months" (Gibson & Rafter, 2006, 48). Furthermore, cranial abnormalities found in criminals, he stated, "corresponded to characteristics observed in normal skulls of the colored and inferior races" (Gibson & Rafter, 2006, 48). Lombroso made the mistake of mixing race with inferiority and inferring from cranial anthropometry the mental or psychical state of mind and moral capacity of humankind.

******

Race and the racial theory of white supremacy was a consistent theme in the works of Lombroso and reflected a widely held belief system in Europe and America. The Positivists' belief in the inferiority of non-whites was closely affiliated with the theory of atavism and arrested development in evolution. Lombroso also equated race with poverty and criminality: "The notion of crime is indistinct among the savage races." Non-whites were considered inferior morally, physically and psychologically due to their arrested development in the evolutionary process. They were described as still in a savage or primitive state of nature, which normalized their deviance as acceptable behavior. Their physiognomy was defined as typically distinctive in a degenerative way. Lombroso tended to mix physiognomy and physiological characteristics together, thus the determination of character by physical features was often intermixed with the functional attributes of being human (Lombroso, 1911/2012, 128; Gibson & Rafter, 2006, 91, 114).

Nevertheless, Lombroso argued that all the traits of criminality "prove that the most horrendous and inhuman crimes have a biological, atavistic origin" (Gibson & Rafter, 2006, 91). Lombroso did not shy away from confusing race with ethnicity in labeling with a sweeping stroke of the pen Bedouins, Gypsies, Negroes, Albanians, Greeks, and indigenous people of southern Italy as examples of criminal types (Gibson & Rafter, 2006, 90; Lombroso, 1911/2012, 223). In short, "European criminals bear a strong racial resemblance to Australian aborigines and Mongols" (Gibson & Rafter, 2006, 57). Lombroso asserted that the biological defects he observed where a manifestation of racial origin, which is another extension of the theory of arrested development.

While Villella and many other criminals Lombroso studied were not from Africa, there was a perception in northern Italy that the south was not much more than a colony of Africa inhabited by savages (Lumley, 1997, 87-88). This bias unquestionably influenced Lombroso's work and analysis. The racial overtones of his analysis are not unique to the European mindset of the day, and they were often repeated, in particular from a less than inclusive nationalist perspective. This mindset was forged over the clash of civilizations during the conquest of Africa and the Middle East by European nations in the 19th century. The African empires of Great Britain, Germany, France, and Belgium were at their height during the 19th century. Their attitude toward the race of peoples in Africa and Arabia permeated all of Europe including Italy. It was all too easy to see in the hugely popular Darwinian theory the supremacy of the white man in the process of natural selection. That point of view was called "scientific racism," the word "science" extended a facade of legitimacy and authority in support of the favored European belief system.

However, scientists also applied race theory to some groups of whites that were deemed regressive and criminal. Lombroso did not acquit any race from harboring a criminal type; rather, he argued that every race harbored the criminal type. These groups included, according to Lombroso, the Irish, various "tribes" in Russia and India, gypsies, Jews, virtually all southern Italians, and certain others in France and elsewhere in Europe. He attempted to qualify his inclusion of Jews, his own heritage, by emphasizing that they were still less criminal than gypsies and that their reputation was in essence an unfair label. Lombroso and the Positivists systematically confused race with ethnicity and biology with culture as illustrated above (Lombroso, 1911/2012, 21-42, 223,

228; Gibson & Rafter, 2006, 48, 114, 115, 118-119, 230; Rafter & Gibson, 2004, 48; Lombroso, 1891/2015, 133-135).

******

To Lombroso, heredity was the primary biological means in the evolutionary chain for regressive or atavistic traits to pass from generation to generation. Alcohol was also closely associated with genetic degradation. Lombroso often cited the Juke family as an excellent example of the generational effects of atavism. The Jukes were not the only family history that Lombroso used to illustrate the degenerative effects of atavism. He reported on similar hereditary atavistic characteristics found in several other crime family histories as well. Lombroso concluded that regressive traits of atavism led to criminal behavior and all too readily exemplified an atavistic criminal class. These regressive traits were both biological and neurological with physical stigmata and insanity marking the hereditary influence through generations of a family.

Once Lombroso expanded his research beyond biological determinants for criminality, he identified a variety of environmental and social causal factors for crime. This approach reached its ultimate conclusion with the posthumous publication of *Crime: Its Causes and Remedies* in 1911, which was also a testimonial summary of Lombroso's life work published in the United States specifically for the American market. One of the most significant social factors Lombroso described was the abuse of alcohol within the environment of Italian cities in particular. Alcohol not only contributed to individual biological and mental degradation potentially effecting generations, but it was also a serious threat to the national health and the progress of civilization. Lombroso did not personally imbibe distilled spirits, beer, or wine from early adulthood; he associated alcoholic beverages with crime, social disorder, and dysfunctional families.

Alcohol was a precursor to the commission of thousands of crimes reported in statistics that Lombroso collected from a variety of European countries. It also had a detrimental effect on the brain and heredity. He concluded that "distilled alcohol stimulates the brain perversely, provoking a tendency to crime and suicide." Wine, in his view, was even worse (Gibson & Rafter, 2006, 122). The "perverse" effect of alcohol, Lombroso noted, was the result of inhibitions or restraints failing under the influence of alcohol allowing deviant behavior free reign. There was no room for doubt in Lombroso's opinion that "drunkenness causes crime" (Gibson & Rafter, 2006, 277). He also argued that alcohol was a cause of insanity (Lombroso, 1911/2012, 93).

The common denominator in all criminal pursuits of pleasure was alcohol. In a very insightful passage, Lombroso described the relationship of alcohol to crime,

> The criminal finds no greater pleasures than those offered by drinking and gambling. However, the passion for alcohol is very complex, being both a cause and an effect of crime. Indeed, alcohol is a triple cause of crime. First, the children of alcoholics often become criminals, and second, inebriation gives cowards the courage to undertake their dread deeds, as well as providing them with a future justification for their crimes. Furthermore, precocious drinking seduces the young into crime. Third, the tavern is a common gathering place for accomplices, where they hatch their plots and spend the proceeds. For many it is their only home. The innkeeper is their banker, with whom criminals deposit their ill-gotten gains (Gibson & Rafter, 2006, 67-68).

Temperance supporters in America and England used the same arguments. Lombroso believed that alcohol was a contributing factor to degeneration and arrested development in the evolution of man. He believed that incarceration provided a healthy cure for alcoholism by depriving the criminal of the source of his affliction and giving him a chance to become sober. Lombroso also made suggestions to prevent alcoholism by limiting the hours of sale, raising taxes on alcoholic beverages, restricting the issuances of licenses, and prohibiting purchases on credit. Lombroso also promoted the use of hospitalization to insure treatment of alcoholism, even if it meant "permanent detention" (Lombroso, 1911/2012, 274).

The clinical effect of alcohol and intoxication on the brain's center for controlling behavior was not yet understood in the late 19th century. Lombroso and medical researchers of his day surmised correctly that there was a pathology associated with alcohol and the brain, but the science of how the brain functioned under the influence eluded them. In autopsies scientists could see physical degradation of the brain, but little else. They also, of course, did not yet understand the genetic effect of alcohol, only that alcohol altered human behavior and the regressive nature of heredity among alcoholics. In addition to alcohol being readily available in the city, Lombroso cited the presence of other "stimulants" including tobacco and opium as contributors to crime and indolence. He actually considered tobacco as the gateway drug to alcohol, hashish, and opium and morphine (Lombroso, 1911/2012, 102-103).

Lombroso recognized a "nexus between alcohol and crime" and recidivism; the nexus was both "social and pathological" (Gibson & Rafter, 2006, 318; Lombroso, 1911/2012, 90, 96). Alcohol was, in his estimation, the "aggravating" factor to criminal behavior (Gibson & Rafter, 2006, 318). Lombroso reported from his findings that "crimes most associated with drinking" were "assault, sex crime, and political rebellion" followed by murder and assassination, and finally arson and crimes against property (Gibson & Rafter, 2006, 318). The urban environment he concluded created more opportunity for crime and alcohol abuse. The problem was acerbated by the flow of the rural poor migrating to the industrialized cities looking for work and never really escaping poverty. Alcohol inevitably contributed to the decay of society. He wrote in the second edition of *Criminal Man* that the "progress of civilization" multiplied both the wants and needs by a "hundred fold:" "Civilization thus increases rates of alcoholism and progressive paralysis in the madhouses, and it fills the prisons with offenders against property and public morality" (Gibson & Rafter, 2006, 120-121; Lombroso, 1911/2012, 67, 89, 90).

******

The relationship of civilization and urbanization to crime was a recurrent focus of attention in Lombroso's publications. In general he equated the term "civilization" with cities and urban environments, and the term "progress of civilization" as a reference to modernity in the political, economic, cultural, and legal/penal institutions of society. The urban environment was conducive to criminal activity and organized crime due to the proximity of people, the greater availability of goods and opportunities, high levels of poverty, and among other determinants, the ready availability of alcohol and other stimulants. Lombroso reported a correlation between poverty and the lower classes with crime as a product of urbanization and industrialization. Using statistics from several countries, Lombroso was able to show an association between density of population and higher rates of crime, particularly for property crimes, abortion, infanticide, and prostitution (Lombroso, 1911/2012, 53, 72-75, 219-220; Gibson & Rafter, 2006, 120-121, 235).

Additional data on immigration led Lombroso to conclude that immigration from poorer countries also resulted in higher crime rates. He noted the same affect with migration within a country as in the case of Italy: it was migration from the rural southern regions to the industrial cities of the more urban north. In order to reduce immigrant crime, Lombroso proposed that a process of selection for entry should be created to favor the "respectable" who had some means of support and "manual" skills. A growing urban population put stresses on the supply of foodstuffs to the cities. Lombroso cautioned that volatile fluctuations in the cost of food staples and decreases in supply in cities assured an increase in property theft and some violent crimes such as assault (Gibson & Rafter, 2006, 122; Lombroso, 1911/2012, 63-64, 66-67, 250).

The density of population found in cities coupled with alcohol not only contributed to a greater frequency of both property and personal offenses, but Lombroso explained it also contributed historically to political unrest and even revolution or insurrection. Lombroso was a student of history and often cited history to further validate his findings, and the threat of revolutionary political or economic upheaval was a concern to him. The threat of insurrection or revolution was greatest when food was in short supply or when the "man of genius" exerted his persuasive influence and persona in the public sphere of affairs. War and economic distress raised the serious risk of revolution and the breakdown of law and order (Lombroso, 1911/2012, 59, 85, 100, 134, 220, 227; Lombroso, 1891/2015, 239, 243, 334-335).

Criminals were afforded more anonymity and greater profits in cities compared to the countryside. Cities also provided a fertile ground for youth gangs and organized crime. From history, Lombroso related that criminal associations or enterprises were fairly common in urban centers. Abandoned children on city streets were also prone to organize gangs to facilitate theft. However, organized crime was not unique to cities alone, in rural southern Italy the Mafia and Camorra were prominent. The density of population common to cities contributed to opportunities for property crimes and prostitution, which was primarily an urban problem uncommon to rural Italy. But civilization was not without means to defend itself and had already Lombroso noted,

> started curing the plagues it has caused with asylums for the criminally insane, cellular prisons, industrial factories, the savings banks available at post offices and workshops, and charitable organizations that protect homeless children, thus preventing crime practically from the cradle" (Gibson & Rafter, 2006, 121).

Lombroso made an interesting observation on the proliferation of newspapers in cities as indirect contributors to crime. His concern centered on extensive reporting of crime and the potential for imitation, or for the desire of certain criminals to become famous and the center of attention for their crimes. He even worried about the tendency to sensationalize criminal behavior in novels. Lombroso did not propose censoring the press and literary creativity, but the notoriety given to crimes deeply concerned him (Gibson & Rafter, 2006, 81, 89, 141, 85-89, 316, 342; Lombroso, 1911/2012, 53, 54, 57, 59-60).

The growth of cities as the vanguard of "civilization" Lombroso explained, was the perfect environment for the expression and actuation of deviant behavior and mental illness. Cities also were the most prominent sites for prisons, which Lombroso believed were but little more than breeding grounds for criminality, providers of enhanced criminal "education," and perpetuated recidivism. The intermixing of hardened criminals with novices to crime resulted he claimed in a learning environment for more successful criminal activity upon the novice's release from prison. Lombroso forecast that prison education would facilitate the use of the railroad, telegraph, explosives, cipher messages, and even the review of court cases in the commission of crimes and revolution.

******

Lombroso opposed the introduction of elementary education in prisons unless it was accompanied by "special training designed to correct the passions and instincts rather than to develop the intellect" (Lombroso, 1911/2012, 114, 115; Gibson & Rafter, 2006, 334). He feared that without the "special training," education would only produce a more intelligent criminal and recidivist. As a psychologist, it is probable that Lombroso had in mind a curriculum for "special training" that addressed self-worth and impulse control. In the place of traditional education, Lombroso favored prison education that focused on vocational skills, with the hope that the released inmate would seek honest employment (Gibson & Rafter, 2006, 139, 335; Lombroso, 1911/2012, 114, 116).

Public education was closely associated with "civilization" and "progress," but Lombroso warned that even education created "needs and aspirations" without always providing the "power to gratify them" (Lombroso, 1911/2012, 117; Gibson & Rafter, 2006, 75). This sentiment is remarkably close to Robert Merton's Strain Theory, which says that, unable to satisfy wants and needs, even a law-abiding person could become a criminal. Lombroso failed to explain in this circumstance the internal conflict between Beccarian choice theory and determinism. Lombroso's solution included provision of employment opportunities appropriate to the level of education earned and moral education in schools.

He stated that public education should be denied the born criminal in order to avoid instruction that might be used to facilitate criminal offenses to greater success. Lombroso suggested that with the "advances of criminal anthropology" it was now possible for elementary teachers to identify the "incurable signs of inborn criminality," which included "physiological and craniological anomalies" and deny education to such children. He considered this early intervention an important measure of social defense. Refusing to allow education to be used for the enhancement of criminal skills was an unrealistic proposal. The problem of implementation of such a policy is where the details matter, and unfortunately, Lombroso did not elaborate on just how a policy of denying education to youths could be accomplished fairly. Today the very premise upon which Lombroso framed his argument would be considered unjust and a denial of equal opportunity, particularly in the context of rehabilitation (Lombroso, 1911/2012, 114, 301; Gibson & Rafter, 2006, 294, 334, 335).

Aside from the potential problems associated with education, Lombroso recognized that it also served to elevate society and create positive opportunities for individuals. In addition to enhancing individual opportunity and success, education had "an indisputable influence upon crime in changing its character and making it less savage" thus reducing "its severity" (Lombroso, 1911/2012, 111, 329; Gibson & Rafter, 2006, 121). That "indisputable influence" he explained changed the type of crime from the most violent to the less serious, from murder and assault to property, fraud, prostitution, and political crimes. Using statistics, Lombroso found what he believed to be a correlation between recidivism, education, and illiteracy. While criminality and illiteracy tended to decrease in the general population with the widespread increase of public education, especially in the middle class, illiteracy rates among criminals, commonly members of the lower class, actually increased. Thus education appeared to have little effect on recidivism, already a highly recognized problem in Italian society.

What Lombroso perhaps failed to consider were the social-economic changes taking place between classes in society. The suspected increase of illiteracy and crime in reality reflected the differential between a growing middle class in contrast with an increase in poverty and lower social status among the less fortunate, which contributed to an increase in crime. Lombroso struggled with this social phenomenon and concluded, "in sum, it is not possible to say that education decreases crime, nor can it be said that it increases it. When education is spread through all classes, it is in fact beneficial, reducing crimes among those with middling [elementary grade] education" (Gibson & Rafter, 2006, 76).

Lombroso associated public and private education with the rise of the middle class, which had the beneficial effect of reducing crime through gainful employment. He placed great emphasis on what he considered the primary purpose of education, to teach moral values and the development of character. He believed that education focused too much on form and not substance, facts and not context or cause and effect. A social defense against deviance and criminality required in his impression a well-rounded education centered on moral development. Even though Lombroso considered himself a man of science, he had little faith that developments in science and technology could "add a jot to morality" (Gibson & Rafter, 2006, 75, 76; Lombroso, 1911/2912, 105-106, 108, 111, 112, 114-116, 301).

******

Although illiteracy was a common characteristic of the criminal class, Lombroso found that criminals had their own way and method of oral and written expression. He was fascinated with both the "jargon" and "literature" of criminals. Criminals had their own lexicon, often associated with archaic words (example, *arton* for bread), attributes of something (example, *jumper* for goat), and onomatopoetic words that imitate what they denote (example, *tic* for watch). Once again Lombroso found in this pattern of language a connection with the atavistic or primitive man, "criminals speak differently because they feel differently; they speak like savages because they are savages" (Gibson & Rafter, 2006, 78). Furthermore, the use of secretive jargon or slang facilitated the planning and commission of crimes.

Lombroso was perhaps the first to recognize the difference between learned behavior, illiteracy, and the role of education in the making of criminal man. He noted in *Criminal Man* (1876) that different kinds of crimes required different skills, and that these abilities might seem extraordinary, but in reality were simply the result of repetition, and thus learned behavior. Even an "idiot" might seem especially skilled and even "learned" from "repeating a movement continuously" (Gibson & Rafter, 2006, 76). Nevertheless, Lombroso argued that educated men could fall prey to criminal behavior. On this thought, Lombroso recognized that education "may be the servant of good, but it may also be the servant of evil," it increased power but not necessarily virtue (Lombroso, 1911/2012, 114).

Even the arts were not exempt from the temptation or allure of crime. Lombroso argued that artists and writers were prone to crime because many of them gave way freely to their passions. To artists even more than writers, Lombroso ascribed crimes inspired by "love and professional jealousy." He also linked poetry to brigandage historically, citing Robin Hood as an example among others. This was in contrast to men of science, who "more clearly realize than others that crime is not only unjust and illogical but also fruitless, always returning to haunt the criminal himself" (Gibson & Rafter, 2006, 74).

On the matter of unemployment, Lombroso was somewhat ambiguous. He argued that the unemployed were largely either criminals who did not seek employment (they had an aversion to work) or individuals laid off because of their own choice to strike. Little room was left in his conclusion for the temporary worker or those laid off when the job was completed. There appeared to be little sympathy for the unemployed, and to answer his own question, "Does unemployment notably affect crime"? Lombroso's answer was simply no, unemployment was not a "major cause of violent crime." Perhaps, but his response does not address non-violent property crimes. Only a few paragraphs further in *Criminal Man*, Lombroso unequivocally stated that the poor, conceivably including the unemployed, would resort to theft and even violence if necessary to feed their families — a reversion to the survival of the fittest. In conclusion, Lombroso argued that industrialization was an even greater cause of crime than poverty, and that wealth and poverty were still potential causes of crime in the urban environment (Gibson & Rafter, 2006, 320-322; Lombroso, 1911/2012, 205).

Lombroso raised a rhetorical question in the fifth edition of *Criminal Man*, "when is crime the result of wealth?" He chided researchers for focusing only on poverty as a causal factor for crime and not considering the question of wealth. Industrialization and commercialization of urban centers contributed to inequalities of wealth. Lombroso believed that these inequalities as much as poverty contributed to urban crime rates. Wealth could, he surmised, corrupt and lead to excessive vanity and indulgences, alcoholism, sexual abuse, and fraud, "if not balanced by an elevation of character and broad religious and political ideals, acquisition of wealth leads to harm rather than good" (Gibson & Rafter, 2006, 321). Echoing Spencer, Lombroso concluded that wealth could lead to either "virtue or vice" (Gibson & Rafter, 2006, 320-322; Lombroso, 1911/2012, 51, 132, 134).

Virtue resided in the person and not their accumulated wealth. The emphasis on leading a moral life whether rich or poor once again reflected Victorian proprieties regarding social norms. It also reflects in greater measure the upbringing of Lombroso and his middle class lifestyle centered on family. He did not practice his Jewish faith but was raised to respect God's law and the moral principles inherent in the Torah. Lombroso expressed indignation in the injustice of the wealthy being able to flaunt the judicial system and avoid conviction or prison terms because they had the influence of their fortune and social status to insulate them. Lombroso exclaimed satirically that the rich "represented what was really modern," because their crimes were formulated with "cunning" while the poor typically resorted to violence. Circumstances for the commission of crime by either the rich or poor was not lost on Lombroso, but he still reverted to evolutionary theory to explain that the wealthy by use of their intellect were the more advanced, while the poor represented atavism and regression. The rich were driven by vanity and "fatal ambition" to "surpass others" but suffered their own degeneration in syphilis, indolence, and alcoholism (Lombroso, 1911/2012, 50, 133, 134, 136).

******

Although statistics were limited, Lombroso found the connection between religion and criminal behavior of great interest. He recognized that the subject of religion and criminality was complex, but still worthy of study. In fact Lombroso and Ferri both explored the question or connection between religion and criminal activity. Following his interview of 700 convicted criminals Ferri contributed the primary conclusions to their study. Of the 700 felons, only one was an atheist while the others were predominantly Catholic, with the remainder Protestant. The general conclusion of their study was that criminals or those about to commit crimes were not inhibited by their religious beliefs, and for some, religion provided assurance of forgiveness. In a perverse way, religion not only provided the cover of forgiveness for criminal acts but because of that assurance, an inverted permission to commit crime. Several quotations from Ferri's interviews illustrate the criminals' premise: "It is God who gives us the instinct to steal," or, "Crimes are not sins, for the priests also commit them," and another, "I have sinned, it is true, but in confession the priest will pardon my bad deeds." Criminals thus used religion to excuse their crimes. Lombroso postulated that the number of criminals and normal citizens who attended church were essentially equal. Religiosity was characteristic to both criminal and normal citizens in society (Lombroso, 1911/2012, 138-139; Gibson & Rafter, 2006, 323-324).

******

Certainly one of the first specialized studies of its kind undertaken, led Lombroso to expound on the close association of crime to the effects of climate, geography, orography, temperature, and the seasons. Lombroso had always been fascinated with climate, in particular to the warm spring and summer days of his youth spent in the region of Veneto with the northern mountains as a backdrop. His mentor, Paolo Marzolo, had taught him at the university to explore nature and to look for relationships between man and the natural world. In 1865 Lombroso published a monograph, "Studies of Medical Geography," a research project on national health divided into three sections. The first section was a study of mental pathologies related to meteorology, followed by a second section devoted to the relationship of food and drink to health. The third section of the monograph focused on the link between physical and mental illness and race. Returning home from military service in 1866 Lombroso learned that his monograph had been awarded a Lombardo Institute prize. He followed this publication with additional monographs over the next several years focusing specifically on the influence of meteorological conditions on the human mind, race, and criminality. These works essentially provided the blueprint for his life work with the natural world at its center. Lombroso always believed that meteorological conditions had a direct bearing on criminal activity and the mind (Lombroso-Ferrero, Chap. V, 4, 20; Chap. VI, 7; Chap. X, 14; Chap. XVII, 12).

Lombroso was not the first to recognize the influence of meteorological phenomena, the seasons, or physical geography on human behavior. Many of his statistics were sourced from the research of Guerry. But Lombroso provided perhaps the most extensive collection of statistical and anecdotal evidence coupled with his own experiments and observations published to date. The first two chapters of *Crime: Its Causes and Remedies* published posthumously in 1911 were dedicated to his findings regarding meteorology and the natural environment related to human physiology and criminal activity. Other references to Lombroso's environmental research can be found in his many publications, but this particular volume provided his cumulative knowledge on the subject. Lombroso made a special connection between temperature and barometric pressure on geniuses, who he believed were especially susceptible to meteorological influence (Lombroso, 1891/2015). The idea that man was a creature of his natural environment was an easy extension for Lombroso to make based on his belief in evolution and natural selection. Mankind, including the born criminal, was primarily the result of the forces of nature. Humankind and the natural world were in a symbiotic relationship regardless of the consequences.

Temperature, Lombroso determined, had a direct influence on human physiology and psyche. Heat, he noted, made people irritable and thus more prone to commit violent criminal acts. Heat and geography to Lombroso were also closely related, "the number of crimes increases as we go from north to south, and in the same measure as the heat increases" (Gibson & Rafter, 2006, 14). Lombroso deduced that there was an inverse relationship between temperature and density of population to homicide. While lesser crimes involving mostly property offenses were more common in the moderate temperature of northern Italian cities, homicide and other crimes against persons were more frequent in rural southern Italy where hotter temperatures prevailed. Among the correlates of temperature, density of population, and homicide, Lombroso concluded that temperature was the primary variable. He also determined that crimes spiked in hotter years. Although Lombroso was familiar with the presence of law enforcement and the justice system in both northern and southern Italy, he did not include law enforcement as a variable in his research question or compare different sizes of population density (Lombroso, 1911/2012, 3, 8, 13, 16).

In contrast to regions of moderate temperature, tropical climates contributed to physical and mental inertia. Lombroso reported further that excessive heat produced a lethargic population easily manipulated by despots. The colder temperatures of northern Europe and the Arctic tended to focus attention on the expenditure of energy necessary for the acquisition of food and provision of warmth. In these areas, Lombroso argued, survival tempered the mind and consumed the energy "that would otherwise have been available for the social and personal activity of the individual" (Lombroso, 1911/2012, 3). Cold of the winter months had a similar effect on reducing crime across Europe. The spring and summer months recorded the highest rates of crime including rape, insurrection, and other violent crimes, whereas, crimes against property trended up during the winter months when the nights were longer (Lombroso, 1911/2012, 6-7).

******

In terms of the time of day recording the highest frequency of crimes in general, Lombroso reported night hours were favored by criminals, especially for burglaries. Lombroso noticed from his studies that storms and other atmospheric disturbances agitated the insane. He deduced that they were sensitive to changes in barometric pressure and the rise of a full moon, which were factors he speculated that criminals shared in general. One unexplored time-frame for the commission of crime was the preferred day of the week, otherwise Lombroso's research was broad in scope and rather thorough for the resources and scientific procedures available to him (Lombroso, 1911/2012, 4-6, 8-12).

Crime statistics correlated with the orographic and geographic landscape provided Lombroso and his readers with another perspective on the nature of crimes committed. Using Italy as his primary point of reference and 54 years of statistical data, Lombroso concluded that the number of reported cases of rape in the mountains and hill country totaled approximately 33 percent of all recorded crimes; however, in "level country" the percentage jumped to 70 percent. He recognized that the greater number of rapes on the plains represented the greater density of population and opportunity for rapists. The number of crimes committed against property closely aligned with the plains and population density as well, with the exception of parts of southern Italy, Calabria, and coastal areas in particular (Lombroso, 1911/2012, 17-18).

Lombroso reported that the frequency of commission for all categories of crimes against persons were 50 percent in the plains, 47 percent in the hill country, and 43 percent in the mountains. The geographic portrait of crime composed by Lombroso can only be taken at face value since no explanation was provided on how the statistics were complied, who reported the crimes and were non-reported crimes considered as a margin of error, categories of crimes need more specificity, and among other things, the total percentages do not add to 100 percent. Considering the incomplete data and the statistical tools and procedures available, Lombroso's effort to synthesize large quantities of data are admirable. The general conclusion that can be taken away for his effort that more crimes were committed in the plains where large cities were located seems logical and contemporary to our own time (Lombroso, 1911/2012, 18).

CHAPTER 8
Social Defense and Criminal Justice Reform

"It is no longer enough to repress crime: we must try to prevent it."
—Cesare Lombroso, 1906

Very early in his university training, Lombroso decided that he wanted to benefit mankind and his new nation by exercising a pragmatic approach to finding cures for medical problems ranging from cretinism and pellagra to insanity. Lombroso believed as early as 1863 that certain illnesses and insanity in particular were more hereditary than acquired. Even before the conclusion of his military experience in the 1860s Lombroso had begun to make a connection between insanity and criminal behavior. It was not a great stretch of creative deduction to surmise that criminal behavior was like a disease and diseases had natural causes, and natural causes were inheritable. It was but a short leap to determine that insanity and criminality could be hereditary and in fact primitive in origin. Lombroso determined that natural born criminals were precocious, and precocity was a "distinguishing feature of savage people" (Lombroso, 1911/2012, 177). The theory of evolution provided the pathway to link natural causes, heredity, and primitive traits with Lombroso's discovery of the born criminal (Lombroso-Ferrero [ca. 1914]; Unpublished manuscript, Chap. V, 6, 11; Chap. IX, 1; Lombroso, 1911/2012, vii, 172; Gibson & Rafter, 2006, 99).

While Lombroso and his daughter Gina gave different dates for his discovery of the median occipital fossetta in the skull of Villella, it is clear that Lombroso's post military career provided him the opportunity to advance his study of the biology and pathology of criminal man. Lombroso created criminal anthropology to assist the criminal justice system in determining a defendant's level of dangerousness to society and accordingly suggest an appropriate punishment. He claimed that the real value of criminal anthropology was that it "not only identifies criminals but also saves innocents from punishment" (Gibson & Rafter, 2006, 351; Lombroso, 1911/2012, 437). By understanding the nature of the criminal, Lombroso hoped to change the Italian government's criminal justice policies to provide society with an appropriate means of defense. Lombroso understood social defense to include measures of crime prevention and criminal justice reforms that addressed the heart of the problem, the atavistic born criminal. Criminals and their deviant behavior in the commission of crimes posed a serious danger to society that Lombroso believed could be successfully addressed by application of criminal anthropology:

> The science of criminal anthropology has evolved to the point of offering both a theory of crime and practical applications of that theory. It can make useful suggestions in the struggle against crime, in contrast to traditional legal philosophy, which becomes ever more theoretical and has less and less to say about defending society. The new positivist criminology has also demonstrated its usefulness in the daily practice of psychiatry and forensic medicine (Gibson & Rafter, 2006, 350).

Criminal Justice Reform

The first priority for Italian justice, Lombroso argued, was the need to make a 180-degree turnabout from the existing model of Italian justice, which was built on the Beccarian concept of free will. Lombroso considered the power of choice a figment of imagination for born and habitual criminals. Implementing the concept of free will was in his view a mere exercise in theoretical contrivance and metaphysical futility, "daydreaming of a free will that never was" (Gibson & Rafter, 2006, 337). The Beccarian model of justice emphasized to Lombroso "abstract violations of juridical order" and not the "pressing social necessity" (Lombroso, 1911/2012, 361). In Lombroso's estimation public opinion and tradition perpetuated a broken criminal justice system. The existing Italian penal code and judicial philosophy focused on compensation, retribution, and determinate sentencing for commission of crimes. It was a system based on the principle of one-size-fits-all: if an individual committed a crime, there was a specific punishment for that type of offense; "the great truth of the present and the future, for criminal science, is the individualization of penal treatment" (Lombroso, 1911/2012, vii). Lombroso did not question the right of the state to punish offenders, but he believed punishment should be proportionate to the crime. For all but the incorrigible criminals, Lombroso favored indeterminate sentences (Lombroso, 1911/2012, 386).

The criminal justice system failed, Lombroso explained, to consider the individual or actor of the crime and the potential biological, medical, and psychical causes for criminal behavior. This failure also doomed any rehabilitation effort, which Lombroso believed was only at best lip service to the principle. Lombroso noted that prison did not rehabilitate; on the contrary, it provided an educational environment for the commission of more successful crimes in the future. Prisons provided opportunities for criminal association and for some a place of refuge and a surrogate home (Lombroso, 1911/2912, 209, 382). Reform of the guilty, Lombroso explained "is always or nearly always an exception, while the prison not only does not improve him but even makes him worse" (Lombroso, 1911/2012, 382). The victim was also lost in the existing criminal justice process, but most important to Lombroso was the seeming dis-concern for the public's safety: "We must have in view [the] welfare of society more than the punishment of the criminal and the criminal and his victim more than the crime" (Lombroso, 1911/2012, 385; Gibson & Rafter, 2006, 153).

Recidivism, Lombroso argued, was a by-product of the failure of the current system: "It is well known that among true criminals, successful reform is always, or nearly always, the exception, while recidivism is the rule" (Gibson & Rafter, 2006, 93). In contrast to the claim that "education is a panacea for crime," Lombroso complained that education was "in fact one of the causes of recidivism, or at least one of its indirect causes" (Gibson & Rafter, 2006, 108). The skills and crafts taught in prison Lombroso warned only enhanced the criminal's expertise for commission of additional crimes, and in some cases turn the criminal from one type of crime to another, for example the thief becomes a forger. He also argued that religion, contrary to what some claimed, was also a false panacea for crime. Lombroso was convinced that rehabilitation could not take effect on a criminal who was "naturally predisposed" to crime. The judicial system seemed, in his estimation, to ignore the problem of repeat offenders by simply meeting out the same sentence to the same individual time-after-time. Lombroso referred to repeat offenders as incorrigibles that required a different approach from the periodical repeat appearance in court and prison for the same offender (Gibson & Rafter, 2006, 108, 141, 338, 347; Lombroso, 1911/2012, 208, 245, 292, 387).

By the use of anthropometric methodology, Lombroso insisted that the criminal anthropologist could determine guilt or innocence in cases where evidence was circumstantial or non-existent and thus eliminate presumptive decisions. Lombroso was often called as an expert witness in court to help determine whether the party at trial was guilty or innocent. Criminal anthropology Lombroso stated, "has become a precious tool for proving, for example, what part a suspect played in a particular crime or which individual among a group is the true ringleader" (Gibson & Rafter, 2006, 350). Lombroso forecast the day when the technical expertise of the criminal anthropologist would replace "the empty rhetoric of defense attorneys" in the courtroom (Gibson & Rafter, 2006, 231). He offered as suitable evidence of the applicability of criminal anthropology two examples in the fifth edition (1896-1897) of *Criminal Man*:

> Maria of Lucera was found dead on June 19, 1886, at the age of sixty-six. . . . She was face down on the mattress, with a bloodied, broken nose. Suspicion immediately fell on her two stepsons, M. and F., who had bad reputations, had been seen in the area on that day, and had something to gain by her death because she was about to disinherit them. I was summoned to the court to provide an expert assessment of the case. According to the testimony of C., suffocated shouts were heard coming from the room of the victim on the night of the seventeenth. One of the suspects, the stepson M., had previously been sentenced for carrying arms, and he had swindled the victim of a large portion of her inheritance as soon as his father died. When a girl had rejected his advances, M. said he would like to strangle her as he had his mother; furthermore, he had threatened his brother over the division of their inheritance. Moreover, M. was named as the murderer by his brother F., who was less criminal and less inclined to evil.

> Criminal anthropology served admirably on this occasion in deciding which of the two brothers was guilty. M. represented more completely the criminal type, exhibiting huge jaws, swollen sinuses, extremely pronounced cheekbones, a thin upper lip, large incisors . . . tactile insensitivity . . . and left-handedness. All of these physical anomalies, except the swollen sinuses and pronounced cheekbones, were absent in his brother F. for these reasons, M. was deemed more criminal in his tendencies and convicted (351).

In the second case, Lombroso offered an example of determination of innocence:

> Criminal anthropology not only identifies criminals but also saves innocents from punishment. In one such case a three-year-old girl was raped and contracted syphilis. Her mother offered the names of six suspects who were arrested. All lived in the same building, had frequent contact with the child, and denied raping her. After studying them, I pointed out to the judge one in particular: he had obscene tattoos on his arms, Negroid physiognomy, and an altered field of vision that we traced to a recent case of syphilis. The confession followed shortly (351).

The use of physiognomy to determine guilt or innocence raises the question of whether justice was served or not in these two examples provided by Lombroso. Certainly the admission of guilt by M. in the first case to a third party and his threats to his brother F. provided strong but not conclusive circumstantial evidence. The case of rape in the second case and one of the defendants having syphilis also provided strong circumstantial evidence. Aside from the confession, interesting questions not addressed by Lombroso center around the scope of the dragnet for suspects and the culpability of the mother and whether or not she was a prostitute who had multiple johns visiting the settlement house. The racial overtones of Lombroso's assessment of defendants also raise serious questions. In today's terms Lombroso would have relied on DNA evidence, but his reliance on the criminal anthropologist's profiling skills was the 19th century's equivalent to DNA.

******

The judicial process in Italy was held in contempt by Lombroso, he believed that juries and judges could be easily corrupted and compromised. The use of juries Lombroso claimed was an "institution that is atavistic in its ineffectiveness and corruptibility" at least as practiced in Italy (Gibson & Rafter, 2006, 187; Lombroso, 1911/2012, 248). Too often he alleged, the "ignorance of most jurors" or their willingness to "barter away justice" resulted in a large number of acquittals (Gibson & Rafter, 2006, 335, 336; Lombroso, 1911/2012, 353). Jurors also were too easily persuaded due to their lack of education, public opinion, or by the rhetorical skills of the defense attorney. In addition, Lombroso noticed an increase in the rights of defendants, which he believed was misplaced justice for the true criminal type. He believed that sequestering jurors and the adoption of public education like in England and the United States would promote informed jurors and improve the criminal justice system's accountability. Lombroso argued that in England and America the public believed and practiced the principle of public service and duty, which made their jury systems more effective, the same spirit of service was lacking in Italy (Lombroso, 1911/2102, 353, 354, 356; Gibson & Rafter, 2006, 337).

Wealth, Lombroso noted, played an important part in the determination of guilt or innocence, whether by a jury, judge or magistrate, "poor men — unless by accident or pardon — enjoy no real justice compared with the rich, who find ways of escaping or reducing their sentences" (Gibson & Rafter, 2006, 187). The unequal application of justice, Lombroso declared, had a detrimental effect on national morality:

> Corruption of juries becomes a great incentive to immorality among the poor. Lower-class defendants, seeing that justice is anything but equal for all, feel free to revenge themselves against the society that condemns them (Gibson & Rafter, 2006, 336).

Although Italian judges and law professors claimed the universality of "the laws of justice," Lombroso doubted that the practice of justice ever lived up to its high claim of fairness (Gibson & Rafter, 2006, 187; Lombroso, 1911/2012, 134, 36). The only true universal law in nature according to Lombroso was crime, not justice. The influence of wealth in the judicial process echoes through history to our present day. Lombroso predicted, based on history, that the perpetuation of social inequality put Italy at risk for revolution, which he hoped could be avoided with governmental reforms (Lombroso, 1911/2012, 229-231; Gibson & Rafter, 2006, 170-171).

Lombroso took exception to the use of royal pardons, which he called an "atavistic practice" that virtually circumvented the whole judicial processes and negated its effect. Expressing his mistrust of the judicial system, Lombroso exclaimed that, "the origins of justice often lay in the caprice of kings or priests or in popular anger" (Gibson & Rafter, 2006, 336). The frequent granting of pardons by the king of Italy was contrary to Lombroso's sense of fairness and the rule of law. This practice was especially disheartening to the poor, Lombroso argued, when the recipient of a pardon was usually a member of the wealthy upper class:

> How can we say that justice is equal for all, that it is destined to bring the disturbed juridical condition into equilibrium, and that it is based upon fixed, immutable laws, free from all personal influence, when all that is needed to blot out the whole thing is a simple stroke of the pen — the signature of a man who may be the

best man in the country, but is after all only a man? (Lombroso, 1911/2012, 358; Gibson & Rafter, 2006, 336).

Lombroso did not propose that the use of the power to pardon should be abolished, just used with more circumspect judgment. He was convinced that pardoned criminals, regardless of wealth or status, were the real winners and would simply recidivate, what we would call today a perpetual revolving door. The use of pardons, Lombroso warned, lead to a sense of impunity to judicial penalty (Lombroso, 1911/2012, 220).

******

Judges and magistrates, Lombroso asserted, should be subject to public election rather than appointment by the national legislature, which was the existing practice. He believed that legislative appointment in contrast to popular election deprived judges of,

> a power and independence so great as to allow them, upon compliant of a citizen whose rights are infringed, to pronounce null and void laws which do not conform to the constitution (Lombroso, 1911/2012, 327).

Lombroso admired the English and American legal systems and the practice of elections by what he assumed to be an educated public, but no system is perfect. Of course there were risks to public elections that Lombroso did not ignore since any elected official could be tempted to allow their independence to be purchased (Lombroso, 1911/2012, 220). More than revocation of royal pardons and court independence, Lombroso believed the whole Italian criminal justice system and even the government needed reform in order to assure judicial freedom and fairness.

A federal form of government based on the American constitutional model, Lombroso advocated, would empower the judiciary to protect the constitutional rights of the individual and guard the balance between federal and state government power. Lombroso quoted Spencer who said: "The future of society politically lies in decentralization," to Lombroso the concentration of power afforded great opportunities for abuse and corruption (Lombroso, 1911/2012, 326). The parliamentary form of government, Lombroso, argued was prone to corruption and "parliamentary immunity" protected its members. He believed that the rule of law was best served in allowing, cities to administer their own affairs freely, according to their importance, to elect their own officers, to have charge of the courts of first instance, secondary education, the police, the prisons, the means of communication [and in doing so] you will eliminate a great cause of injustice and abuses (Lombroso, 1911/2012, 326).

Lombroso firmly believed that decentralization of power would level the playing field between rich and poor in terms of both governance and procedural justice. While his concerns regarding the concentration of government power in the hands of the wealthy primarily focused on the travesty of political crimes, Lombroso's deeper concern was with the lack of judicial independence from Parliament. It was too easy in the existing system to perpetuate injustice.

Lombroso also believed that the introduction into the existing parliamentary and legal system of a mediator and social aid society advocates would be beneficial to protect the interests of the poor and the underclass at the parliamentary and judicial levels. Similar to the Roman tribunes, these advocates would serve as the voice of reason to call-out injustices in the law or its court application to members of Parliament. Lombroso's proposal was not for a peacemaking form and practice of alternative justice, rather, for a system of checks and balances on behalf of society. The Italian judicial system did not provide public defenders or guarantee legal representation. The employment of counsel was an individual matter, which of course greatly hampered the poor in obtaining the services of counsel (Lombroso, 1911/2012, 327, 328).

The "increasing tendency" of the courts to show deference to the defense Lombroso claimed threatened to overwhelm society with recidivists and new offenders. Lombroso lamented that the growing trend of disregard for justice gave "every opportunity of defense to the criminal . . . while nothing is done to increase the security of society and the certainty of the repression of crime" (Lombroso, 1911/2012, 361). The right of appeal was another problem, Lombroso upheld the right, but challenged the practice of basing judgments in the appellate court "upon matters of form" such as a misspelling of a word rather than on the facts of the case (Lombroso, 1911/2012, 328, 357, 358).

Lombroso did not demand or advocate for immediate change in the practice of justice, he recognized that change should be incremental. He often admonished that revolution was not a favorable course of action because too often it resulted in tyranny, and tyrants were often men of genius whose own ambition outweighed the interests of society (Lombroso, 1891/2015, 329, 334, 335). Lombroso also described another form of potential revolutionary conflict that reflected the racial divide between the Italian north and south. He believed that the more backward and darker skinned "race" of the south was susceptible to revolution due to disagreement with the enforcement of national law (Lombroso, 1911/2012, 325). Specifically, Lombroso made the case that brigandage was common in southern Italy and its depredations required special legislation and enforcement. One irony not lost on Lombroso was that while he supported regional or local semi-autonomy from the national seat of government, he also recognized the risk of usurpation of power by the regional political majority or a charismatic "genius." In the case of a large part of southern Italy, the balance of power was exercised by brigands, including the Mafia and Camorra (Lombroso, 1911/2012, 212, 221, 223; Gibson & Rafter, 2006, 354).

******

The right of society to punish criminal behavior, Lombroso explained was based on two principles: 1) natural necessity; and 2) the right of self-defense (Lombroso, 1911/2012, 379). Crime was a natural phenomenon that by its very existence required from society an appropriate response. Rather than focusing on retaliation for punishment and applying it with a broad stroke, Lombroso proposed that punishment should address the individual level of dangerousness to society. The complex nature of each offender, more than the type of offense, required a specialist to determine the level of dangerousness posed, that specialist to Lombroso was the criminal anthropologist:

> The purpose of punishment should not be the infliction of pain on the criminal, but the well-being of society and restitution to the victim. Punishment should be proportional less to the gravity of the crime than to the dangerousness [of] the criminal. . . . Crime is like an illness that requires a specific remedy for each patient. It is the job of criminal anthropology to establish the relationship between criminals and their punishment (Gibson & Rafter, 2006, 341).

The criminal anthropologist would serve the court proceedings as an expert witness. Lombroso described a system of differentiation that varied punishment with the type of offender, ranging from the born criminal to habitual criminals and all degrees of dangerousness between. Based on his research of criminal types and their crimes, Lombroso created a scale of applicable punishments (Lombroso, 1911/2012, 379, 381, 385).

The most serious and dangerous offender was the born criminal. Lombroso found no redeeming qualities in the born criminal who were prone to commit violent crimes due to their savage nature. The born criminal Lombroso argued was "refractory to all treatment," simply, there was no cure for this unique criminal type, but for the safety of the community, life imprisonment or capital punishment were the only viable means of social defense. They posed a danger not only to common society but even the prison population. Lombroso suggested that these individuals should be interned for life in special prisons or colonies reserved for incorrigibles maintained in isolated valleys, islands, or in agricultural colonies in the countryside employing forced labor (Lombroso, 1911/2012, 432; Gibson & Rafter, 2006, 145).

Lombroso proposed that the use of these more severe special prisons and the death penalty would "eliminate the eternal clients of the criminal justice system who pose a danger to society" (Gibson & Rafter, 2006, 231). He did not consider the immediate recourse to the death penalty necessary for the first offense; however, "repeat bloodthirsty crimes" committed for a third or fourth time left no other choice than to resort to capital punishment. Lombroso agreed with Ferri that to be effective, capital punishment had to be used enough to become "repugnant to modern society:" "It is enough that it should remain suspended, lie the sword of Damocles, over the head of the more terrible criminals" (Lombroso, 19111/1202, 427). Capital punishment was to be used as a last resort and hopefully would provide a level of deterrence. Lombroso also recommended that born criminals should be prohibited from sexual intercourse, he did elaborate on whether castration was the preferred method for men, neither did he suggest sterilization for the female born criminal (Gibson & Rafter, 2006, 197).

> In defense of the death penalty against concerns raised by critics, Lombroso responded: To claim that the death sentence contradicts the laws of nature is to feign ignorance of the fact that progress in the animal world, and therefore the human world, is based on a struggle for existence that involves hideous massacres. Born criminals, programmed to do harm, are atavistic reproductions of not only savage men but also the most ferocious carnivores and rodents. This discovery should not make us more compassionate toward born criminals (as some claim), but rather should shield us from pity, for these beings are members of not our species but the species of bloodthirsty beasts. . . . Sadly, born criminals are impervious to every social cure and must be eliminated for our own defense, sometimes by the death penalty (Gibson & Rafter, 2006, 348, 354).

Lombroso did make one exception for the immediacy of the death penalty — he believed it was especially necessary in the part of Italy under the influence of brigandage, the Mafia and Camorra (Lombroso, 1911/2012, 424, 426-427, 432-433; Gibson & Rafter, 2006, 145, 348, 354). Imprisonment for life was an option Lombroso argued for all career or incorrigible criminals regardless of "whether biologically abnormal or not" (Gibson & Rafter, 2006, 146). Recidivism was a problem that Lombroso often addressed in his writings. Recidivists he noted were a harmful threat to "themselves and their offspring" and therefore required incarceration (Gibson & Rafter, 2006, 146). Lombroso did not believe life imprisonment for recidivists was any more unjust than internment of the insane in mental hospitals. But Italy had not yet, he determined, provided for either class of criminal on the scale required. The judicial fate for the congenital criminal was life imprisonment or death by hanging.

******

Very early in his studies of criminals Lombroso came to the conclusion that born criminals and to a varying degree, many other criminal types suffered mental illness and usually also suffered from epilepsy. For the criminally insane and epileptic criminal, Lombroso believed that the best solution to provide for the safety of the community and the individual himself was placement in an asylum. Prison was too harsh and unjust a punishment he believed, he argued society had relegated these unfortunates to languish in prisons where they were at great personal risk:

> Only criminal insane asylums can provide an alternative to prison for those unhappy beings whose crimes have arisen our morbid psychological impulses rather than inner perversity. For judges, criminal insane asylums provide an answer to the eternal conflict between justice for the insane and defense of society (Gibson & Rafter, 2006, 343).

Lombroso was not in his words, "advocating a sentimental pity that might threaten the well-being of others. Criminal insane asylums are more a precautionary than humanitarian measure" (Lombroso, 1991/2012, 148). He firmly believed that dangerous mentally ill criminal types should be housed in asylums and only released when they had been "cured." From his own experience, Lombroso did not hold great hope for recovery from insanity. Lombroso asserted that all categories of insanity suffered at some level from a degenerative mental pathology (Gibson & Rafter, 2006, 247; Lombroso, 1911/2012, 369-370; Lombroso-Ferrero, 1911/2015, 112).

To the insane criminal type, Lombroso added the subcategories of alcoholic, hysterical, and mattoid criminals. Like epilepsy these designations were really ancillary conditions to the basic mentally ill individual. Lombroso recognized alcoholism as a disease and a contributor to neuropathology, but he also noted that the condition or desire for alcohol could be inherited. The sufferer of hysteria, and the mattoid who was given to delusions, had an inherent pathology that could pass from generation to generation as well. Although Lombroso did not explicitly describe the form of punishment for these individuals, it is reasonable to assume that since they were at one stage or another of mental illness, a mental hospital or asylum would be appropriate for them. There was no real cure for these individuals known to Lombroso, but aside from the neurotic mattoid, none were seriously dangerous (Gibson & Rafter, 2006, 277-287).

Lombroso explained that moral insanity was a condition common to most if not all criminal types. The condition as defined by Lombroso was the literal absence of a moral conscience or sense due to a lack of moral values being taught at home or in the schools. The born criminal was inherently immoral since all he knew was the struggle for survival and the savage state of mind. The insane were in a similar arrested state and incapable of learning moral values. All other criminal types in Lombroso's classification scheme had a diminished capacity for morality. Lombroso considered moral insanity as both a cause and effect of criminal behavior. He never ascribed to the argument that morally grounded individuals could choose to commit a crime, choice was never an option for Lombroso, rather, there was always some physical and psychical or environmental cause for crime.

Punishment by Criminal Type

The criminaloid and occasional criminal acted as good citizens for the most part until external circumstances drove them to commit a crime. They were less degenerate and showed little or no stigmata compared to the born criminal. In his classification of criminal types, Lombroso considered the criminaloid to be a subtype of the occasional criminal. The only real difference between the two was the fact that criminaloids, Lombroso explained, were predisposed to crime and only needed a motive or opportunity. Compared to the criminaloid, the occasional criminal was the least degenerate and represented what Lombroso called a "pseudocriminal," one who generally committed crimes involuntarily. The occasional criminal was a literal victim of his environment driven to crime by circumstances outside his control. Lombroso described the occasional criminal's crimes as typically minor, or misdemeanors in our terminology today (Gibson & Rafter, 2006, 289, 291-294; Lombroso, 1911/2012, 373, 374).

Lombroso recommended that occasional offenders should only be fined or required to pay restitution: "A prison sentence serves no purpose for occasional criminals who commit minor offenses and are not essentially dangerous" (Gibson & Rafter, 2006, 346). Women who committed prostitution, abortion and infanticide, Lombroso also labeled as occasional criminals, but his preference was for their actions to be de-criminalized. But under the existing laws, he recommended for their infractions probation or judicial warnings, cutting of hair and confiscation of their finery, and even committal to a nunnery as options. Lombroso did not consider them a serious threat to society or hardened recidivists. For the criminaloid, Lombroso believed that the appropriate punishment for a first offense committed alone should be a suspended sentence, accompanied by bail, a judicial warning, and restitution for damages. Lombroso also noted that if the defendant could not pay restitution, he should be required to provide forced labor. Prison should only be used, Lombroso continued, if the criminaloid refused to work. The occasional offender and criminaloid were generally non-repeat offenders, thus their sentences were more compatible, Lombroso believed, with their level of dangerousness (Lombroso, 1911/2012, 376; Gibson & Rafter, 2006, 344, 347, 418).

Another pseudocriminal type described by Lombroso was the latent criminal. Latent criminals suffered a neuropathic disorder that allowed them to disguise their "depraved instincts" with wealth or position. The only real difference with the mattoid was the latent criminal's ability to mask their criminal tendencies. Lombroso does not ascribe a specific penalty for the latent criminal, but perhaps we can assume that their neuropsychological disorder and a recommendation by the criminal anthropologists would result in their transfer to a mental institution. A singular, non-atavistic type of criminal was responsible for crimes of passion in Lombroso's classification scheme. Lombroso essentially defined "passion" as impulsive behavior typically triggered by matters of love or defense of honor. Lombroso's punitive recommendations for the passionate criminal included fines, judicial admonition, or exile separating the offender from the victim (Lombroso, 1911/2012, 376, 412; Gibson & Rafter, 2006, 105-107, 313, 314, 346).

Politicians and other professionals, including doctors, lawyers, and priests among others, who committed crimes could also be found in the criminaloid, latent, passion, or mattoid subcategories of the occasional criminal. Lombroso made the case that the nature of their crime and their criminal type should dictate their form of punishment, but it should not be harsh. However, Lombroso makes an interesting observation that political criminals often make contributions to society, which should mitigate their sentence: "If there is any crime that merits neither the death penalty nor even serious punishment, it is political crime" (Gibson & Rafter, 2006, 346). He concluded that "many" political criminals were insane and the mental hospital was more appropriate than "the prison or scaffold" (Gibson & Rafter, 2006, 346). Criminals who were repeat offenders Lombroso labeled habitual criminals who needed to be sentenced in a similar progressive fashion as the criminaloid. However, a pattern of recidivism would warrant a prison sentence for the habitual criminal (Lombroso, 1911/2012, 412, 419-420; Gibson & Rafter, 2006, 346).

******

Without categorizing to type or subtype, Lombroso outlined several additional infractions that he considered either civil or misdemeanor offenses. Defamation of character was punishable under the Italian penal code, but Lombroso argued that the matter of truth should judge the act. It should be enough Lombroso said for the defendant to furnish proof of fact, but if his accusations were false, than a retraction should be sufficient to close the case. On the matter of adultery, Lombroso agreed that it was immoral, but should only be subject to church canon law and not civil law. In contrast to ecclesiastical authority over divorce, Lombroso believed that the provision for civil divorce laws would reduce or even prevent adultery (Gibson & Rafter, 2006, 332, 333; Lombroso, 1911/2012, 418). In the case of assisted suicide, Lombroso dismissed penalties for aiding a suicide, quoting Ferri, Lombroso concluded, "who does not see that the real and voluntary consent of the victim removes every excuse for interference on the part of the state?" (Lombroso, 1911/2012, 415).

In cases of complicity to crimes by adults, Lombroso recommended that instead of considering the accomplice's participation or role in the crime, the criminal justice system should consider the individual as belonging to the "most dangerous classes" and punished accordingly with imprisonment (Lombroso, 1911/2012, 419). For the crime of homosexuality or what Lombroso also called sexual inversion, he described two case types: 1) in the first case the practitioner of homosexual behavior exhibited in college or the barracks may reform by personal choice of celibacy when proximity to members of the same sex is removed; and 2) in the second case of individuals who "are born such" should be confined because they, "are a source of contagion and cause a great number of occasional criminals" (Lombroso, 1911/2012, 418; Gibson & Rafter,

2006, 273, 274). Lombroso encouraged young men to marry in order to reduce in his belief the number of rapes. Even the marriage of the clergy was proposed by Lombroso in order to reduce the number of sexual crimes, particularly pedophilia (Lombroso, 1911/2012, 246; Gibson & Rafter, 2006, 332).

For the crime of dueling, Lombroso argued was a moral question and morality should not be legislated. He believed that both parties to a duel were really victims of circumstance generally involving honor and unless one of the duelists was a known criminal, there should be no punishment (Lombroso, 1911/2012, 416). For minor offenses including thefts of small value, "a simple reparation to the person injured, with a reprimand or a conditional sentence, would suffice" (Lombroso, 1911/2014, 418, 419; Gibson & Rafter, 2006, 273-274). For lesser offenses in general Lombroso favored the use of probation versus prison sentences. Prison and life terms to Lombroso should be reserved for the incorrigibles, the death penalty should be reserved for only the most dangerous criminals. He also suggested for minor offenses the use home detention, forced labor without imprisonment, corporal punishment, fines, judicial reprimand, and security (bond) for good behavior (Lombroso, 1911/2012, 388-390; Lombroso-Ferrero, 1911/2015, 114).

The Prison Experience

In addition to the individualization of punishment, Lombroso had high praise for the prison graded system practiced in Ireland. The Irish system was modeled after Alexander Maconochie's proposed marks system for convicts on the Island of Tasmania off the coast of Australia in the mid-1830s. The British penal colony on Tasmanis focused on strict corporal punishment, which Maconochie proposed was ineffective and resulted in a high rate of recidivism. The Irish penal system was developed in the 1850s by Sir Walter Crofton based on Maconochie's proposal with a special focus on the reform measures of training and performance; training for gainful employment and performance of good behavior.

At the core of the system was a three-phase program starting with a period of solitary confinement, usually nine then eight months. This was followed by confinement in a single cell and a period of congregate work, which allowed the prisoner to advance in levels of privilege based on "marks" earned for good behavior and industry and actually receive some financial compensation for his work. The final period of confinement was served in an open cell under minimal supervision, where the prisoner had to demonstrate dependability and employability. Release to a "half-way" house following internment was conditional based on good behavior and employment. Following release from the "half-way" house, the prisoner was checked on periodically by an "inspector," which is today's equivalent to a probation officer. Upon proof of residence and continued employment with a good conduct record the prisoner was then "paroled." The common prison design in Italy at the time was the congregate model, where prisoners were housed in common with a large yard and mess hall.

Lombroso described with approval the Irish system in the second edition (1878) of *Criminal Man*. He noted in particular the reduction of recidivism and rates of crime in Ireland and gave credit to the mark system employed. To his psychologist's pragmatic mind, Lombroso recognized a win-win situation for the prisoner as well as society and its defense:

> The Irish system favors the application of criminal psychology by permitting gradual movement toward complete liberty and turning the prisoner's perpetual dream into an instrument of discipline and correction. Moreover, it offers a way to overcome public resistance to the early release of prisoners. (Gibson & Rafter, 2006, 144).

Because congregate prisons were "schools for crime," Lombroso promoted the use of the cellular prison in order to isolate prisoners. In 1892 the Italian Minister of Interior presented Lombroso with a model of the Eastern State Penitentiary in Philadelphia, which featured the panopticon whose design resembled the giant hub and spoke system of a wheel, with the main hub featuring management and surveillance. The radial spokes from the hub housed the prisoners in individual cells.

Museo di Antropologia Criminale "Cesare Lombroso," University of Turin, Italy

The panopticon Cesare Museum model of the Eastern State Penitentiary in Philadelphia.

The purpose of the design was to isolate prisoners, a decided move away from the Maconochie model prison. The design was the origin of the modern penitentiary. The panopticon prison design originated with the English philosopher and social theorist Jeremy Bentham in the late 18th century (Gibson & Rafter, 2006, 141; Lombroso, 1911/2012, 222, 331; Bianucci and et al, 2011, 55; Beirne & Messerschmidt, 2000, 69-72).

The prison Lombroso envisioned would "forget about improving literacy," which would only enhance prison communication, rather, "we must institute gymnastics and other obligatory labor to develop the physical and mental energy that is nearly always lacking in criminals" (Gibson & Rafter, 2006, 142). Even more important than "molding prisoners' minds" and training in useful trades, was the need to develop "their feelings:" All people, especially the unhappy, need to have an interest and purpose in life" (Gibson & Rafter, 2006, 142). To this Lombroso would add an appreciation for "design and color" in order to develop a "sensitivity to beauty that is in turn linked to an understanding of what is good" (Gibson & Rafter, 2006, 142).

******

Lombroso was consistent in his references to "beauty," which was a reflection on his joy of growing up in northern Italy with the backdrop of mountains, plentiful sunshine, and the beauty of the natural world around him. In the world of nature he had found solitude and purposeful meaning to spur his reading and writing. He sought in his prison and asylum reform proposals and actions to promote in the inmates a renewed respect for the natural world around them. Lombroso the psychologist considered that the role of prison for non-incorrigibles was to provide a training school for a life free of crime. According to Gina Lombroso-Ferrero (1911/2015), her father's goal for criminal anthropology was to "redeem" as many criminals as possible and justify their existence, "in the eyes of mankind and in the scheme of nature" for the purpose of "social safety" (116, 118; Lombroso, 1911/2012, 302).

Lombroso concluded his formula for rehabilitation with the belief that: "Work must be the purpose and pastime of every prison. It will awaken inmates' drowsy energies and prepare them for productive labor after release. Work is also an instrument of . . . discipline" (Gibson & Rafter, 2006, 143). For those prisoners who showed promise, Lombroso favored a reduction of sentence and earlier release. He opposed the use of contractors being allowed to use prison labor because they ignored "moral improvement" (Gibson & Rafter, 2006, 144). Lombroso's model prison featured the moral and physical development of the individual over the excessive use of punishment and forced and meaningless labor. He recommended that all prison assignment to labor should be tailored to the "strength and abilities of the prisoner" (Gibson & Rafter, 2006, 144). Lombroso was optimistic that for the non-incorrigibles: "We can cure and educate criminals by action rather than words and be encouraging good behavior rather than spouting theories" (Gibson & Rafter, 2006, 143). Of course the incorrigibles including gang and organized crime members could not be "cured" and should be kept in solitary, confined to avoid their contamination of other prisoners.

Social Defense

Social defense was much more than adjudicating adults, Lombroso understood that the roots of crime aside from the born criminal ran much deeper in the social fabric. The rapid growth of Italian cities put enormous strain on social institutions including families. Poverty was on the rise along with crime rates leading to homeless and neglected children and young adults. Lombroso reported in 1878 that Italy had 3,770 reformatories for youths. While Lombroso admitted that there were a handful of well-managed reformatories, but as a system the Italian reformatories failed miserably. The institutions in general were overcrowded and organized on the congregate prison system with no individual cells (rooms) for sleeping, educational opportunities were minimal, the teaching of work skills was inadequate, and there was no separation by age or criminal history (Gibson & Rafter, 2006, 137, 139).

*****

The same condemnation Lombroso made regarding adult prisons also applied to the reformatories, they were schools for criminality: "Anything that increases reciprocal contact increases criminality" (Gibson & Rafter, 2006, 137). The environment of these institutions favored insolence and gang development. Although establishment intentions were benevolent, Lombroso believed that most reform schools caused more damage than good. The primary problem stemmed from overcrowding which increased contact, overwhelmed teachers, and decreased supervision, but more than that, the boys become mere numbers in a bureaucratic system resulting in the "material impossibility of reform" (Gibson & Rafter, 2006, 137, 138). A further problem centered on Italian civil law that allowed parents to send an unruly child to the reformatory without even sharing in the cost of provision for the child. Lombroso recommended changing the law to at the very least force well-to-do parents to pay a "hefty daily fee proportional to their income" (Gibson & Rafter, 2006, 139; Lombroso, 1911/2012, 320).

A good part of the problem involved mixing older boys who were past the age of being "corrected and molded" with juveniles of younger age. The older youths, he argued, are, "naturally drawn to evil because of the violence of their passions, their minimal education, and their lack of judgment" (Gibson & Rafter, 2006, 137). It was not a healthy environment to have them in the proximity of more impressionable minors who naturally looked up to their older peers:

> The idea that reformatories protect the young from bad influenc-
> es is an illusion. While they do impede contact with vagabonds
> and slightly depraved companions on the outside, they house a
> far worse crowd that has already entered the web of the criminal
> justice system. Thus the young are subjected to an atmosphere of
> concentrated vice at an age when they are particularly susceptible
> to crime (Gibson & Rafter, 2006, 138).

An additional concern involved bringing minors to the urban reformatories from the countryside where contact with delinquent youths was minimal. Their exposure to hardened youths will provide, "all they need in the way of bad influence" and will expose them, "to a learning process that would otherwise never have taken place" (Gibson & Rafter, 2006, 138). Lombroso suggested that it actually might be better to place young offenders with rural families, "who could isolate them from big city corruption" (Gibson & Rafter, 2006, 139).

Resolution of the reformatory problem was complex, Lombroso realized, and required a firm commitment from society to change the existing institutional order, "state welfare, needs new forms," he admonished (Gibson & Rafter, 2006, 139). What was needed he suggested were "industrial schools" or "agricultural schools" where young men could learn a trade and taught "respect of property, the love of work, and the sense of beauty" (Gibson & Rafter, 2006, 139; Lombroso, 1911/2012, 302, 307, 309). In short, he exhorted that he, "would permit reform schools . . . only in exceptional cases and for a small number of individuals [not to exceed 100], these to be classified according to age, aptitude, and morality" (Lombroso, 1911/2012, 313; Gibson & Rafter, 2006, 137).

Lombroso also proposed the use of criminal anthropology to identify youths that for example had asymmetrical and small heads, and other physical stigmata indicating a potential born criminal. These youths, he recommended, upon arrival at the reformatory should be separated from other "normal" children and, "directed toward careers [trade crafts and general labor] more suited to their temperament" (Lombroso, 1911/2012, 439). These youths should, he proposed, be indoctrinated with moral values and given medical treatment, and perhaps even be encouraged to emigrate, which sounds remarkably close to today's term, displacement. Without much enthusiasm, he stated that a cure might even be found for them (Lombroso, 1911/2012, 438-439).

*****

The model that Lombroso had in mind was the Elmira Reformatory for 16-30-year-old males in New York State. Technically named the Eastern New York Reformatory, the institution was founded the same year that Lombroso published his first edition of *Criminal Man* in May 1876. The reformatory was founded and under the management of Superintendent Zebulon. The two men evidently corresponded because Lombroso notes that Brockway credited him as his source of inspiration and Lombroso received at least one annual report. Brockway's "Elmira System" involved the principles that Lombroso advocated, including a classification system based on criminal record and moral aptitude, separation by age, and rewards for good behavior. Inmates also received pre-classification psychological screenings and physical exams.

At the core of the program youths were taught a trade, attended classroom instruction, wore a uniform and participated in military drills, and had a daily exercise regimen. The program also instituted a parole system based on merit. Discipline also included corporal punishment, which in later years with reported abuses combined with a growing rate of recidivism forced the resignation of Brockway in 1900. On paper and early execution it was a model system much admired by Lombroso. However, it proved to be a penal-science and bioscience experiment gone awry (Pisciotta, 1994; Lombroso, 1911/2012, 394-396; Gibson & Rafter, 2006, 342-343, 346; Lombroso-Ferrero, 1911/2015, 106-107; Lombroso-Ferrero, [ca. 1914]. Unpublished manuscript. Chap. XII, 14).

One preventive measure for juvenile delinquency promoted by Lombroso was the Ragged School concept first adopted in the 1820s in England. Similar Children Aid Societies also were developed in America. Because of the growing number of disconnected youths from families and educational opportunities, in a society that lacked social services Lombroso advocated for Italian society to adopt the Ragged School program of intervention. The schools provided housing, basic care including clothing and food, and education. He also supported the idea of Day Reformatories for Children between the ages of 6-12 for parents who could not care for their children during work hours. Children would be fed and given a preliminary education. The concept is the forerunner of day care centers in America today. Lombroso also recommended adoption for orphans to help remove them from the danger of the street. Basically, Lombroso wanted children to be cared for by the state or philanthropic organizations in order to keep them off the streets and away from criminal influences (Lombroso, 1911/2012, 315, 318, 319-320).

Of all the institutions for juveniles, perhaps the one closest to Lombroso's heart and mind was the orphanage founded and managed by the priest Don Bosco (1818-1888) at the Roman Catholic Basilica of Our Lady Help of Christians in Torino, only a few miles from Lombroso's home. Bosco established at the church an educational mission and home for orphaned boys in the city. His orphanage was more a refuge than reform school. Children were provided shelter, food, and clothing, all the basic necessities. Bosco forgo punishment for religious instruction, the teaching of moral values and the power of reason, and the understanding that they were loved. The students were also exposed to music, games, and morally sound plays. Reason, religion, and kindness were the cornerstones of his "Preventive Education System" (Lombroso, 1911/2012, 314 315). Bosco's vision is today a worldwide missionary effort.

All the efforts to save lost children were not lost on the Lombroso family. At the urging of daughters Paola and Gina, Lombroso in 1896 established a School and Family day center in Torino for children after school. The regimen of education and provision of food and clothing, along with music and games was similar to Bosco's program. Within a year there were four centers in the city under the management of Gina and Paola until the city agreed to take over the endeavor (Lombroso-Ferrero [ca. 1914]. Unpublished manuscript. Chap. XVII, 5).

There were several very basic elements that Lombroso emphasized in all his reform recommendations for both adult prisons and youth facilities. Chief among these elements or values for instruction were morality, employment skills, respect for people and property, and educational attainment. As a pragmatist, Lombroso was not overly optimistic about reform achievements, but he held firmly to the ideal that change was possible. The goal of incarceration at least for incorrigibles was to reduce recidivism. The role of reformatories and other programs of refuge were to both train for an adult life free of crime and thus prevent further increases in levels of national crime. Prisons, Reformatories, Ragged Schools, and other youth oriented facilities for training life skills all served a preventive purpose in the larger scheme of criminal justice.

While youth facilities were largely proactive efforts at prevention, prisons provided society immediate reactive relief and also served the questionable role of preventive deterrence.

Modern Policing

Before adjudication and institutionalization, and the preventive steps taken to protect juveniles from criminal influences stood the imperative role of policing or law enforcement to protect society. Again, Lombroso applied his pragmatic mind to the larger problem of crime prevention in the urban environment. Lombroso understood that a social defense against crime required the use of new technologies in policing, urban design and planning, and social legislation. In the fifth edition (1896-1897) of *Criminal Man* and *Crime: Its Causes and Remedies* (1911) Lombroso described many crime prevention ideas. Several measures he proposed were forerunners of the Crime Prevention Through Environmental Design (CPTED) concept developed in the United States in the 1980s, for example, he proposed wide avenues and adequate street lighting. He believed that these measures would prevent robberies, thefts, and rape better than police (Gibson & Rafter, 2006, 331).

Some of Lombroso's proposals to prevent or reduce crime within a social context reflected his interest in socialism during the 1890s. Legislation Lombroso suggested should limit the hours of work for children and better regulate prostitution. Such measures would protect children from exploitation and reduce assaults, thefts, and other crimes in addition to better control of venereal diseases often associated with prostitution. Several social-economic measures he believed would reduce crime and labor strikes, including: "Reasonably priced housing for workers, workman's compensation, and civil responsibility on the part of business owners" (Gibson & Rafter, 2006, 331). Regarding the political order, Lombroso observed that a "truly liberal government discourages insurrections and anarchist violence, just as freedom of the press impedes political corruption and civil rebellion" (Gibson & Rafter, 2006, 331).

******

Police were at the core of Lombroso's social defense for the prevention of crime. He had a firm belief in the efficacy of utilizing science and technology in law enforcement. Alternately, Lombroso called his vision for efficient policing the Modern Police System or Scientific Policing. His suggestions were not original in most cases, but he was an advocate for their use in Italian policing. Bertillon's development in Paris of combining a criminal's side and front facial photographs with anthropometry biometric measurements added on a single card, and later the creation of composite photographs to help identify recidivist criminals was a top priority for Lombroso. He had met Bertillon at the first international criminal anthropology conference held in Paris in 1888. Lombroso used a number of Bertillon supplied photo cards and composite photographs in his publications. He recognized the value in being able for witnesses and officers to identify a recidivist criminal for arrest or for booking. Lombroso also recommended with the same enthusiasm the adoption of Galton's fingerprint technology (Gibson & Rafter, 2006, 331; Lombroso, 1911/2012, 250; Lombroso-Ferrero [ca. 1914]. Unpublished manuscript, Chap. XIII, 11). In the use of photographs and fingerprinting, Lombroso saw the value of identification with "scientific accuracy."

In addition to promoting the use of photography, Lombroso also encouraged law enforcement to utilize the telephone, telegraph, and railroads in the apprehension of criminals and sharing information across jurisdictions. Lombroso recommended the utilization of signal boxes, used in America, so that officers would not have to leave their beat. Also from American policing, Lombroso advocated for the use of detectives to investigate crimes, and for businesses to install the recently invented electric burglar alarm. Although he did not invent the plethysmograph (kymograph), which was an early but dissimilar form of the polygraph, Lombroso recommended its use to determine guilt or innocence. The device supposedly made its determinations based on the flow of blood to the brain, whereas the modern polygraph bio-electrically measures stress to questions of guilt or innocence (Lombroso, 1911/2012, 250-252, 254).

Another crime fighting tool Lombroso recognized was the press. In the press, he saw the advantage of mass circulation and recognition. The publication of a criminal's photograph and information could be a real benefit to police apprehension. Although Lombroso did not suggest that police should carry a card with the physical characteristics of the born criminal listed for identification, he did encourage the public's awareness of the characteristics, including teachers. Lombroso did recommend that officers have ready access to composite photographs of recidivists for quick identification. He was in essence promoting an early form of profiling, and encouraging early detection of criminals as social misfits. Lombroso's embrace of social engineering would identify and remove from society the menace of the born, insane and habitual criminals. In the 1930s Germany would take the program one step further from incarceration to extermination (Lombroso, 1911/2012, 253-254).

******

Lombroso's police proposals had an international scope to them, which revealed his comprehensive thinking on the subject of crime suppression and public safety. He encouraged greater cooperation among nations to identify and arrest criminals. To accomplish this goal, he advocated for international extradition treaties and the development of an international register. His support for an international register was only a decade away from the creation of INTERPOL. Lombroso believed that all nations would benefit from the creation of a centralized criminal register. He also recommended that a country deporting a criminal should provide a warning to the country of return, and notice to neighboring countries when a criminal absconded from a member of the international treaty. The sharing of identifying information about criminals was an important element for modernizing crime control in Italy and all of Europe (Lombroso, 1911/2012, 251). Lombroso would live to see some of his judicial and penal reforms instituted by a Socialist Parliament prior to his death.

CHAPTER 9
Decline

> *"Oh, dear, I am tired of life, tired to fight,*
> *fed up and disgusted with man."*
> —Cesare Lombroso

riminal Man, in its five editions, was Cesare Lombroso's magnum opus. While he continued to work on various projects — as well as defend his research in the pellagra fight — Lombroso's career began a decline after 1880. He suffered personal and professional defeats, and the depression that haunted him as a young college student resurfaced. Shortly before his death, Lombroso embarked on the study of a phenomena that would cast a pall over his earlier work.

While working on the first edition of *Criminal Man*, Lombroso was comfortably seated in academe at the University of Pavia. He was happy there, but he did not have full professor status, despite his work. At the University of Torino, where many of Lombroso's colleagues taught, including Moleshott, a full-professorship opened.

They informed Lombroso that the position could be his, but that *Criminal Man* was not sufficient enough work to secure it for him. One can interpret that as not scholarly enough, or perhaps not within the rails of mainstream academia. A Dr. Magirani wrote Lombroso suggesting that he could secure the position if only he would do a little extra work. "My colleagues will refuse once more to elect you if you do not prepare some work of legal medicine on the

corpse, it is on that point that they fired you [from his earlier stint at Torino],"
Magirani, who supported Lombroso for the position, added that his own and
Lombroso's "honor" were at stake (Lombroso-Ferrero, Chap. X, 5.).

Such was a knife in Lombroso's academic heart. He had devoted his career
to criminal anthropology, had endeavored to validate the field, and had published in it. Now the offer from Torino carried with it the not-so-veiled contempt of ensconced academia.

Lombroso bristled at the demand. His daughter, Gina, said, "he was not very
willing to do it. . . . If Torino [did] not want him, he [would] stay in Pavia"
(Lombroso-Ferrero, Chap. X, 5).

Lombroso at first felt like declining the offer. He and his family liked Pavia,
much as he had in his youth (Lombroso-Ferrero, Chap. X, 5). Still, a college
professor — then or now — aspires to full professorship. It is a stamp of approval, a culminating point. And Lombroso wanted it.

Throughout early 1876, while he finished edition one of *Criminal Man*, defended his work on pellagra, and talked with new aspirants to the field of criminal anthropology, Lombroso vacillated on the Turin post. Then he relented.

In late spring and early summer, as daughter Gina recalled, Lombroso
"work[ed], measure[ed], [and] look[ed] through the microscope." Then, "with
a few monograph[s] on the 'legal medicine of the corpse," Lombroso won the
full professorship. He began his tenure at Torino on September 2, 1876 (Gina
Lombroso-Ferrero, Chap. X, 6).

Moving from Pavia to Turin, however, was traumatic. The family was used to
a large apartment in Pavia, plus Lombroso had laboratory space for his collections. In Turin, he had to take a much smaller apartment, which he promised
his family was "sunny and near the university." Gina noted that both were true,
as it was close to the college and faced fully south. As for space, there was none.
Lombroso brought his two daughters, Gina and Paola, sons Arnaldo and Leo,
and wife Nina, who was pregnant with another son. They lived among luggage,
boxes — and a few skeletons for which Lombroso had no room. "What a bad
year!" Gina later remembered (Lombroso-Ferrero, Chap. X, 9).

Lombroso discovered the situation in Turin was worse than a cramped living space. The University refused to let him teach a free course in psychiatry,
which had become one of his passions, and the asylum in Turin banned him
from practicing medicine there, even as a volunteer physician. He was dis-

heartened (Lombroso-Ferrero, Chap. X, 8). Lombroso must have thought that his uncle, Giacomino Levi, was correct when he had warned him not to take the Torino post. "I do not know why you absolutely want to come to Torino," he said (Lombroso-Ferrero, Chap. X, 8).

Gina always suspected that the professionals in Torino were jealous of the notoriety that *Criminal Man* was beginning to bring Lombroso. Leone Metchnikoff, an editor at *Dielo* magazine, had recently written "I think that the work of Lombroso will remain in the story of the evolution of our time and civilization. The social consequences of Lombroso's theory will be enormous" (Lombroso-Ferrero, Chap. X, 4).

With a hostile faculty and hidebound administration, why would Lombroso want to go to Turin? For the full-professorship, certainly, but there was more. In an inaugural lecture, Lombroso explained to a class of students exactly why he came. His old Italian patriotism was central to his reason:

> I did it because this town gave to all us new Italians the first hope when still adolescent, and to us a youth it gave us the hospitality and the pleasures of feeling free for the first time, and triumphant a little later. And now in this town the first to lose all traces of that great plague of Italy — regionalism (Lombroso-Ferrero, Chap. X, 7).

Lombroso's move harkened back to the heady days of revolution, independence, and unification. Those thoughts and feelings would never be far from him. They gave him purpose, and drove his greatest of researches. His quest for the discovery of the cause of pellagra was for all humankind, to be sure, but also for the betterment of Italy. So was his work into the causes of criminal activity. With his studies, new Italy could be first among European nations to pinpoint and begin to "cure" the plague of crime. If Lombroso's lifework could validate Italy, then so too could Torino, the seat of Piedmont-led unification, validate Lombroso.

Gina was never convinced. She saw the move to Turin further wear down her father, who was already tired from his work and academic fights. Her father found himself "without a laboratory, without clinics, without patients, without access to prisons, to asylums, with no possibility to see insanes [sic] or criminals," she wrote (Lombroso-Ferrero, Chap. X, 8).

To Gina, moving to Turin was like a "terrible exile, in a prison." And she would always dispute her father's romanticized image of Turin. "Unhappily, the fact will show . . . that the plague of regionalism is worse in the new [Turin] than in the old. In the cradle of Italian freedom, it was not enough to have fought for its independence and to have brought glory and honors to have the right of full citizenship" (Lombroso-Ferrero, Chap. X, 7).

In Turin, Gina discovered what would be one of the prime missions of her life — to support to her father. Even at the age of 4, in 1876, she understood that she had a unique ability to prop up her father when he dipped into periods of depression. "I became the preferred one," she wrote. "I began to love father with the affection I had, concentrating in him all my filial and motherly affection" (Lombroso-Ferrero, Chap. X, 9).

She continued, "I understood that my mission was to laugh, to fill the house with joy even when daddy was most desperate. To jump at him and kiss him so much until he would smile. To make him speak about this work, his struggles, his hopes . . . ." (Lombroso-Ferrero, Chap. X, 9). In the midst of a university town full of academics, Professor Cesare Lombroso discussed with his little children "pellagra, criminal[s], geniuses, insanes [sic]." Gina said that what she and her siblings did "not understand with our heads, we understood with our heart[s]" (Lombroso-Ferrero, Chap. X, 9).

Both Lombroso daughters, Gina and, to a lesser extent, Paola, hewed close to their father. Gina, as already noted, became a medical doctor and writer. She ably interpreted her father's sometimes rambling prose, and she wrote the unpublished biographical manuscript that forms the backbone of this biography. Having realized her "mission" at age 4, Gina never left it.

****

Lombroso made it through his trying first year as a full professor in Turin; then things began to change for him. The second edition of *Criminal Man* began to bring him wider notoriety. "From this moment on, the name of Lombroso started being known as the exclusive scientific field out in the whole world," Gina said. "The Criminal Man entered in novels, in works of art, in newspapers" (Lombroso-Ferrero, Chap. XI, 2). Gina did not mention which novels included her father's work, but the trend certainly continued. Joseph Conrad, in his 1907 novel *The Secret Agent*, had characters involved in an anarchist bomb plot discuss briefly Lombroso and his criminal types. One of them, in great disagreement with the classification of degenerates, suddenly spits out that, "Lombroso is an ass!" (Conrad, *Secret Agent*, Chap. III, paragraph 26). Leo Tolstoy, who had met the aging Lombroso, uses the scientist's findings in *Resurrection*; Bram Stoker, in *Dracula*, says Lombroso would target the dread Count as a criminal because of his appearance. In the narrative, vampire hunt-er Van Helsing asks Mina Harker, whom the Count has bitten, to describe him. "The Count is a criminal and of the criminal type," she says. "Nordau and Lombroso would so classify him" (Starr, *Dracula*).

The German scientific community praised the book, and German Chancellor Otto von Bismarck (who himself had led the unification of the new German state in the 1860s) sent Lombroso his compliments. Professor Vorwort von Kirchenheim hoped that Germany would adopt the penal reforms that Lombroso suggested, and which Italy would oppose (Lombroso-Ferrero, Chap. XI, 7).

Gina said *Criminal Man* made her father a "celebrity." People from as diverse places as South America, India, and Japan came to Turin to see the scientist. She noted that the visitors must have been "astonished" when they arrived, "dressed perfectly," to find the renowned Lombroso working out of a too-small lab and living in an apartment with worn furniture that he had brought from Pavia (Lombroso-Ferrero, Chap. XI, 7).

Lombroso enjoyed the many young psychiatrists and budding anthropologists who flocked to him; enjoyed stirring their enthusiasm and shepherding them in the new academic field. Among them were Ferri and Garofalo, with whom he inaugurated a new academic journal, the *Archivio di Psichiatria, Antropologia Criminale Scienze Penali.* Lombroso enjoyed serving as procurements editor, copy editor, and publisher for the journal (Lombroso-Ferrero, Chap. XI, 15-17).

Lombroso's academic colleagues, however, did not share enthusiasm for his notoriety. The University of Turin frequently offered a series of free courses for the public. Lombroso's, and those of some of his young followers, were often full; other professors faced empty lecture halls. In 1880, some of them charged Lombroso with making students pay him for the free courses. He had not, of course, and an investigation cleared him. But the incident impressed Lombroso that he was "surrounded by enemies" (Lombroso-Ferrero, Chap. XI, 23, 24).

Personal tragedy also hounded Lombroso. That same year, 1880, and within a week of each other, both of his parents died. In her unpublished biography, Gina Lombroso-Ferrero spends no time on the death of Aronne Lombroso, but recall that she always harbored a hatred for the man whom she thought so inadequate to be her father's father.

As for the death of Zefora "Nina" Levi Lombroso, however, Gina expounded. Gina elevated Zefora to the level of a saint, saying she had "for the sake of her children had voluntarily left her land which now was so bitter against her most beloved son" (Lombroso-Ferrero, Chap. XI, 24).

In 1882, Lombroso suffered another loss. His second son, Leo, died of diphtheria contracted from a visitor to the Lombroso home. Lombroso must have blamed himself the child's death. He later would confide in Gina that he knew the visiting friend had the disease, but he could not bear to turn him away (Lombroso-Ferrero, Chap. XI, 25).

Conferences, Conflict, and Trials

A series of academic arguments and personal trials marked the next phase of Lombroso's life. Just as he discovered as he moved to Torino, a popular book was no guarantee of academic support. A series of professional conferences drove that home.

As an acknowledged leader of the "Italian school" of criminology, Lombroso led the creation of the International Congress of Criminal Anthropologists. He organized the first meeting of the Congress in Rome in November 1885. There Lombroso elucidated his theories of "born criminals" and their classifications, Ferri stressed crime as "degeneration," and others supported Lombroso's work.

French researchers, however, argued against Lombroso's findings. Edward Lindsey, historian of the conference, reported that "Professor [Alexandre] Lacassagne thought that the atavistic and degenerative theories as held by the Italian school were exaggerations and false interpretations of the facts, and that the important factor was the social environment" (Lindsey, 578).

The Rome Conference showed a division between French and Italian researchers, but the next conference in 1889 — in Paris — showed a major breach and animosity between the schools of thought. There, Lombroso outlined the work of the Italian school since 1885, and he placed special emphasis on the role of epilepsy in criminality. But French professor Leonce Pierre Manouvrier put aside academic decency when he charged that "Lombroso's theory [was] nothing but the exploded science of phrenology" (Lindsey, 578). Manouvrier said that both honest men and criminals possessed the anomalies that Lombroso outlined, and they possessed no physical differences. Lindsey reports that "Garofalo, [Dimitry] Drill, Lacassagne, and [Mortiz] Benedikt opposed Lombroso's theories in whole or in part." M. G. A. Pugliese stressed social surroundings as more important in criminality than biological traits (Lindsey, 579).

According to Havelock Ellis, "Lacassagne pointed out that we too often forget the factor of misery in the production of crime [including social misery]." Garafalo argued that social class — both high and low — had bearing on criminal behavior. Professor Paul Brouardel said "crime should not . . . be regarded as the result of any single isolated cause, physical, moral, or social, but of all those causes at once" (Ellis, 76).

Lombroso defended his findings, admitting that he may, at times, have been too "rash" in his theories. That, however, was only because biological factors and atavism in crime had so long been ignored. He said that he was always ready to give up an indefensible position. Of course, Lombroso did not think his was (Ellis, 76).

Before the Paris conference adjourned, members appointed, at Garofolo's urging, a seven-member committee to conduct a study of 100 criminals and 100 non-criminals to, essentially, check Lombroso's work (Gina Lombroso-Ferrero commented that typology plan was only a result of Manouvrier and company realizing that Lombroso's categorization plan was gaining ground.) (Lombroso-Ferrero, Chap. XII, 9). The Paris committee planned to present findings at the Brussels conference in 1892. The research, however, was too cumbersome, and the committee did nothing (Lindsey, 579).

Dr. Emile Houze and Dr. Leo Warnots, of the University of Brussels, refuted Lombroso at the Brussels meeting, which the Italian school boycotted. Their paper, entitled "Does There Exist an Anatomically Determined Criminal Type?" answered with an emphatic "No!" (Lindsey, 579).

Lindsey writes, "They concluded that the proposed type designated by Lombroso as the born criminal was not a real type; that the division of individuals into criminals and non-criminals was purely arbitrary and not a scientific classification, and that a certain number of criminals present pathological and degenerative characteristics but that these do not constitute a special category of degenerates" (Lindsey, 579).

The Paris and Brussels conferences were but an ugly precursor to an even more difficult trial for Lombroso. Ever enthusiastic to research and write on different topics, Lombroso found himself embroiled in 1894 in an academic's nightmare — a charge of plagiarism.

The incident began in 1893, after the Brussels conference, with a publisher named Hoepli encouraged Lombroso to write a treatise on graphology, or the study of handwriting as a way to ascertain one's personality. Lombroso agreed, and he collected numerous books for study. Some of them required translation, including one written by a dentist in Rouen. Lombroso took them to a translator for transcription, but the man carelessly mixed the graphology notes in with other of Lombroso's work (Lombroso-Ferrero, Chap. XVII, 1).

When, in 1894, Lombroso began his own writing, he mistakenly used the dentist's material as some of his own work on the handwriting of asylum patients. The book went to press with Lombroso unaware that he had passed off another's work as his own.

In 1895, Lombroso received a letter from Hoepli informing him that the dentist had filed suit against him and Lombroso. Gina and Lombroso traveled to Milan where they spoke to an attorney, who advised them that the suit was an attempt to blackmail Lombroso and that they should ignore it. They did.

When Hoepli's brother found out about Lombroso's decision, he was furious. He tried to convince the professor to change his mind, but Lombroso would not. Hoepli was in France, and, after the experiences of the Paris and Brussels conferences, Lombroso thought "all French hated him [and] that anything done in France would come out against him" (Lombroso-Ferrero, Chap. XVII, 2).

With Lombroso thus in absentia, a judge in Rouen found in favor of the dentist. It remained for some sentenced to be levied against Lombroso and Hoepli. Gina took it on herself, as her father's secretary and de facto protector, to visit both France and Milan to work out the legal details of the case. In the end, Lombroso had to pay 300 lire to the dentist.

When the ordeal was over and Gina was back home in Turin, she and her father were walking along a bridge when he asked her the results of the sentence. Exhausted, she told him. The conferences and the plagiarism had worn down both of them, and Gina admitted that for a fleeting moment she considered throwing both herself and her father in the river below them. Then Lombroso wearily said, "Oh, dear, I am tired of life, tired to fight, fed up and disgusted with men." Then, as if he was reading Gina's mind and rejecting her dark thoughts he added, "But I want to finish the [new] edition of *Criminal Man* before I die" (Lombroso-Ferrero, Chap. XVII, 6). The professor simply went back to work.

The incident showed Gina yet another aspect of her complex father. "I had never understood that complete [ability] my father had to forget disagreeable things. I was every time surprised and sometimes I suffered when I had to discover it over and over again" (Lombroso-Ferrero, Chap. XVII, 6).

With that ever-present resilience, Lombroso prepared for the meeting of the criminological conference in Geneva. If his French detractors had their way, the conference would be the final undoing of the Italian school. Edward Lindsey asserts that congress members thought they had settled the Lombroso issue at the third conference. At the end of the Brussels conference, Manouvrier and his confederates pushed for the next conference, in 1896, to be held in Geneva, Switzerland. Switzerland was home of Professor Ladame, a friend of Manouvrier, and they expected him to control the conference to the detriment of the Lombrosians. Ladame was no supporter of the Italians and, according to Gina Lombroso-Ferrero, thought that criminal anthropology was "finished since '89 because of the question of the type of delinquent and of atavism." He was all in favor of "debaptising [sic]" the Italian school of thought (Lombroso-Ferrero, Chap. XII, 7).

Ladame might have been in the Manouvrier camp, but Switzerland, while it produced no academic practitioners of the Italian New School, had plenty of government officials who supported it. Naturally, they had a stake in causes and correction of criminal activity, just like Italy. They included Swiss President Adrien Lachenal; Albert Dunant, counsellor of State; and Gustav Cernavon, Swiss first justice. Collectively they had adopted the philosophies and advice of the New School.

Lachenal opened the Geneva conference with a speech that recounted the history of criminal anthropology and its academic infighting. Discord characterized the Rome and Paris conferences, he said, and in Brussels "there seemed to be more harmony in between the different systems discussed" (Lombroso-Ferrero, Chap. XII, 8).

Lachenal continued, "Your work is not limited to the discoveries of biology and to [theoretical] considerations. It is now at the turning point . . . where it can become a strong and useful help to the social defense against vice and crime. You cut and it is the job of the legislator to sew. It is now in the hands of Society, the State, and the Parliaments and the people to build a penal organization" that could separate asylums from prisons and "ameliorate and eliminate" elements that endangered society (Lombroso-Ferrero, Chap. XII, 9).

Lombroso-Ferrero admits that the Lombrosians at Geneva were "bad strategists," but they had a fortunate alliance in the Swiss government officials. Once the idea that criminals might be "nearer the insane than the normal man," she said, the matter left the realm of researchers and theorists and entered that of society and its representatives (Lombroso-Ferrero, Chap. XII, 10).

To be sure, plenty of Lombroso's adversaries were present at Geneva. However, once they saw the tenor and trajectory of the conference, "they just disappeared" (Lombroso-Ferrero, Chap. XII, 10).

Geneva was not all French-school capitulation, though. Professor Zagrewski, "an old and venerable Russian magistrate," and a devout anti-Lombrosian, asserted that doctors — whether medical or psychiatric — should not involve themselves in criminal study. Such was the reserve of social and political entities. Lombroso's chief surrogate, Enrico Ferri, gave a "brilliant exposé" of Positivist doctrine, "showing how they did not stop at anatomic facts but went far in the social, psychological, and juridical camp" (Lombroso-Ferrero, Chap. XII, 11).

President Lachenal closed the conference with a rousing reaffirmation of Italian Positivism. The Italian school was back, driven by the "strong impulsion" of Lombroso. "Nothing can stop it anymore" (Lombroso-Ferrero, Chap. XII, 13).

Not only was the Geneva Conference a success for the Italian school, it gave Lombroso a chance to realize a personal wish. He had long admired the work of Russian author Leo Tolstoy. After the Geneva Conference, Lombroso's Russian supporters beseeched him to visit Moscow for the General Conference of Medicine in 1897. Lombroso agreed, although somewhat reluctantly because of his health.

He began the trip with a party of fellow travelers, but in Budapest he wanted to rest a day or two while the others went on. He checked into a hotel, but after the first night discovered he had lost his billfold and wallet. When word got out that the author of *Criminal Man* was alone and in need in their city, his fans and supporters in Budapest found the hotel and feted him for several days! (Lombroso-Ferrero, Chap. XVIII, 7).

Journeying on, Lombroso made it to Moscow and the conference. While there, he expressed his desire to meet Tolstoy, and he was escorted to the author's estate. The *prospect* of meeting Tolstoy was more satisfying than *actually* meeting him. They could not understand each other and had little in common. Yet, even with what little understanding they had, they managed to argue. Tolstoy did not agree with the concept of the born criminal. Lombroso determined he could not engage Tolstoy "in debate without irritating him." When it came to a discussion of punishments, Tolstoy shouted "All this is nonsense! All punishment is criminal" (Mazzarello, "Lombroso and Tolstoy").

In the end, Lombroso came away more impressed with the author's home and wife than the man himself. Lombroso's daughter Gina wrote that her father was "always more convinced that Tolstoy was a living confirmation of his theories of genius" (Lombroso-Ferrero, Chap. XVIII, 10).

Tolstoy went further. He wrote in his diary of Lombroso's visit that "He is an ingenuous and limited old man." When Tolstoy wrote *Resurrection* he makes reference to Lombroso. The book's main character, Dimitry Nekhlyudov researches criminal deviance in a series of books, including some of Lombroso's and becomes more "disappointed" the more he reads. Later, Lombroso's theories are not admitted in a courtroom; one jurist notes that their author is "a very stupid fellow" (Mazzarello, "Lombroso and Tolstoy").

Travel was also problematic as Lombroso prepared to journey to the Amsterdam criminal anthropology conference in 1901. Gina Lombroso-Ferrero recalled that "Amsterdam is 35 hours away from Turin and it was just by luck and great good will that he [Lombroso] arrived there" (Lombroso-Ferrero, Chap. XX, 3). Lombroso had long suffered from angina pectoris and arteriosclerosis as well as "a pseudo Basedow [goiter], complicated since 1900 by an ateromasy of the aorta." The professor was sensitive to extremes of heat and cold and to changes in sea level. "He had always been sensitive to the pressure, and he had now become a real barometer," Gina wrote. The trip to Amsterdam would be arduous, but he wanted to go. "His desire was to be present [at] the congress of anthropology, which he thought would be the last one, so we decided he should go and we [presumably Gina and the rest of his family] should go with him" (Lombroso-Ferrero, Chap. XX, 4).

They made many stops along the way — Lucerne, Zurich, Frankfort, and Cologne — and arrived exhausted. The conference, however, was worth the trip. Gina realized that they were correct in making the trip. The amicability of the Amsterdam conference was a treat for Lombroso. The conference included many "wonderful, interesting discussions without [a] fight, [something that was] so rare in his life" (Lombroso-Ferrero, Chap. XX, 4).

Still, some controversies remained in Amsterdam. Researchers again debated the social causes of crime, as well as "sexual inversion and perversion." The acrimony of earlier conferences, however, was absent, although not permanently so (Lindsey, 580).

When the congress returned to Italy, on Lombroso's home turf of Turin in 1906, many of the old arguments resurfaced. Not having to weather the exhaustion of travel, the Father of Criminal Anthropology again took up the fight. He used an argument from a different field of social inquiry, and one that would satisfy many — and anger as many others — today. Lindsey writes:

> Lombroso . . . drew an ingenious parallel between the homosexual individual and the criminal. Specialists, he said, distinguished between the occasional and the insane homosexual, and, finally, those born inverted, who, from their earliest years experience an attraction toward persons of the same sex and often exhibit special characteristics. He thought it strange that authorities such as Nacke, Lacassagne, Gross, and Krafft-Ebing should refuse to credit the existence of born criminals and yet affirm the congenital character . . . of the born homosexual (Lindsey, 581).

Simply, Lombroso and many of his colleagues accepted that many people were born with homosexual tendencies. If that was so, why was it so difficult to accept the same about criminals? Not all of them, for Lombroso had gotten to the point of acknowledging occasional and political criminals, but many of them. The argument was controversial and typically Lombrosian; well-fitting since the 1906 conference would be Lombroso's last.

Lombroso's Last Work

Amid the discord caused by his move to Turin, the academic infighting of the conferences, and the ordeal of the plagiarism case, Lombroso worked on what would be the final project of his life. It saw Lombroso go from the abnormalities of the criminal mind to the mysteries of the spirit world.

In the 19th Century, spiritualism followed war as surely as did advances in weaponry and medicine. With young soldiers falling in the Crimean War, the wars of Italian and German unification, and the Franco-German War, grieving Europeans by the thousands sought to somehow communicate with their dead loved ones. Likewise in the United States after the devastating Civil War, which claimed the immediate deaths of 630,000 Americans and contributed to the later deaths of countless others (Nartonis). Perhaps driven by the deaths in his own family, perhaps by his innate, unceasing curiosity, Cesare Lombroso became caught up in the mania of European spiritualism.

Lombroso began inquiry into the world of spiritualism gradually, and as a skeptic. "If ever there was an individual in the world opposed to spiritism [which he called spiritualism] by virtue of scientific education, and . . . by instinct, I was that person," he said (Lombroso, *After Death*, 1). Lombroso noted that he entered his researches with an eye to supporting his own theories and belief in materialism. "I had made it the indefatigable pursuit of a lifetime to defend the thesis that every force is a property of matter and the soul an emanation of the brain" (Lombroso, *After Death*, 1).

In 1882, the same year young Leo died, Lombroso agreed to observe, as a neurologist, the case of the 14-year-old daughter of a prominent Italian citizen. The girl, whom Lombroso referred to only as C.S., had periodic spells of blindness, paresis of her legs, and lack of muscular control. But what got Lombroso's attention, and his agreement to consult, were periods of sleepwalking in which the girl showed increased strength and activity doing household chores and playing music. She also exhibited a change in personality, displaying "a virile audacity and immorality" (Lombroso, *After Death*, 3). But, while blindness ensued in these episodes, the girl remarkably displayed the power to see through her nose and left ear lobe! (Lombroso, *After Death*, 3). Lombroso noted that the girl's sense of smell was also "transposed" to the point that she could detect smells through her chin (Lombroso, *After Death*, 4). Ultimately, C.S. showed minor predictive abilities.

His interest piqued, Lombroso began researching historical incidents of somnambulism with odd behaviors, of thought transmission, and clairvoyance. He found enough anecdotal evidence to begin building a case for what he called "hypnotic phenomena." Recall that much of the evidence he collected in his work on criminal anthropology was also anecdotal — and thus problematic. One of the incidents which Lombroso himself verified was that of a "Madame V" who was attending a Florence theater in November 1882. During the performance she cried out, saying her father was extremely ill. She fled the theater. At home, she found a telegram saying that her father in Turin was dying. A second telegram soon arrived saying the man had died. Madame V, said Lombroso, "was subject to hysteria" (Lombroso, *After Death*, 25).

Lombroso also lumped into this pile of evidence the story of an Italian army officer, a Lieutenant Perrino. Perrino, assigned to the fight against brigandage in southern Italy, awoke one morning from a premonition in which he saw himself "bound to a tree, with his orderly, and the two [had] been shot by brigands." On Perrino's next foray, brigands ambushed his squad and killed most of them. Lombroso wrote that "he and his orderly . . . were tied together, bound to an oak tree, and both shot at the same time" (Lombroso, *After Death*, 33). It can be no coincidence that Lombroso, who spent so much time in Calabria on new Italy's brigandage front, picked that story as one of his foundational points of evidence.

These collected anecdotes and his own smattering of observances were enough to change Lombroso's mind on spiritualism. As he wrote:

> There is enough in all these observations to enable us to conclude that there exists an immense series of psychical phenomena that completely elude the laws of psycho-physiology, and that have solely this feature in common and this certainty, — that they take place more readily in individuals subject to hysteria, or who are neuropathic, or who are in the hypnotic or dreaming condition, just at the moment, in fact, when the normal ideation is more or less completely inactive, and in its stead the action of the unconscious dominates, which is more difficult to subject to scientific examination of any kind (Lombroso, *After Death*, 38).

For the next several years, Lombroso conducted experiments on "the limits of suggestion in the waking state, and the influence of a permanent magnet upon suggested sensations" (Kurella, 168). Lombroso biographer, Hans Kurella, said it was "most remarkable" that Lombroso, so attuned to objective observations, "should concern himself with matters so little accessible to objective observation as the reaction to hypnotic procedures and the examination of suggested ideas in hypnotized and hysterical subjects" (Kurella, 168).

In short, Lombroso observed phenomena that he could neither deny nor scientifically test. His positivist tendencies took over; if he observed the phenomena, then it must be true. Combined with "the materiality of the performances of hypnotized persons," Lombroso adopted the "credulous assumption that there existed a peculiar material condition of the brain substance as the cause of all these . . . phenomena" (Kurella, 168).

Thus primed, Lombroso was to fall under the sway of one of craftiest "mediums" in Europe — Eusapia Paladino. Born in 1854, Eusapia (as she was commonly and simply known) spent her adult years touring Europe, capitalizing on the notion of contacting the dead to perform séances and commune with spirits in the afterlife. Her demonstrations included levitations of tables at which she sat and chairs she sat upon; phantom limbs appearing from the midst of her own body; strange scratching or writings appearing on sheaves of paper; and facial or hand impressions, presumably of ghosts, appearing in boxes of soft clay. Eusapia, always with an accompaniment of men as assistants, appeared in Italy, Germany, France, England, and later in the United States.

Her demonstrations were part of what historian Simone Natale calls a brand of Victorian entertainment. "The rise of the spiritualist movement [was] a religious and cultural phenomenon . . . closely connected to the contemporary evolution of the media entertainment industry." Mediums essentially gave performances to willing audiences. Even though many of those performances occurred in private households, "séances integrated numerous elements what were connected to forms of domestic entertainment in nineteenth-century households, such as amateur prestidigitation tricks, parlor theaters, table games, and rational amusements" (Natale, 1-3).

Upon a challenge from one of Eusapia's supporters, Lombroso began observing her in 1892. While others would later expose her as a charlatan who used tricks of light, convulsive movements, and simple furniture manipulation, Lombroso and a host of other observers were taken in (Lombroso would have had a particular preoccupation with death during his long series of Eusapian observations. In 1894 his oldest son, Arnoldo, died of typhus at the age of 20.) (Lombroso-Ferrero, Chap. XII, 12).

Ultimately, Lombroso observed Eusapia in seventeen séances in Milan in 1892. He attended them with fellow scientists Alexandre Nikolayevich Aksakoff, who published *Psychische Studien*; Charles Richet; Giorgio Manganelli; Giorgio Finzi; G.B. Ermacora, Angelo Brofferio; Dr. G. Gerosa; Giovanni Schiaparelli; and Carl DuPrel (Evans, 178). The group attempted to "control" the sessions by providing their own tables for the séances, and by holding onto Eusapia's hands and feet (Lombroso, *After Death*, 41).

In their first séance, the table moved. Lombroso said this was "the more remarkable in that the medium was always seated at one end of the table, and because we never once let go of her hands and feet" (Lombroso, *After Death*, 41). At their second séance, the experimenters attached a dynamometer to the table. If it moved, they could then detect how much force had been applied to it. A hanging device, the dynamometer displayed the weight in pressure of the table attached to it; if the table rose, the pressure on the dynamometer would *decrease* by the amount of pressure applied. When the table did indeed rise, dynamometer reading steadily decreased until it could register no more and was, in fact, laying horizontally on the table (Lombroso, *After Death*, 43).

In other séances, the scientists observed lateral movements of the table, then full levitation. They attempted to weigh Eusapia in her chair, then see if the scale registered a difference in weight as she apparently levitated. In five attempts, they got "two curves of the phenomenon." Lombroso added that it took all of the scientists standing on the platform of the scale to move the weight beam as they had seen Eusapia do (Lombroso, *After Death*, 47).

In other instances, the group reported seeing hands appear as silhouettes before cardboards they had smeared with phosphorescence and hung behind Eusapia; saw Eusapia in her chair rise up and set down on the table; they felt objects in the room touch them; Schiaparelli twice had his glasses removed and placed on the table.

Lombroso made those observations in 1892. He made more observations of Eusapia in 1895 and as late as 1907, and he followed the results of scientists examining her "phenomena." While the positivist relied on observations, Lombroso augmented that with the wonders of technology as he and colleagues invented various experiments and toted experimental contraptions to séances.

Among the devices that Lombroso and his colleagues wielded at various séances were a cardiograph, which would record movement on a cylinder when a stethoscope membrane pulsed. The researchers intended it measure the presence of any spirit Eusapia conjured. They also used a Desprez register, which used electric pulses and a hidden telegraph key to record movement on a cylinder enclosed in a bell jar, and a manometer, which used water and air pressure against mercury in a tube to record movement on a cylinder.

In the end, Lombroso categorized some 40 evidences in five different classes in what he called "The Resume of the Eusapia Phenomenon." Those included:

Class I: Mechanical phenomena, which consisted of movements of the table, rappings on the table, movements of curtains around the séance cabinet, and movements of Eusapia's garments.

Class II: Mechanical phenomena caused without the contact by the medium, including "independent levitations of the table," "undulations, inflations, and flinging" of cabinet curtains, spontaneous movements of objects within the cabinet; and movement of chairs, including those upon which the scientists were sitting.

Class III: Alterations of the gravity of bodies, which Lombroso says are the "least sure cases." They include changes in the weight of the medium's body, levitation of the medium, wind rushing from the séance cabinet, intense cold in the cabinet, chilly puffs of air emanating from Eusapia's head and body, sounds of musical instruments, and sounds of human voices.

Class IV: Materializations, such as apparent human hands and limbs that touched the observers, and "complicated actions of materialized forms" which "advance towards the observers, touch them, and handle them, draw them close and grasp them, or push them away, caress them, attract and kiss them."

Class V: Luminous phenomena, which included glowing points or "little flames" and clouds or "dim white mists" (Lombroso, *After Death*, 90-101).

Lombroso admitted that Eusapia played many "crafty tricks" during her séances, "for example, freeing one of her two hands, held by the controllers, for the sake of moving objects near her" (Lombroso, *After Death*, 102). No doubt Lombroso contributed much of her craftiness to the region of her birth — Minervino Murge in southern Italy, very near Calabria from where so many of Lombroso's criminal specimens hailed. When he noted that "her culture is that of a villager of the lower order," one expects to find her in a list of "born criminals" (Lombroso, *After Death*, 111).

But Eusapia possessed many characteristics that Lombroso admired. While she lacked "good sense and . . . common sense," she had a "subtlety and intuition of the intellect in sharp contrast with her lack of cultivation." Eusapia could be sly and mysterious, but also had a "most keen visual memory" (Lombroso, *After Death*, 111).

Even though these characteristics could definitely point to someone quite capable of manipulating — tricking — an audience, Lombroso believed her trance-state behavior. "She first becomes pale, turning her eyes upward and her sight inward," he wrote. Her hands and feet took on "movements of flexure or extension, and every little while [became] rigid." She laughed out loud, underwent seizures, used words uncommon for what Lombroso perceived as her social station. She sometimes spoke in a foreign language and might "pass into a state of ecstasy" (Lombroso, *After Death*, 113).

Lombroso continued:

> After a séance Eusapia is overcome by morbid sensitiveness, hyperesthesia, photophobia, and often by hallucinations and delirium (during which she asks to be watched from harm), and by serious disturbances of the digestion, followed by vomiting if she has eaten before the séance, and finally by true paresis of the legs, on account of which it is necessary for her to be carried and to be undressed by others (Lombroso, *After Death*, 115).

Lombroso also claimed belief in the spirits — or phantasms — that Eusapia conjured in her séances. "The facts relating to the activity of phantasms are so numerous and so well proved that we can permit ourselves to construct their biology and their psychology," Lombroso wrote. The spirits were indeed ghostly, but, hewing to Lombroso's materialistic bent, they had form and substance. "Phantasms are covered with a white woven stuff, extremely fine, sometimes doubled, tripled, and even quadrupled. They seem to draw it out from the clothes of the medium." Spirits, he wrote, sprang from the "material substance of the medium," who at times gained weight as the phantasms appeared (Lombroso, *After Death*, 329-331).

In more than 350 pages, Lombroso never admitted that Eusapia's séances could have been completely broad theater. Yes, she could be a trickster, but, especially when in a trance, Eusapia was not faking. In fact, in the final two pages of *After Death*, Lombroso makes a huge academic leap in an attempt to wrap her in science and place her on a pedestal of materialism.

Lombroso tied his tenuous theory to the phenomena of the trance itself. He wrote:

> The special conditions of the trance (in which . . . by the paralysis of certain centers certain others are intensified) give to the medium at a stated moment extraordinary faculties, which she certainly did not have before the trance and which ordinary persons do not have. Above all, the action of the unconscious is intensified. Those centers which seem dormant in the ordinary life come into activity and predominate (Lombroso, *After Death*, 355).

Lombroso concluded that the special abilities of the medium, when in a trance, "happen because with the power of the medium there is associated another power that has, even though transiently, those gifts that are denied to the living; namely, the ability to read the future, to extemporize artistic powers, and the like" (Lombroso, *After Death*, 356). In short, the material of the medium's brain was plastic, subject to change in the midst of a trance and able to take on supernatural powers.

Simply, Lombroso had seen the strange phenomena. Having seen them, his positivist attitude mandated he explain them. However, as with so much of his work on criminal man, his scientific vocabulary could not exactly articulate his theories. He had seen something, but what it was he could not exactly say.

But, neither could he dismiss the medium's séances as sheer antics, the type of chicanery that he had so frequently accused the Romagna of. One modern internet site goes so far as accusing Lombroso of sleeping with Eusapia; thus he could not condemn her (Eusapia Paladino, Rational Wiki, http://rationalwiki. org/wiki/Eusapia_Palladino#cite_note-15, accessed 6/13/ 2017).

Lombroso biographer Hans Kurella has a more sophisticated explanation for his belief. Kurella spends much of the last few pages of his biography apologizing for Lombroso's interest in spiritualism. He suggests that Lombroso was so scarred by allegations during the pellagra controversies that he and his work were fraudulent that, when observing Eusapia, he could not bear to allege fraud against her. "It was this experience which made it psychologically impossible for him, when he came to study occult phenomena, to take into consideration the possibility of fraud" (Kurella, *Modern Man*, 173).

Lombroso's daughter, Gina, also sought reasons why her father dabbled in studying the occult. In her unpublished manuscript, she blamed his foray on ill health. Lombroso, she said, wrote *After Death* in the midst of attacks of angina pectoris. She wrote that:

> Arteriosclerosis had wrecked [his] digestive system, always very delicate, by now it upset also his sleep, which had [been] always wonderful and long and very restful. Now he could not eat and sleep regularly, many times it happened that he could not sleep all night and felt sleepiness during the whole day (Lombroso-Ferrero, Chap. XXII, 8).

However, there may be another interpretation of Lombroso's interest in spiritualism, and it does indeed tie in with other factors of his life. As noted, spiritualism was rampant in late 19th-century Europe. Even England's Queen Victoria had dabbled in it, which gave the craze added validity. Andrzej Diniejko, D. Litt., a writer in Victorian culture, notes that spiritualism played to female mediums, such as Eusapia, because Victorians recognized women as "more spiritual than men." Women "had allegedly a better predisposition to spiritual perfectibility" (Diniejko, "Victorian Spiritualism," accessed June 15, 2017). Alex Owen, in *The Darkened Room. Women, Power and Spiritualism in Late Victorian England*, agrees. He notes that spiritualism attracted many female believers and practitioners because the movement held "possibilities for attentions, opportunity, and status denied elsewhere." Such fits Eusapia perfectly. Spiritualism, writes Owen, was a "movement which privileged women and took them seriously" (Diniejko, "Victorian Spiritualism," accessed June 15, 2017).

Such a social and cultural phenomenon would have attracted Lombroso for two reasons. First was the fact that spiritualism was indeed a *social phenomena*, just as was crime and its causes. To study it, to find its causes, motivations, and implications would have been, to Lombroso, on par with his study of criminality. Its exploration could again put Italian science and psychiatry on the academic map.

The fact that spiritualism drew so many female actors would also have attracted Lombroso. Remember that he was the product of a universe of strong women. His mother, Nina, organized her life so that her Jewish children could receive an education in a Catholic world, and she continually encouraged Lombroso to strive further. His daughters, Gina and Paola, supported his endeavors and, to one extent or another, followed his academic lead. Both married men who contributed to Lombroso's own work. Gina herself became a medical doctor and was her father's best, most ardent supporter. It was Gina, who at age four, recognized the need to buttress her father during his moments of depression. Gina, of course, wrote the unpublished manuscript upon which much of this study is based. Of course, a downside to so many strong women structuring Lombroso's life and story is that the men involved — namely, his father and sons — recede from importance. Rarely are they mentioned, and, as Kurella noted, when Gina mentions her grandfather, Aaronne, it is with contempt and no little measure of hatred.

Nevertheless, Lombroso was a product of strong women. "He was definitely female oriented," said psychology professor Mark Aldridge. "He looked up to them. Got strength from them. Got comfort from them." Aldridge suggests that Lombroso may have had something of a neo-Freudian Oedipal complex — not the classical Freudian complex suggesting a desire for sex with one's own mother, but a lesser complex indicating a comfort with and desire to be around strong women (Aldridge, interview with Jones, Butler, June 13, 2017). Interestingly, when Eusapia asked him to envision a dead relative during a séance, Lombroso pictured his mother in his head, not one of his two deceased sons (Lombroso, *After Death*, 122).

"He likes the association with strong women," said Aldridge. "It transmits power to him."

Lombroso's life certainly indicates periods of powerlessness in his life, such as his loneliness during his early days in college, and his inability to break into the rigid — and male dominated — academic world of Turin without doing extra, mundane, and uninteresting research. In this regard, with Lombroso's own history and makeup, his interest in spiritualism is not unusual.

One other factor remains, and it has to do with the ever-present danger of foisting modern ideas onto historical subjects. Twenty-first century human beings, accustomed to seeing CG effects on screen, playing video games, have information come instantly into their handheld devices, tend to regard such ideas as ghosts, spirits, and phantasms as quaint, as elements of fun on Halloween or a good fright in a horror movie. However, Victorians regarded spiritualism as fact. It was wrapped in theater and ballyhoo, to be sure, but they perceived its core elements as true. How could people levitate? How could limbs grow from the midst of a medium's body? The photographs that Lombroso included in his book, *After Death*, are laughable today, but he obviously considered them quite serious.

To Lombroso, spiritualism required inquiry, just as criminal behavior, just as pellagra and cretinism. In 1891, with so much furor over mediums and séances, Lombroso's interest in spiritualism would not have cast him as an outlier. Remember that many other researchers accompanied Lombroso to Eusapia's séances, and conducted work on their own. When Kurella and Gina Lombroso-Ferrero wrote their biographies of Lombroso, the spiritualism craze was receding (although World War I would, understandably, cause another spike in its popularity). It is not surprising that they downplayed his interest in spiritualism, even apologized for it.

Lombroso's conclusions, while readers today would regard them as silly, were the product of his time and the limits of scientific understanding. The same applies to his ideas of "the born criminal," even though a century of eugenics, Nazism, and racial profiling cast them into disfavor and tended to brand Lombroso as crazy.

****

After Death — What? was Lombroso's final book. He spent much of 1908 finishing the book and correcting proofs, although he did not feel at all well. His depression returned. Gina noted that his periods of happiness now lasted only "a few hours," while sadness lasted "long months" (Lombroso-Ferrero, Chap. XXII, 11).

Lombroso home office, note the skull of Villella on his desk.

Museo di Antropologia Criminale "Cesare Lombroso," University of Turin, Italy; Photographer: Randall Butler

The family decided to summer in England, where Lombroso could spend time on the beach yet be away from Italy's sultry climes. He enjoyed visiting London, where he had never been. "But he did not feel well at the sea place we had taken for the summer, he could not stand the wind, the sadness of the country, the regularity and monotony of the village, he much preferred the sun, although so hot and oppressing, of our lovely Italy" (Lombroso-Ferrero, Chap. XXII, 11).

Gina's notes of Lombroso's last days are, perhaps understandably, confused. Still, she was away from Turin for much of early October. Lombroso, agitated and wanting to get out and about unable to, suffered great melancholy. Hearing that his old friend was ill, Max Nordau visited Lombroso frequently. "The company of Nordau was probably the last joy he had," Gina wrote (Lombroso-Ferrero, Chap. XXII, 12).

On October 16, 1909, Lombroso sent a telegram to Gina's son, Leo, named for her deceased brother. The note was a birthday greeting, "but it was a letter of farewell, too," said Gina. "Very upset, I left the 18th for Torino, we arrived at 6 o'clock in the evening." Lombroso was up waiting for her (Lombroso-Ferrero, Chap. XXII, 12).

Lombroso cried. "I waited for you, Gina, now I can die happy" (Lombroso-Ferrero, Chap. XXII, 13).

He lay down on a couch and asked Gina to help him go to sleep as she did when she was a child, "with my arms around his neck and my face next to his." Lombroso slept a few minutes then awoke, seemingly feeling better. He drank a cup of milk, and, characteristically attempted to work. "[He] looked at the translation I had prepared for the U.S. of . . . *Criminal Man*, [and] changed a few words (Lombroso-Ferrero, Chap. XXII, 13).

He said that he had finished the preface to *After Death — What?*, and he noticed a look of doubt about the project on Gina's face. He smiled. "It is a secret I will penetrate soon," he said (Lombroso-Ferrero, Chap. XXII, 13).

Meanwhile, some bound copies of his books arrived, and Lombroso wanted to write dedications in them. He did not have a pen, and Gina told him to wait until the next day. He insisted, however, saying, "No, no, you never know." When he finished, he went to bed (Lombroso-Ferrero, Chap. XXII, 13).

His immediate family was all together: his wife, Nina; their last surviving son, Ugo; Gina, her husband, Guglielmo, and their son, Leo; and Paola Lombroso-Carrara and her family. Lombroso went to sleep, but woke up after mid-night asking for broth. Nina took him some but panicked when he could no longer swallow. The family gathered back around his bedside, and Lombroso returned to sleep. "As we left him, sleeping calmly, regularly as he had not done for years," said Gina. "His breath got rare[r] and rare[r] until it died away, without a notion . . . [as] his soul passed to infinit[y], as quietly as a river ends in the sea" (Lombroso-Ferrero, Chap. XXII, 13).

Museo di Antropologia Criminale "Cesare Lombroso," University of Turin, Italy; Photographer: Randall Butler

Cesare and his beloved daughter Gina.

CONCLUSION

Cesare Lombroso had directed that his body be donated to science — to his own laboratory at Turin, in fact — for study. When word spread of his death, a large crowd of people arrived to accompany his body to the school.

"It was a lovely October day [with] birds and [the] sweet scent of autumnal flowers" wrote Gina Lombroso-Ferrero (Lombroso-Ferrero, Chap. XXII, 14).

Lombroso's desire to have his remains open for study, it turns out, was not just an extension of his scientific work. It was also manifestly part of the Italian patriotic fervor that drove enlistment in the army and much of his earlier work.

Silvano Montaldo notes that Lombroso's orders were in line with the "ideals of the Italian Risorgimento [as part of a] collective task for the construction of a new Italy" (Montaldo, "Relics," 184). Montaldo continues:

> Within the national movement, the bodies of great figures of the past assumed a strong symbolic value. As early as 1848, but especially after the Unification of Italy, the remains of conspirators, fighters and leaders, but also of the artists whose works had given voice to the spirit of the nation, were subjected to thanato-political practices.

In short, Lombroso's act of donating his body to science enshrined not only as an Italian scientist, but also as an Italian revolutionary, patriot, and member of the *Risorgimento*. Even if his theories of criminal man passed away, his remains would stand testimony to his work.

Gina, Lombroso's emotional support and staunchest advocate, also remained a testament to his work. She devoted herself to interpreting his work, writing, among other things, a brief summary of *Criminal Man* (which often does a better job of explaining its tenets that Lombroso's original works) and the unpublished biography of her father to which this current book is so indebted.

Indeed, Lombroso has needed a spokesperson over the last century. Eugenicists, white supremacists, and other have co-opted Lombroso's work and cast it in bad light.

In general, they, and most of Lombroso's critics stop short of a true understanding of his research. They grasp Lombroso's initial conclusion that criminals are "born," thus creating the class of "criminal man." But they fail to realize that Lombroso evolved in his thinking. In fact, he ultimately accepted that environment also played a role in the development of criminal behavior.

Detractors also fail to credit Lombroso with understanding that *science* — that cornerstone of the Enlightenment — could help define the nature of criminality. Lombroso was, to be sure, outpacing the limits of 19th-century science, instinctively reaching for something that the crude instruments of his time could neither record nor interpret.

Lombroso could not have known, nor elucidated, was that he was on the cusp of DNA causality — verifiable hereditary factors — in criminal behavior. He was knocking at the door of biological determinism within a medical model framework.

Gina Lombroso-Ferrero sums up her father's work well. Acknowledging that he often worked by impulse and instinct, she said that Lombroso "did not feel he had to shut the generous impulses of his heart, to isolate himself in the cold of the anatomic world, he did not abandon entering the new field, the generous impulses [of] his heart" (Lombroso-Ferrero, Chap. XXIII, 9).

The end of Lombroso's life was marked with a peaceful transition to eternity but it would be inaccurate to say that the impact he made to criminology ended with his life as well. In fact, over 100 years after his death, we find ourselves reinterpreting his works and the impact his life had on his writings and focus as an academic field of study. This book highlighted the major events of Lombroso's life as told often by those closest to him; this should have highlighted the importance that his personal life had on his writings and wishes to unmask the criminal mind. It goes without saying that we are only beginning to understand his struggles in the context of the era and times that surrounded him. The hope of the authors is to make a small contribution in this realm in order to inspire others to advance knowledge through the study of historical events and the lives of those that inspired for the birth of criminology as a field of study. It is only through this effort that we will achieve a complete understanding of the father of criminology; a most remarkable man, father, scholar, and physician.

BIBLIOGRAPHY

Abel, E.L. (2015). Images in psychiatry: Benedict-Augustin Morel (1809-1873). Retrieved from http://ajp.psychiatryonline.org/doi/full/10.1176/appi.ajp.161.12.2185.

Albrecht, A. (1910). Cesare Lombroso. A glance at his life work. *Journal of The American Institute of Criminal Law and Criminology,* 1 (2), 71-83. Retrieved from http://www.jstor/stable/1133036?seq=3#page_scantab_contents.

Aldridge, M, Ph.D. Interview with Randall Butler and R. Steven Jones, June 13, 2017.

Allen, F.A. (1960). Raffaele Garofalo (1852-19334). In Mannheim, H. (Ed.), *Pioneers in criminology* (pp. 318-340). Chicago, IL: Northwestern University.

Becker, P. (2006). The criminologists' gaze at the underworld: Toward an archaeology of criminology writing. In Becker, P. & Wetzell, R.F (Eds.), *Criminals and their scientists: The history of criminology in international perspective* (pp. 105-133). New York: Cambridge University Press.

Beirne, P., & Messerschmidt, J. (2000). *Criminology* (3rd Ed.). Boulder, CO: Westview press.

Bellamy, R. (Ed.). (1995). *Beccaria: On crimes and punishments and other writings* (R. Davis, Trans.). New York: Cambridge University Press.

Bianucci, P., Cilli C., Giacobini, G., Malerba, G., & Montaldo, S. (Eds.) (2011). "Cesare Lombroso," *Museum of Criminal Anthropology Visitor's Guide.* (P.W. Christie, Trans). Torino, Italy: Edizioni Libreria Cortina.

Blim, M. (1998). Contemplating the palm tree line. In Schneider, J. (Ed.), *Italy's "southern question:" Orientalism in one country* (pp. 279-284). New York: Oxford University Press.

Bondio, M. G. (2006). From the "atavistic" to the "inferior" criminal type: Impact of the Lombrosian theory of the born criminal on German psychiatry. In Becker, P., & Wetzell, R.F. (Eds.), *Criminals and their scientists: The history of criminology in international perspective* (pp. 183-205). New York: Cambridge University Press.

Bretherick, D. (2015). The 'born criminal'? Lombroso and the origins of modern Criminology. *BBC History Magazine*, October 9, 2015, pp. 1-7. Retrieved from http://www.historyextra.com/article/feature/born-criminal-lombroso-origins-modern- criminology.

Browne, J. (1989). *The voyages of the Beagle: Charles Darwin's journal of researches*. New York: Penguin.

Buttafuoco, A. (1993). On 'mothers' and 'sisters': Fragments on women/ feminism/ Historiography. In Kemp, S., & Bono, P. (Eds.), *The lonely mirror: Italian perspectives on feminist theory*. New York: Routledge.

"Cesare Lombroso." *JewishEncyclopedia.com*. Accessed March 23, 2016.

Cilli, C. Personal communication, March 21, 2017.

Collier, M. (2003). *Italian Unification, 1820-1871*. Essex, England: Heinemann.

Conrad, J. *The Secret Agent*, 1907; transcribed to Project Guttenberg, https://www.gutenberg.org/files/974/974-h/974-h.htm, accessed June 17, 2017.

Craig, G.A. (1971). *Europe Since 1815*. New York: Holt, Rinehart, and Winston.

Curi, E. "Lombroso e Verona," Retrieved from www.societaletteraria.it. Accessed February 17, 2017.

D'Agostino, P. (Apr. 2002). Craniums, criminals, and the 'cursed race': Italian anthropology in American racial thought, 1861-1924. *Comparative Studies in Society and History*, 44 (2), 319-343.

Darwin, C. (1871/2014). *Descent of man* (Reprint). CreatSpace Independent Publishing Platform.

Davis, J.D. (1955). "Phrenology: Fad or science." New Haven, CT: Yale University Press.

Dickie, J. (1997). "Stereotypes of the Italian South, 1860-1900," 114-147. In Lumely, R., & Morris, J. (Eds.), *The New History of the Italian South: The Mezzogiorno Revisited*. Devon, UK: University of Exeter Press.

Diniejko, A. "Victorian Spiritualism," The Victorian Web, http://www.victorianweb.org/victorian/religion/spirit.html, accessed June 15, 2017.

Doyle, D.H. (2002). *Nations divided: American, Italy, and the southern question*. Athens, GA: University of Georgia Press.

Ellis, H. (1890/1911). *Criminal Man* (Reprint). Memphis, TN: General Books.

Evans, H.R. (1897). *Hours With the Ghosts: Or, Nineteenth Century Witchcraft*. Laird and Lee, E-book edition, http://bit.ly/2sR7dJz. Accessed June 20, 2017.

Evans, J.E. (2016). *The pursuit of power: Europe, 1815-1914*. New York: Viking.

Ferri, E. (1908/2017). *The Positive school of criminology — three lectures given at the University of Naples, Italy on April 22, 23, and 24, 1901* (Reprint). (E. Untermann, Trans.). San Bernardino, CA: Filiquarian Publishing.

Francis, M. (2007). *Herbert Spencer and the invention of modern life*. Ithaca, NY: Cornell University Press.

"Francesco Siacci." Retrieved from http://www.history.mcs.st-and.ac.uk/bibliographies/aiacci.html.

"Frederick Engles, Ludwig Feuerbach and the end of classical German philosophy, part 2: Materialism." Retrieved from https://www.marxists.org/archive/marx/works/1886/Ludwig-feuerbach/ch02.htm.

Galton, F. (1869). *Hereditary Genius*. Retrieved from http://galton.org/books/hereditary-genius/.

Garland, D. (1985). The criminal and his science: A critical account of the formation of criminology at the end of the nineteenth century. *The British Journal of Criminology, 25* (2), pp. 109-137.

Garland, D., & Sparks, R. (2000). Criminology, social theory, and the challenge of our times. In Garland, D., & Sparks, R. (Eds.), *Criminology and social theory* (pp. 1-22). New York: Oxford University Press.

Gatti, U., & Verde, A. (2012). Cesare Lombroso: Methodological ambiguities and brilliant intuitions. *International Journal of Law and Psychiatry, 35,* 19-26.

Gibson, M. (2002). *Born to crime: Cesare Lombroso and the origins of biological criminology*. Westport, CT: Praeger.

Gibson, M. (2006). Cesare Lombroso and Italian criminology: Theory and politics. In Becker, P., & Wetzell, R.F. (Eds.), *Criminals and their scientists: the history of criminology in international perspective* (pp. 137-158). New York: Cambridge University Press.

Gibson, M., & Rafter, N.H. (Eds.). (2006). *Criminal man* (M. Seymour, Trans.). Durham, NC: Duke University Press.

Gibson, Mary. "Cesare Lombroso, Prison Science, and Penal Policy." In Knepper, P., & Ystehede, P.J., (Eds.), *The Cesare Lombroso Handbook*. New York: Routledge, 2013.

Gilmour, D. (2011). *The pursuit of Italy: A history of land, its regions, and their peoples*. New York: Farrar, Straus and Giroux.

Granieri, E., & Fazio, P. (2012). The Lombrosian prejudice in medicine: The case of epilepsy, epileptic psychosis, epilepsy and aggressiveness. *Neurological Sciences, 33,* 173-192.

Grazi, Alessandro. (November 2015). David Levi, A Child of the Nineteenth Century, in Portrait of Italian Jewish Life (1800s-1930s). In Tullia C., Cristina P. (Eds.), *Quest. Issues in Contemporary Jewish History, Journal of Foundazione CDEC,* (8).

Gribaudi, G. (1997). Images of the south: The *mezzogiorno* as seen by insiders and outsiders. In Lumley, R., & Morris, J. (Eds.). *The New History of the Italian South* (pp. 83-113). Devon, UK: University of Exeter Press.

Gutek, G.L., (Ed.). (2004). *The Montessori Method: The Origins of an Educational Innovation: Including an Abridged and Annotated Edition of Maria Montessori's The Montessori Method*. New York: Rowan, Littlefield.

Hagins, Z.R. (2013). Fashioning the 'born criminal' on the beat: Juridical Photography and the police municipal in Fin-de-Siecle Paris. *Modern and Contemporary France,* 21, 281-296.

Hibbert, C. (2008). *Garibaldi: Hero of Italian unification* (3rd Ed.). New York: St. Martins Griffin.

Horn, D.G. (2003). *The criminal body: Lombroso and the anatomy of deviance.* New York: Routledge.

Horn, D.G. (2006). Making criminologists: Tools, techniques, and the production of scientific authority. In Becker, P., & Wetzell, R.F. (Eds.), *Criminals and their scientists: The history of criminology in international perspective* (pp. 317-336). New York: Cambridge University Press.

Huxley, J. (Ed.). (2013). *Origin of species: 150th Anniversary Edition.* New York: Signet.

Jalava, J. (2006). The modern degenerate nineteenth-century theory and modern psychopathy research. *Theory and Psychology,* 16, 416-432.

Jensen, R.B. (1989). Police reform and social reform: Italy from the crisis of the 1890s to the Giolittian era. *Criminal Justice History,* 10, 179-200.

Judson, P.M. (2016). *The Habsburg empire: A new history.* Cambridge, MA: University of Harvard Press.

Kalfus, S. (2010). Darwin's evolution and positivism. Retrieved from https://scienceleadership.org/blog/darwin-s_evolution_and_posivitism.

Klein, D. (1973). The etiology of female crime: A review of the literature. *Issues in Criminology,* 8 (2), 3-30.

Knepper, P., & Ystehede, P.J. (Eds.). (2013). *The Cesare Lombroso Handbook.* New York: Routledge.

Kushner, H. (2011). Cesare Lombroso and the pathology of left-handedness. *The Lancet,* 377 (9760), 118-119.

Kurella, H. (1911/2012). *Cesare Lombroso: A modern man of science* (Reprint). San Bernardino, CA: Forgotten Books.

Lambert, T. (2016). A history of science and technology in the 19th century. Retrieved from http://www.localhistories.org/victech.html.

Lindesmith, A., & Yale, L. (1937). The Lombrosian myth in criminology. *American Journal of Sociology,* 42 (5), 653-671.

Lindsey, E. "International Congress of Criminal Anthropology: A Review." *Journal of Criminal Law and Criminology.* Vol. 1, Issue 4, March 1911. 578-583.

Lombroso, C. (1909/1988). *After Death — What? Researches into Hypnotic and Spiritualistic Phenomena* (Reprint). Translated by William Sloane Kennedy. Northamptonshire, England: The Aquarian Press.

Lombroso, C. (1911/2012). *Crime, its causes and remedies* (Reprint). Lexington, KY: Forgotten Books.

Lombroso, C. (1891/1892, March 30). [Letter to Felix Alcan]. (S. Lapini-Lozzi, Trans.). Copy in possession of Dr. Alex del Carmen.

Lombroso, C., (1891/2015). *The man of genius* (Reprint). London, England: FB & Ltd.

Lombroso, C. *The Savage Origin of Tattooing*. L.M. Publishing (n.d.).

Lombroso, C., and Guiseppe Pelaggi. *In Calabria, 1862-1897* (1898). Print version, Catania, 1898; e-book version, http://bit.ly/2sQ0QGB, edited by Viale Rosale Rubbettino, 2009, accessed June 17, 2017.

Lombroso, C., & Ferrero, W. (1909). *The female offender* (Reprint). New York: D. Appleton and Company.

Lombroso-Ferrero, G. (1911/2015). *Criminal man: According to the classification of Cesare Lombroso briefly summarized by his daughter Gina Lombroso- Ferrero* (Reprint). CreateSpace, An Amazon.com Company.

Lombroso-Ferrero, G. (ca. 1914). "Cesare Lombroso." Unpublished manuscript. Museum of Criminal Anthropology. Turin, Italy.

Lombroso, Cesare. (April 1896). The Savage Origin of Tattooing." *Popular Science Monthly*, 48.

Lord, J.R. (1912). A pioneer in criminology: Notes on the work of James Bruce Thompson. Retrieved from http://bjpsych.org/content/59/245/354.

Lyell, J.H. (April 1913). A pioneer in criminology: Notes on the work of James Thomson, of Perth. *The British Journal of Psychiatry,* 59 (245), pp. 364-371. Retrieved from http://bjpsychap.org/content/59/245/354.

MacDonald, A. (1893/2010). *Criminology: With and introduction by Cesare Lombroso* (Reprint). Cambridge, MA: Harvard School Law Library.

Mason, E. (2015). The 'born criminal'? Lombroso and the origins of modern criminology. Retrieved http://www.historyextra.com/article/feature/born-criminal-lombroso-origins-modern-criminology.

Mannheim, H. (1955). *Group problems in crime and punishment: And other studies in criminology and criminal law.* London, England: Routledge and Kegan Paul Limited.

Mazzarello, P. (2011). "Cesare Lombroso: An anthropologist between evolution and degeneration." *Functional Neurology,* 26 (2), 97-101.

Mazzarello, P. (2001). "Lombroso and Tolstoy: An Anthropologist's Unwitting Gift to Literature." *Nature,* 409 (6823), 983.

Melossi, D. (2000). Changing Representations of the Criminal," In Garland, D., & Sparks, R. (Eds.), *Criminology and Social Theory*. New York: Oxford University Press.

Merriman, J. (2004). *A history of modern Europe: From renaissance to the present* (2nd Ed.). New York: W.W. Norton & Company.

Mishra, P. (2017). *Age of anger*. New York: Farrar, Straus & Giroux.

Moffit, T.E. (Oct. 1993). Adolescence-limited and life-course-persistent antisocial behavior: A developmental taxonomy. *Psychological Review*, 100, 674-701.

Montaldo, S. Interview with Dr. Randall Butler, September 20, 2016.

Montaldo, S. (2013). The Lombroso museum from its origins to the present day. In Knepper, P., & Ystehede, P.J. (Eds.), *The Cesare Lombroso Handbook* (pp. 97-111). New York: Routledge.

Montaldo, S. (2017). "The relics of two 19th century scientists: Carlo Giacomini and Cesare Lombroso." In Beretta, M. Conforti, M., & Mazzarello, P. (Eds.), *Savant Relics Brains and Remains of Scientists* (pp. 183-199). New York: Science History Publications USA.

Morris, J. (1997). "Challenging *meridionalismo*: Constructing a new history for southern Italy." In Lumley, R., & Morris, J. (Eds.), *The new history of the Italian south: The Mezzogiorno Revisted* (pp. 1-19). Devon, UK: University of Exeter Press.

Munthe, C., & Radovic, S. (2015). "The return of Lombroso? Ethical aspects of (visions of) preventive forensic screening." *Public Health Ethics*, 8, 270-283.

Nartonis, D.K. "The Rise of 19th-Century American Spiritualism, 1854-1873." *Journal for the Scientific Study of Religion*. 2010. 49(2): 361-373.

Natale, S. (2016). *Supernatural Entertainments: Victorian Spiritualism and the Rise of Modern Media Culture*. University Park: Pennsylvania State University Press.

Nordau, M.S. (1892/2016). *Degeneration* (Reprint). San Bernardino, CA: Jefferson Publishing.

Nordau, M.S. (1895/2012). *The conventional lies of our civilization* (Reprint). San Bernardino, CA: Forgotten Books.

Noyes, W. (1888). The criminal type. *Journal of Social Science*, (24), 31-42.

Nye, R.A. (Sept., 1976). Heredity or milieu: The foundations of modern European criminological theory. *Isis*, 67 (3), 334-355.

Paoletti, C. (2008). *A Military History of Italy*. Westport, Connecticut: Praeger Security International.

Pec, R. "Dreaming About Dreams." Mieux-Etre.org. http://www.mieux-etre.org/Rever-sur-les-reves.html. Accessed March 7, 2017.

Petrusewicz, M. (1998). Before the southern question: "Native" ideas on backwardness and remedies in the kingdom of two Sicilies, 1815-1849. In Schneider, J. (Ed.), *Italy's "southern question:" Orientalism in one country*, (pp. 27-49). New York: Oxford University Press.

Petrusewicz, M. (1997). The demise of *latifondismo*. In Lumley, R., & Morris, J. (Eds.), *The New History of the Italian South*, (pp. 20-41). Devon, UK: University of Exeter Press.

Pick, D. (1989). *Faces of degeneration: European disorder, c. 1848-1918*. New York: Cambridge University Press.

Pisciotta, A.W. (1994). *Benevolent repression: Social control and the American reformatory-prison movement*. New York: New York University Press.

Pomata, G. (1993). Premise: A figure of power and an invitation to history: Epilogue: To room nineteen. In Kemp, S., & Bono, P. (Eds.), *The lonely mirror: Italian perspectives on feminist theory* (pp. 155-169). New York: Routledge.

Popper, K.R. (1972). *Objective knowledge: An evolutionary approach*. Oxford, England: Clarendon Press.

Porter, T.M. (1986). *The rise of statistical thinking 1820-1900*. Princeton, NJ: Princeton University Press.

Procter, C. (2014). *The history of Italy, from the fall of the western empire to the Commencement of the wars of the French revolution* (Reprint). San Bernardino, CA: CreateSpace Independent Publishing Platform.

Rafter, N.H. (2006). Criminal anthropology: Its reception in the United States and the nature of its appeal. In Becker, P., & Wetzell, R.F. (Eds.), *Criminals and their scientists: The history of criminology in international perspective*, (pp. 159-181). New York: Cambridge University Press.

Rafter, N., & Gibson, M. (Eds.). (2004). *Criminal woman, the prostitute, and the normal woman*. Durham, NC: Duke University Press.

Rafter, N., Posick, C., & Rocque, M. (Eds.). (2016). *The criminal mind: Understanding biological theories of crime* (2nd ed.). New York: New York University Press.

"Rudolf Virchow:" Famous Scientists. Retrieved from http://www.famousscientists.org/rudolf-virchow/

Schneid, F.C. (2012). *The Second War of Italian Unification, 1859-61*. Oxford: Osprey Publishing.

Scott, P. (1960). Henry Maudsley (1835-1918). In Mannheim, H. (Ed.), *Pioneers of criminology* (pp. 208-231). Chicago, IL: Northwestern University.

Sellin, T. (1960). Enrico Ferri (1856-1929). In Mannehim, H. (Ed.), *Pioneers of criminology* (pp. 361-384). Chicago, IL: Northwestern University.

Sellin, T. (1926). A new phase of criminal anthropology in Italy. *Annals of American Academy of Political and Social Science,* 125, 233-242.

Simon, J. (2006). Positively Punitive: How the Inventor of Scientific Criminology Who Died at the Beginning of the Twentieth Century Continues to Haunt American Crime Control at the Beginning of the Twenty-First. *Texas Law Review,* 84, 2135-2172.

Spencer, H. (1864/2017). *The Principles of Biology, Vol. 1* (Reprint). Lexington, KY: Forgotten Books.

Starr, D. "Dracula Was the Original Thug." *Slate: The State of the Universe.* October 30, 2012. Accessed June 17, 2017.

Stewart-Steinberg, S. (2007). *The Pinocchio Effect: On Making Italians, 1860-1920.* Chicago: University of Chicago Press.

Thio, A. (2004). *Deviant behavior* (7th Ed.). New York: Pearson Education.

Tolstoy, Leo. (1904). *Resurrection.* New York: Charles Scribner's Sons; transcribed to Google Books, http://bit.ly/2sdR7rO, accessed June 17, 2017.

Vine, M.S.W. (1960). Gabriel Tarde (1843-1904). In Mannheim, H. (Ed.), *Pioneers of criminology* (pp. 292-304). Chicago, IL: Northwestern University.

Vold, G.B., Bernard, T.J., & Snipes, J.B. (1998). *Theoretical criminology* (4th Ed.). New York: Oxford University Press.

Wetzell, R.F. (2000). *Inventing the criminal: A history of German criminology, 1880-1945.* Chapel Hill, NC: The University of North Carolina Press.

Wolfgang, M.E. (Winter 1961). Pioneers in Criminology: Cesare Lombroso (1825 [sic]-1909)." *Journal of Criminal Law and Criminology,* 52, (4), 361-391.

Wolfgang, M.E. (1960). Cesare Lombroso (1835-1909). In Mannheim, H. (Ed.), *Pioneers of criminology* (pp. 232-291). Chicago, IL: Northwestern University.

Zimmern, H. (April 1897). David Levi, Poet and Patriot. *The Jewish Quarterly Review,* 9, (3), 363-402.

INDEX

moving from Pavia to Turin, 194–196
ordeals, 200
Paris conference, 199–200
"The Resume of the Eusapia Phenomenon," 208
travel problems, 203
degenaracy role, 87, 110
degeneration, 55, 96
Del Grego, Samson, 5–7
Descent of Man, 48
determinants to crime, 152–167
abandoned children, 159
alcohol, 156–158
born criminal and epilepsy, 153
celibacy, 154
civilization influence, 154, 158
climate, 154
environmental, 153
fatal ambition, 164
heredity, 156
illiteracy, 162
immigration, 158
insanity, 153
mental, 153
meteorological conditions influence, 165
moral insanity, 153
orographic and geographic landscape, 166
physical, 153
physiognomy, 154
population, 159
race and the racial theory, 154–155
social-economic changes, 161
temperature, 165
urbanization, 154, 158
vanity, 164
Diana, F.P., 120
Dickie, John, 34
Diniejko, Andrzej, 211
discovery, 73–77
facial features (physiognomy), 74
tests on sensitivity, 74
DNA evidence, xii
Dracula, 196
drugs use, 93
Dunant, Albert, 201

maternity and, 135, 138
normal versus criminal woman, 129
prevalence, 128
prostitution and, 138–140, 146–147
race and, 134
social-economic environment, 128
female dangerousness, 136–140
Female Offender, The, 85, 122, 125, 134
feminist movement, 117–119
"new woman" movement, 120
Ferrero, Guglielmo, 56, 85, 125–129, 133–138
Ferri, Enrico, 56, 83, 95, 109, 202
Finzi, Giorgio, 207
"Fratelli Bandieri," 9
friends help, 53–55

G
Gall, Franz Joseph, 50, 70
Galton, Francis, 47, 52
Garibaldi, Guiseppe, 28
Garofalo, Raffaele, 56–57, 83, 95, 109
German Materialism, 47
Gerosa, G., 207
Gibson, Mary, xii, 37
Gioberti, Vincenzo, 11
Giordano Bruno; The Religion of The ought; The Man, Apostle, and Martyr, 9
Giovine Italia (Young Italy), 8
graphology, 199–200
Grazi, Alessandro, 3
Greco-Roman descendants, 36
Guarnieri, Luigi, 30
Guerry, Andre'-Michel, 47, 72

H
habitual criminals, 95
Haeckel, Ernst, 52
Haeckel's recapitulation theory, 134
hieroglyphics, 101–102
Hopes of Italy, The, 12
Horn, David G., 97
Houze, Emile, 199
hysteria, 92–93

M

Maconochie model prison, 185
Maconochie, Alexander, 183
Mafia gang, 33–34, 98, 100
Magirani, 193
making of a criminologist, 43–57
    Beccaria, Cesare, 44
    crime prevention concept, 57
    empiricism, 46
    family and assistants, 55–57
    German materialism, 47
    "indeterminate sentences" principle, 57
    influences and practitioners, 48–53
        biogenetic law, 52
        fundamental biogenetic law, 51
        monism, 52
        theromorphisms, 51
        Virchow's discovery, 51
        works of Darwin and Mendel, 48–49
    "isms" movements, 46
    materialism, 44, 46
    mentors and friends, 53–55
        Mantegazza, Paolo, 53–54
        Marzolo, Paolo, 53–54
    nationalism, 44, 46
        Bertani, Agostino, 54
        Nordau, Max, 54–55
        Panizza, Bartolomeo, 54
    positivism, 44, 46
Man of Genius, The, 89, 93, 97, 106
Manganelli, Giorgio, 207
Maniac Pellagra, 60
Manouvrier, Leonce Pierre, 198, 201
Mantagazza, Paolo, 18, 53–54
marks of degeneration, 77–82
Marselli-Valli, Maria, 120
Martyr de la Liberté (Martyr of Liberty), 39
Marzolo, Paolo, 15–16, 24, 49, 53–54, 64, 164
materialism, xiii, 44, 46–47, 60
maternity, 135–136
Mattoids, 93
Maudsley, Henry, 51
Maury, Alfred, 62
Mazzini, Guiseppi, 4, 8–9

CPSIA information can be obtained
at www.ICGtesting.com
Printed in the USA
LVHW051928060819
626729LV00003B/3/P